# Extremism, Free Speech and Counter-Terrorism Law and Policy



This edited collection addresses a number of free speech vs security concerns that are engaged by counter-terrorism law and policy makers across a number of liberal democracies, and explores the delicate balance between free speech and the censoring of views that promote hatred or clash with fundamental democratic values. It does this by looking at the perspectives and level of disagreement between those who consider today's counter-terrorism and extremism strategies to be a soft and liberal approach, and those who believe these strategies disproportionately impact freedom of expression and association, and non-violent political dissent.

The contributors include academics, practicing lawyers, and think-tank analysts who examine whether universities and schools are incubators of violent radicalism and debate, and whether the views of 'extremist' speakers and hate preachers need to be censored. Outside the UK, critical discussion of the regulation of counter-terrorism, extremism, and free speech in other liberal democracies is also offered.

This book will be of great interest to researchers and practitioners with interests in extremism, terrorism, civil rights, and freedom of speech.

**Ian Cram** is Professor of Comparative Constitutional Law, School of Law, Leeds University. His research interests include freedom of expression and constitutional reform. His previous publications include *Terror and the War on Dissent* and *Citizen Journalists: Newer Media, Republican Moments and the Constitution.*

**Routledge Studies in Extremism and Democracy**
Series Editors: Roger Eatwell
*University of Bath* and Matthew Goodwin, *University of Kent*
Founding Series Editors: Roger Eatwell
*University of Bath* and Cas Mudde, *University of Antwerp-UFSIA*

This new series encompasses academic studies within the broad fields of 'extremism' and 'democracy'. These topics have traditionally been considered largely in isolation by academics. A key focus of the series, therefore, is the (inter-)*relation* between extremism and democracy. Works will seek to answer questions such as to what extent 'extremist' groups pose a major threat to democratic parties or how democracy can respond to extremism without undermining its own democratic credentials.

The books encompass two strands:

*Routledge's Studies in Extremism and Democracy* include books with an introductory and broad focus which are aimed at students and teachers. These books are available in hardback and paperback.

**38 When Does Terrorism Work?**
*Diego Muro*

**39 Militant Democracy**
The Limits of Democratic Tolerance
*Bastiaan R. Rijpkema*

**40 Anti-Islamic Protest in the UK**
Policy Responses to the Far Right
*William Allchorn*

**41 Anti-System Parties**
From Parliamentary Breakthrough to Government
*Mattia Zulianello*

**42 Extremism, Free Speech and Counter-Terrorism Law and Policy**
*Edited by Ian Cram*

For more information about this series, please visit:
www.routledge.com/politics/series/ED

# Extremism, Free Speech and Counter-Terrorism Law and Policy

Edited by Ian Cram

Routledge
Taylor & Francis Group
LONDON AND NEW YORK

First published 2019 by Routledge

2 Park Square, Milton Park, Abingdon, Oxfordshire OX14 4RN
52 Vanderbilt Avenue, New York, NY 10017

*Routledge is an imprint of the Taylor & Francis Group, an informa business*

First issued in paperback 2020



*British Library Cataloguing-in-Publication Data*
A catalogue record for this book is available from the British Library

*Library of Congress Cataloging-in-Publication Data*
A catalog record has been requested for this book

ISBN: 978-1-138-54518-2 (hbk)
ISBN: 978-0-367-67095-5 (pbk)

Typeset in Times New Roman
by Wearset Ltd, Boldon, Tyne and Wear

# Contents

# Contributors

**Ashutosh Bhagwat**, Martin Luther King Jr Professor of Law, UC Davis School of Law, California. He joined the UC Davis School of Law faculty in 2011. Prior to joining UC Davis, he taught at UC Hastings College of the Law for 17 years. Bhagwat is the author of *The Myth of Rights*, published by Oxford University Press in 2010, as well as numerous books, articles, and book chapters on a wide variety of subjects, ranging from the structure of constitutional rights, to free speech law, to the California Electricity Crisis. Bhagwat's articles have appeared in the *Yale Law Journal*, the *Supreme Court Review*, the *California Law Review*, the *Administrative Law Review*, and the *University of Illinois Law Review*.

**Ian Cram**, Professor of Comparative Constitutional Law, School of Law, Leeds University. Research interests include freedom of expression and constitutional reform. Member of Board of Editors International and Comparative Law Quarterly; past adviser to the Law Commission; expert witness to House of Commons Select Committee on Political and Constitutional Reform. Monograph publications include *Terror and the War on Dissent*; *Citizen Journalists; Contested Words*.

**Daniel Fenwick** completed his LLB at Kings College, London in 2009, before completing a Masters in Jurisprudence (Mjur) in 2010 and then a PhD in law in 2014 at Durham University (awarded February 2015). His Mjur and PhD topics are within the fields of bioethics and human rights; his PhD is entitled 'A Gewirthian conception of the right to enabled suicide in England and Wales'. He has previously taught at Sheffield University and Durham University in the fields of Jurisprudence, Equity, Land law, and Public law.

**Helen Fenwick**, School of Law, Durham University. Her research interest lies in the field of civil liberties and human rights. Within that field her main interests are in counter-terrorist law and policy, media freedom of expression (in particular contempt law, obscenity law and privacy law), public protest, and the influence of the European Convention on Human Rights on the Human Rights Act. Her current research focuses on counter-terrorist measures, media freedom of expression and judicial reasoning under the Human Rights Act.

She is also acts as consultant for Doughty Street Chambers and is an ongoing Member of the Commonwealth Scholarship Commission in the United Kingdom (2016–23).

**Elana Geddis** was called to the New Zealand Bar. She previously worked for the NZ Ministry of Foreign Affairs and Trade on counter-terrorism issues in a variety of guises, including as a legal advisor to the NZ Mission to the UN in New York from 2001 to 2004, and as the deputy director responsible for the legal team that deals with both counter-terrorism and human rights. She also has been involved in various NZ Law Society working groups that addressed relevant legislative amendments and proposals.

**Andrew Geddis**, Professor of Law, Otago University New Zealand. His research interests lie in the field of public law, rights jurisprudence, and democratic theory, with a particular focus on the legal regulation of elections. Recent publications include, 'From people's revolution to partisan reform: Recent electoral change in New Zealand'. *Election Law Journal*, (2017) 16, no. 2: 222–9. 'The case for allowing aid in dying in New Zealand. *New Zealand Criminal Law Review*, (2017) 3–28; 'Judicial innovation under the New Zealand Bill of Rights Act: Lessons for Queensland? *University of Queensland Law Journal*, (2016) 35(2): 251–82; 'Rights scrutiny in New Zealand's legislative processes. *Theory & Practice of Legislation*, (2016) 4(3): 355–79.

**Keiran Hardy**, Research Fellow on Professor George Williams' ARC Laureate Fellowship on Anti-Terrorism Laws. His research focuses on counter-terrorism laws, cyber-terrorism, the accountability of intelligence agencies, and counter-radicalization and counter-insurgency. Recent publications include 'Executive Oversight of Intelligence Agencies in Australia', in Zachary K Goldman and Samuel J Rascoff (eds.), Intelligence Oversight: A Global View (Oxford, OUP, 2016) with George Williams; 'Online Radicalisation and the Criminal Trial', in Stuart Macdonald, Lee Jarvis and Anne Aly (eds.), Violent Extremism Online: New Perspectives on Terrorism and the Internet (Routledge, 2015); 'What is "Cyber-Terrorism"? Computer and Internet Technology in Legal Definitions of Terrorism', in Thomas M Chen, Lee Jarvis and Stuart Macdonald (eds.) Cyberterrorism: Understanding, Assessment, and Response (Springer, 2014): 1–24 (with George Williams).

**Andrew W Neal**, Senior Lecturer in Politics and International Relations; Co-Director of the Centre for Security Research (CeSeR); Programme Director MSc International Relations. His research interests include International Security, War on Terror, Discourse Theory, Sociological Theory, Cultural Theory, Political Theory, the UK, Britain, Critical Theory, Critical Security Studies, Securitization, Constructivism, Postmodern Governance, Poststructuralism, Scotland, and Scottish Politics. He was principal convenor of the ESRC seminar series 'Security in Scotland, with or without constitutional change', 2013–15. His publications include the 2010 monograph for Routledge, *Exceptionalism and the politics of counter-terrorism: liberty,* *security and the war on terror*, and, more recently, *Security in a Small Nation: Scotland, Democracy, Politics*, (ed.) (Open Book Publishers, 2017).

**Nadine Strossen** is the John Marshall Harlan II Professor of Law, New York Law School, and Immediate Past President American Civil Liberties Union (1991–2008). Nadine has written, taught, and advocated extensively in the areas of constitutional law and civil liberties, including through frequent media interviews. From 1991 to 2008, she served as President of the American Civil Liberties Union, the first woman to head the nation's largest and oldest civil liberties organization. Professor Strossen is currently a member of the ACLU's National Advisory Council, and serves on the Advisory Boards of EPIC (Electronic Privacy Information Center), FIRE (Foundation for Individual Rights in Education), and the Heterodox Academy. When she stepped down as ACLU President in 2008, three Supreme Court Justices (Ruth Bader Ginsburg, Antonin Scalia, and David Souter) participated in her farewell and tribute luncheon.

**Emma Webb** is Director of the Centre for the Study of European Civilisation at *Civitas*. She was formerly a Fellow at the Centre for the Response to Radicalisation and Terrorism. She specializes in European Islamist terror networks, counter-extremism policy, and radicalisation. Her research has focused on non-violent and violent extremism in the UK and Europe, and counter-extremism within educational institutions. Her recent publications include *An Enduring Threat: Europe's Islamist Terror Networks Then and Now* (2016), *Spotting the Signs: Identifying Vulnerability to Radicalisation Among Students* (2017), and *For Our Children: An Examination of Prevent in the Curriculum* (2017). She has spoken on international broadcast media on issues relating to the threat level facing the UK, recent terror attacks in Europe and radicalisation, and has written for the Spectator, the Independent, and the Telegraph. She has a BA in Theological and Religious studies from Trinity College, Cambridge and an MA (Distinction) from Kings College London.

**James Weinstein** holds the Dan Cracchiolo Chair in Constitutional Law, Sandra Day O'Connor College of Law Arizona State University. Research interests include free speech theory, obscenity doctrine, institutional review boards, commercial speech, database protection, campaign finance reform, the relationship between free speech and constitutional rights, hate crimes, and campus speech codes. Professor Weinstein has litigated several significant free speech cases, primarily on behalf of the Arizona Civil Liberties Union. Earlier in his career, he wrote several influential articles on the history of personal jurisdiction and its implication for modern doctrine. Monograph publications include *Hate Speech, Pornography and the Radical Attack on Free Speech Doctrine; Extreme Speech and Democracy*.

**George Williams** is Dean, Anthony Mason Professor, Scientia Professor at the University of New South Wales. He has written and edited 35 books, including Australian Constitutional Law and Theory, The Oxford Companion to the

High Court of Australia, and Human Rights under the Australian Constitution. He has appeared as a barrister before the High Court in many cases over the past two decades, including cases on freedom of speech, freedom from racial discrimination, and the rule of law. He has also appeared in the Supreme Court and Court of Appeal of Fiji, including on the legality of the 2000 coup.

# 1 Introduction

*Ian Cram*

Recent jihadist attacks in the United Kingdom (UK), France, Germany, and Belgium demonstrate the dangers of homegrown terrorism and the need to disrupt the routes by which persons are drawn into committing acts of terrorism. In the UK, the introduction of the Counter-Terrorism and Security Act 2015 placed the 'Prevent' duty, one of the four components of counter-terrorism strategy, on a statutory footing, while in the same year the Counter Extremism Strategy sought to target individuals who justify violence, promote hatred and division, propound alternative systems of law, reject the democratic system and carry out harmful and illegal cultural practices. Terrorist activities in London and Manchester (March to May, 2017) prompted calls for further revisions to Prevent, and the minority administration of Theresa May appears to be inclined to clamp down further on internet communications (see especially the renewed focus on social media platforms) that facilitate the spread of hateful jihadist ideologies. In January 2018, the head of the new Counter Extremism Commission – Sara Khan, a known supporter of Prevent – was appointed and described her first task as compiling 'a comprehensive study of the scale, influence and reach of extremism in this country....' The Commission's tasks include advising the government on new policies to tackle extremism. This entails consideration of whether there is a need for new legal powers and how best to promote 'British values' and community cohesion.

The above strategies are, however, controversial. Indeed, they have polarized expert opinion and debates have been particularly heated across university campuses and local communities. In the case of Prevent, for example, the former Independent Reviewer of Terrorism, David Anderson QC, has noted that Prevent is controversial 'to the point where reputable community organisations refuse to engage with it.'[1] With contributions from a leading international set of scholars, this collection of essays offers a diverse set of analyses of counter-terrorism/ counter extremism policies as they impact across the domain of a number of liberal democracies. The range of questions tackled in this volume includes discussion on whether universities and schools are incubators of violent radicalism; whether the censoring hateful/extremist works as a matter of practice; and whether broadly drafted laws of incitement and encouragement blur the distinction between the 'enemies of the government of the day' and the 'enemies of the democratic state' (and does this matter). Might a shift in policy towards tackling non-violent 'extremism' be problematic insofar as it targets dissenting speech and thoughts that are a long way removed from conduct that is considered to be more than a preparatory step towards a terrorist outrage? How do liberal democracies, with their distinct constitutional and philosophical commitments to human rights and individual freedoms, variously deal with the speech-related issues that affect counter-terrorism law and policy? The aim of this edited collection is to explore the delicate balance between free speech and the censoring of views that either promote hatred or clash with fundamental democratic values. To do so, it will bring together various perspectives and capture the level of disagreement across a range of opinion that extends between: (1) those who consider today's counter-terrorism and extremism strategies to be broadly defensible in that they seek to safeguard national security, combat hateful forms of expression, and defend fundamental democratic values; and (2) those who believe that these strategies disproportionately impact on freedom of expression and association and non-violent political dissent, calling into question the commitment to preserving a liberal democracy. It is hoped that the legal and policy comparisons will help inform future debates concerning the complex relationship between freedom of expression and state security in liberal democracies

Ian Cram's opening chapter sets some perimeters for the rest of the collection by looking at arguments of principle and policy that underpin counter-terrorism inspired restrictions on inciteful expression. He shows that legal provisions such as those found in Part 1 of the UK's Terrorism Act 2006 rest upon both empirical claims (a predicted reduction in the frequency of terrorist incidents) and a desire to address the more oblique harms caused to core liberal norms such as the rule of law. In the aftermath of a terrorist outrage, proponents of a recalibration of the 'balance' between individual freedoms and security frequently can be seen to make the case for incremental downward adjustments to personal liberty. Cram examines the nature of these recalibration claims and questions distributional aspects of the recalibration before setting out what he considers to be principled free speech defences to forms of inciteful expression, which might conduce to a degree of constitutional protection. He concludes by highlighting the speculative basis on which current sets of UK speech restrictions are premised and the diminished political discourse they engender.

Outside the US, proponents of political violence are likely, in the course of their proselytizing, to run foul of incitement to hatred laws. In the aftermath of the publication of the Danish cartoons in 2006, some Muslim protestors, who took to the streets, were charged and convicted on incitement to racial hatred charges.[2] In her chapter, Nadine Strossen considers the basis and impact of hate speech laws in liberal democracies. Her particular interest centres upon the practical consequences of such constraints on speakers and audiences. Strossen asks whether it might not be better if the state directed its energies to consider ways of building resilience in the target audience in order to empower forms of counter-expression. Whatever else it achieves, a 'more-speech' response to hateful expression usefully denies the hateful speaker the label of 'free speech martyr' – a powerful recruiting device in far-right political groupings.

The two succeeding chapters by Andrew Neal (Chapter 3) and Helen Fenwick and Daniel Fenwick (Chapter 4) probe, in their respective contributions, operational aspects of the UK government's Prevent strategy in universities and schools. Prevent requires specified public institutions to have 'due regard' to the need to prevent people being drawn into terrorism. Neal's chapter reviews the evidence on the impact of Prevent on campus, drawing in part on the parliamentary Joint Committee on Human Rights report of 2018. He argues that universities might be considered to enjoy a privileged space of exception in which free speech norms are given more weight than elsewhere in the public sector, where the Prevent duty bites more obviously on expressive interests. He points to section 31(2) of the Counter-Terrorism and Security Act 2015 which requires universities to have 'particular regard to the duty to ensure freedom of speech … and academic freedom'. At the same time, Neal cautions that Prevent's terminological vagueness has created a climate of mistrust on campus' in which Muslim students report a sense of being identified with a suspect community. At root, he contends that Prevent on campus is undermined by the 'pseudo-science of radicalisation', which is said to lack an academically credible basis in scholarly literature.

In the case of schools, the Department for Education guidance, accompanying the statutory duty in Section 26 of the 2015 Act, obliges schools to have regard to disrupting promoters of terrorism and the processes by which individuals are placed at risk of being drawn into terrorism, and who become supporters of terrorist groups and 'extremist ideology'. The latter term is defined as a 'vocal or active opposition to fundamental British values, including democracy, the rule of law, individual liberty and mutual respect and tolerance of different faiths and beliefs'. A multi-agency and voluntary 'Channel' programme exists to 'deradicalize' those identified as being at risk. The chapter by Helen Fenwick and Daniel Fenwick takes as its point of departure the so called 'Trojan Horse' affair concerning a number of Birmingham schools in 2014. The leader of Birmingham City Council was sent an anonymous letter purporting to be from one Islamist to another which set out the means by which schools in Birmingham might be taken over and run on strict Islamic principles. A copy of the letter ended up in the Department for Education in Whitehall and two separate investigations into the substance of the allegations were launched. Fenwick and Fenwick show how the findings of these investigations fed into the drafting of proposals that would ultimately find their way into the Counter-Terrorism and Security Act 2015. Turning to a detailed consideration of the accompanying policy guidance to schools, the authors review the evidence behind claims that Prevent and associated Channel referrals have had a deleterious effect on free speech in schools. Notwithstanding the obvious unease around terms such as 'extremist ideology', it is argued that Prevent has not unduly limited freedom of expression in schools. Particular emphasis is placed on those aspects of the Department for Education's guidance that stress the importance of giving students and pupils the confidence to challenge cultural and political assumptions. The state's active promotion of ideals of equality and non-discrimination is thus considered to offer a 'more speech' solution to the problem of anti-homosexual or sexist forms of expression in the classroom. Fenwick and Fenwick conclude by considering the compatibility of Prevent and the accompanying guidance with the legal framework set by Articles 10 and 17 of the European Convention on Human Rights (ECHR), alongside the High Court's decision in *Butt*. It is suggested that state regulation of expression in schools is likely to benefit from a 'light touch' form of judicial scrutiny, not least on account of the state's strong interest in the inculcation of democratic values in young persons.

Emma Webb's chapter locates UK policy in its wider European context. Noting aspects of governmental initiatives in Denmark, Finland, and France, she focuses upon developments in the Netherlands where counter-extremism and resilience programmes have proved controversial. Problems regarding the transparency and accountability of public bodies entrusted with key aspects of policy delivery are discussed here. In respect of UK policy, the chapter sets out to tackle what the author considers misconceptions and exaggerated criticisms of Prevent. It draws in part on the work of Dame Louise Casey, the former 'Czar' for community cohesion and extremism appointed by the then Prime Minister, David Cameron. As applied to the university sector in the aftermath of *Butt*, Webb highlights those parts of the Prevent Guidance that, far from closing the speech of the non-violent advocates of 'un-British' values, encourages others to challenge such expression in what would be styled a more-speech solution to the problem of anti-democratic, intolerant speech.

A reader interested in the comparative constitutional dimensions of current policy approaches might be forgiven for assuming that, in polities where individual and societal interests in political free speech and association are constitutionally entrenched, attempts by the legislative and executive branches to undermine such core freedoms would almost always be bound to be struck down by the courts deploying a strict or intense standard of constitutional review. The most speech-protective jurisdiction anywhere is that found in the US Constitution and it is here that one would expect that First Amendment norms would nullify legislative/executive order curtailments of speech. During the so called 'war on terror', *Holder* v. *Humanitarian Law Project* was the U.S. Supreme Court's major opportunity to announce clear and protective standards for political expression/association in the context of an ongoing, though non-existential conflict. The outcome, by 6–3, upheld the constitutionality of the 'material support' provisions of US counter-terrorism law as applied to a group of US citizens wishing to provide expert training support to two designated foreign terrorist organizations, namely the PKK (Kurdistan Workers' Party) and the LTTE (Liberation Tigers of Tamil Eelam). The training was intended to train each organization in the use of humanitarian and international law and peaceful political advocacy in national and international contexts. David Cole who appeared for the plaintiffs stated that the ruling had

> potentially grave repercussions.... Under this law, for example, when the Carter Center, run by former President Jimmy Carter monitored elections in Lebanon in 2009, and met with Hezbollah ... to explain what the monitors would look for in a free and fair election, it committed a crime by providing 'expert advice' – a form of 'material support' to a designated terrorist organisation.[3]

In their joint chapter, Jim Weinstein and Ashutosh Bhagwat contend that *Holder* v. *Humanitarian Law Project* mistakenly applied a relaxed degree of scrutiny to the provisions of the material support statute, consequently threatening a return to the diminished levels of protection for political speech witnessed during the trilogy of Espionage Act cases decided in 1919. These decisions are noted for the broad deference shown to the factual assertions of the political branches in the areas of national security and foreign relations. As the authors remark, if in some current or future conflict, the administration is able to point to the dispiriting effect of anti-war campaigners upon serving military personnel (backed by generalized Congressional findings), this would be sufficient, according the majority in *Holder* v. *Humanitarian Law Project*, to deny constitutional protection to the political expression of the campaigners.

The joint chapter by Jim Weinstein and Ashutosh Bhagwat also identifies an important but neglected – as in *Holder* – aspect of the bundle of constraints that are typically located within counter-terrorism laws – i.e. constraints that target associational activities. Ashutosh Bhagwat's sole-authored chapter reviews the response of the U.S. First Amendment and Articles 10 and 11 of the ECHR to challenges to laws restricting freedom of association – on both sides of the Atlantic. One of the themes of his contribution is the absence of judicial coherence when considering constitutional challenges to such laws. Take for example the difficult issues raised by executive designation of 'terrorist' organizations, suffused as they are by an interweaving set of domestic and international political concerns and objectives. Designation allows the executive to take a series of punitive measures against individuals and groups, such as the blocking of assets held within its jurisdiction. As Bhagwat shows, the lower federal courts in the US have regularly rejected First Amendment challenges by donors and donees, deeming that the giving of monies is 'conduct' that facilitates terrorism as opposed to an activity directly linked to the functioning of an association. The denial of a close connection between the act of funding and subsequent activity by the funded association is difficult to sustain. Bhagwat suggests that the reasoning of the federal courts would have carried more conviction if they had acknowledged the linkage between funding and associational activity, but denied First Amendment protection on the basis that the association in question used violence to advance its objectives. The similar failure of the ECHR to specify when, precisely, an individual/group forfeits their Article 11 freedoms on account of having associated with a violent group likewise leaves the contours of this politically important freedom uncertain. The effect, as Bhagwat claims, must surely be to chill otherwise constitutionally protected activity.

The constitutional protections afforded to freedom of expression in the US, the UK, and New Zealand occur through formal legal instruments, either in the form of national human rights statute (UK and NZ) or an express provision of the Constitution (US). In Australia, however, freedom of expression lacks an explicit status – in the case of the freedom of political communication, being left to constitutional implication and techniques of statutory interpretation. In their joint chapter, Keiran Hardy and George Williams analyse an array of counter terrorism laws and policy programmes that impinge on political expression that might well have encountered stiffer constitutional resistance in other polities. Newly created offences, such as 'advocating terrorism' are argued to constitute an extension of criminal liability beyond the law of incitement, while speech that 'urges another' to overthrow the Constitution or the government or use force/violence against a group on grounds of race, religion, nationality, ethnic origin or political opinion is separately made an offence. Other curbs on expression include the absence of a public interest defence for those who disclose information relating to special intelligence operations. New laws requiring communications service providers to retain information regarding the date, time, and location of a phone call, SMS or email could be used to compromise the confidentiality of journalists' sources. These laws might be thought to target speech before it occurs rather than, as happens under the advocacy and urging provisions, already communicated expression. Given the frequency of counter terrorism legislation in recent years, Hardy and Williams devote their attention to the important matter of the adequacy of parliamentary scrutiny. They point to the troubling practice where admittedly problematic legislative provisions are ushered onto the statute book on the basis of a government concession to review these laws once in operation.

Across the Tasman Sea, New Zealand, whilst obviously not wholly immune from acts and threats of politically/religiously inspired violence, is officially considered to be at a much lower risk of a terrorist incident. The chapter by Andrew Geddis and Elana Geddis sets out to contextualize and explain the basis of this risk assessment. Nonetheless some limited legal changes to the country's terrorism laws did occur in the wake of '9/11'. This is explained in part by New Zealand's ready adoption of international norms for combatting terrorism and a desire to keep the population safe from remote risks of terrorist actions. These legal reforms have been implemented against the backdrop of the New Zealand Bill of Rights, which guarantees core civil and political freedoms. While 'unentrenched', and thus capable being overridden by inconsistent legislation (implied repeal), NZ courts are required to give 'rights-friendly' readings of legislation where they are able to do so. One feature of New Zealand's response to the threat of terrorist activity is its partial reliance upon ordinary criminal laws such as film censorship provisions in the case of terrorist propaganda. Where, conversely, special counter terrorism laws have been enacted, such as the Terrorism Suppression Act 2002, which permits the designation of individuals and groups as terrorist entities and limits a range of conduct (including freedom of expression), their efficacy has been questioned. This chapter also provides a useful analysis of the increasing prevalence of closed court procedures in challenges to the withdrawal of passports where a person is suspected of wanting to join terrorists groups outside of New Zealand. Open justice and fair trial concerns have been raised in relation to these procedures. Finally, the protection of intelligence gathering from New Zealand's international partners (the 'Five Eyes') is considered. The Intelligence and Security Act 2017 purports to protect dissent and freedom of expression by asserting that the fact alone of dissent cannot justify the taking of action against an individual or group. However the moment when dissent crosses over into 'violent extremism' or a threat to the operation of the New Zealand government or its sovereignty, thereby authorising security agencies to take covert action, has yet to be established.

## Notes

1 As reported in the *Guardian* www.theguardian.com/commentisfree/2017/jun/05/theresa-may-trusted-counter-terrorism-policy

2 See for example J Bennetto 'Anti-cartoon protestor convicted of inciting racial hatred' the *Independent* (2006) November 10 at www.independent.co.uk/news/uk/crime/anti-cartoon-protester-convicted-of-inciting-racial-hatred-6230199.html

3 D Cole, 'The First Amendment's Burdens: The Place of *Holder* v. *Humanitarian Law Project in First Amendment Doctrine*' (2012) 6 Harv L & Pol'y Rev 147, 149.

# 2 Countering terrorism through limits on inciteful speech

## Principles and problems

*Ian Cram*

> We now want to be able to deal with those who incite terrorism more obliquely, but who nevertheless contribute to the creation of a climate in which impressionable people might believe that terrorism was acceptable.
>
> Rt. Hon. Charles Clarke MP Home Secretary October 26, 2005[1]

> I have been asked on many occasions to speculate on what kinds of phrases might make people fall foul of the provision. The only answer I have felt comfortable giving is where someone says 'Wasn't it a fantastic thing that happened on 7 July?' – knowing that the likely effect is to encourage their audience to engage in acts of terrorism.
>
> Rt. Hon. Hazel Blears MP Minister of State Home Office November 9, 2005[2]

### Introduction

Following the London bus and tube bombings of July 2005, the UK government announced new counter-terrorism legislation which created new criminal offences that allowed the police to deal with: (i) acts preparatory to terrorism; (ii) indirect incitement to commit terrorist acts or disseminate the same in purported alignment with the idea of public provocation to commit an act of terrorism in Council of Europe's Convention on the Prevention of Terrorism,[3] and (iii) the provision or receipt of training in the use of hazardous substances and other terrorist methods.[4] The police were also given powers to hold terrorist suspects for up to three months without charge (a significant increase from the extant 14 day pre-charge detention period).

Prior to the publication of the bill, Prime Minister Blair, in a headline-catching speech made in August 2005, declared that 'the rules of the game are changing.'[5] Mr Blair drew attention to the 'sort of remarks made in recent days' that would be targeted by the new incitement offences. Upon conviction, foreign nationals found to have been 'actively engaging in terrorism' would be deported. The Prime Minister's speech was generally understood to be a reference to website materials published by Islamic militants, including those uploaded by Mohammed Al-Massari, a Saudi dissident then living in London.[6] Until late August 2005, his website broadcast contained footage of the killing of three

Black Watch soldiers in Iraq by a suicide bomber, as well as publishing material that was supportive of Al-Qaeda and Iraqi insurgents. Massari had spoken in the past of Iraqis' entitlement to kill coalition soldiers and other westerners.[7] The website was taken down in late August 2005, at much the same time as Al-Massari fled the UK.[8] The Blair government's response, as set out in the Terrorism Bill, formed part of a broader policy initiative to combat the 'radicalisation' of persons in its Prevent programme. Located within the broader counter terrorism CONTEST strategy,[9] which aims to reduce the risk of exposure to international terrorism, Prevent seeks to tackle the 'radicalisation' of persons by:

> (d)eterring those who facilitate terrorism and those who encourage others to become terrorists – changing the environment in which the extremists and those radicalising others can operate....[10]

Initially developed as non-legally binding policy guidance to relevant agencies and institutions, Prevent has evolved to impose statutory duties on public bodies[11] such as prisons, universities, and schools,[12] which are now mandated to safeguard against the risk that persons are drawn into terrorism.[13] In the case of universities, the statutory duty includes disallowing or monitoring the expression of visiting speakers on the basis that it could aid in the radicalisation of students.[14] At the same time, universities are required to pay 'particular regard' to the importance of countervailing values such as free speech and academic freedom.[15] The 2017 High Court ruling in *Butt* may have ameliorated some of the speech-hostile elements of the statutory incarnation of Prevent, at least in the context of higher education.[16]

Significantly, however, an extension of Prevent beyond a focus upon supporting terrorism and violent extremism to embrace 'non-violent' extremism occurred during the period of the coalition government (2010–15) and Theresa May's tenure of office as Home Secretary. 'Non-violent' extremism is considered by the Home Office to be responsible for the creation of an environment that helps popularize 'anti-British' views, which can then be exploited by terrorists. As the amended 2011 version of Prevent put it:

> We remain absolutely committed to protecting freedom of speech in this country. But preventing terrorism will mean challenging extremist (and non-violent) ideas that are also part of a terrorist ideology. Prevent will also mean intervening to stop people moving from extremist groups or from extremism into terrorist-related activity.[17]

The government's amended policy now indicates that the Prevent duties imposed on public bodies will exist in relation to the peaceful advocacy of whatever is meant by 'non-violent extremism' or 'anti-British values'.[18] At the time of writing, further statutory initiatives to combat the movement of persons from holding extremist views to terrorist-related activity include new proposed offences in the Counter-Terrorism and Border Security Bill. These will allow for 'more effective earlier interventions' against those expressing support for proscribed organizations and the viewing of materials over the internet, which are likely to be useful to a person preparing an act of terrorism. This will be picked up again towards the conclusion of this chapter.

### *Issues of principle*

These developments in the UK raise fundamental issues of principle for all liberal democracies about the legitimacy of restrictions on expressive activity. Can speech restrictions be justifiably imposed on the expression of illiberal viewpoints, such as using force, if necessary, to impose the adoption of the Caliphate or demanding pledges of loyalty to radical Islamic clerics or from an opposing political perspective, the depicting of Muslims as the 'enemy within' and the pressing for mosque closures and the expulsion of Muslims? If so, on what basis? In this contribution to the collection, I begin by looking at the justifications offered by supporters of restrictions on inciteful expression that, at the very least, advocates anti-democratic, illiberal positions, with an especial focus upon indirect or oblique forms of incitement to acts of terrorism. I try here to set out a strong version for the case of restriction, looking at various rationales advanced to support laws of indirect incitement including: (i) claimed consequential benefits of reduced incidents of terrorist-related violence; and (ii) the need to take a symbolic stance against the enemies of democracy, in part to assuage feelings of understandable outrage among the targeted community. Of course, deeper level arguments about the ordering of rival claims to security/public safety on the one hand and personal liberty on the other are implicated in this account. Critical attention will, accordingly, be devoted to ideas of 'balance' and 'recalibration' as they feature in liberty vs security debates. Here, the apparent rationalism of executive claims to be acting in the interest of enhanced public safety is set against a broader institutional context that examines the rigour (or lack of rigour) in parliamentary and independent oversight of downward adjustments of liberty.

What free speech concerns are engaged by incitement to terrorism laws? As a matter of free speech principle, how might restrictions promulgated in the name of counter terrorism be critiqued? Does, for example, a Millian emphasis upon the search for truth and societal advancement condemn incitement laws criminalizing 'pure' advocacy?[19] One especially pressing question here is whether restrictions threaten the self-governing capacities of citizens. A final section of analysis looks at the constitutional treatment of such speech-limiting laws in the constitutions of both the US and the UK. What has been the contribution of the courts in settling questions of the constitutional compatibility of incitement laws? What does this tell us about judicial treatments of underlying security/liberty arguments? Do democracies with entrenched constitutional protections for their rights manage to resist majoritarian encroachments on controversial speech?

Developments in the legal sphere do not occur in a vacuum however. The political and social dynamics that are the initial drivers of law and policy must also be acknowledged. In the immediate aftermath of a terrorist attack, symbolic strikes by legislatures against the websites and other publications of the enemies of democracy may be initially reassuring. After all, why should those who are committed to the destruction of freedoms enjoyed by individuals in democratic states be able to invoke the right to freedom of expression, a core democratic freedom?[20] At the same time, can we be sure that incitement laws are untainted by majoritarian impulses to suppress and/or eradicate the advocacy of alternative ways of living? The US First Amendment scholar, Thomas Emerson, perceptively understood how in a society composed of plural world views, laws restricting expressive freedom had to be applied 'by one group of human beings to another'.[21] Ultimately, we may concur with Emerson on the value of a *speech vs action* distinction in such cases, and that the coercive force of the criminal law ought to be confined to the *actions* of terrorists in preparing, plotting, and executing terrorist atrocities. In any event, the longevity of speech-restricting statutes in this context ought to figure in any critical analysis of democratic states' practices. In the case of the UK's Incitement to Mutiny Act 1797, which was passed to deal with the problem of mutinous sailors considered to be sympathetic to the ideals of revolutionary France,[22] parliament only got round to repealing the legislation in 1998.[23] In the meantime, an amended version of the 1797 Act was used against striking workers and hunger marchers in the 1930s and pacifists protesting against the British military presence in Northern Ireland in the 1970s.[24] Fast forward to the digital era, a new tack in official policy has seen the enjoining of privately-owned digital intermediaries, such as *Twitter* and *Facebook*, to close down forms of 'extreme' speech that is adjudged to be sympathetic to terrorism. Beyond the confines of this chapter, the 'contracting out' of speech regulation nonetheless throws up difficult questions about the accountability of for-profit privately run corporate bodies, whose overriding loyalties are to shareholders and market share growth rather that assisting citizens to play their democratic role in controlling powerful elites.[25]

## The case for restricting inciteful expression in counter terrorism

Alexander sets out a succinct basis for limiting by law speech that encourages members of the audience to commit crimes, including crimes of violence intended to advance a political and/or religious goal.[26] His account starts from the premise that persons generally act for a reason. Many of these reasons may be traced to ideas and thoughts that have been communicated to them by other persons. Within the overall set of communicated ideas are those that set out to persuade the recipient to commit a crime. Included within the overall class of crime-inducing communications are those that concern crimes of violence whose commission will advance, or are believed to advance, an ideological objective. The recipient may not act upon the persuasion immediately, nonetheless laws that strike at the frequency of communications encouraging such crimes may help reduce the total number of terrorist incidents. So here, in empirical terms, the predicted outcome for this class of speech restrictions is fewer incidents of terrorist-related violence. Punishing the speaker may be justified by reference to both reasons of (i) retribution (imposing a penalty that is proportionate to the harm of increased risk of terrorist incident caused by the wrongful speech)[27] and (ii) deterrence (to make it less likely that other speakers will encourage crimes of political violence in the future).

Other writers have pointed to oblique harms caused to the social order and the rule of law by the failure to outlaw indirectly inciteful speech in the terrorism context. These harms occur regardless of whether an actual terrorist event inspired by the words transpires. Kremnitzer and Ghanayim, for example, cite, inter alia, the encouragement that is given to those who would use violence to resolve their political grievances and its deleterious effects upon social order and respect for the rule of law.[28] This concern is present in the UK government's 2005 justification for a new offence of indirect encouragement of terrorism. As the quote from the then Home Secretary, the Rt. Hon. Charles Clarke MP, cited at the beginning of this chapter indicates, indirect encouragement effectively signals in the eyes of some perhaps impressionable persons that violence for political ends is acceptable. Public confidence in democratic values may thus be diminished to the extent that others are free to advocate the desirability of radical, violent change. The toleration of inciteful expression is also likely to induce anxiety among the public and thus lead them to live suboptimal, fear-filled lives. States which fail to clamp down on these problematic speech forms neglect their duties towards these citizens by denying them the right to live in peace, secure from harms of political violence threatened by others. The specific value of criminal law sanctions for indirect encouragement is that it prohibits the sort of communication where, in the context in which the communication is made, members of the audience understand quite clearly what they are being urged to do, even though the speaker stops short of urging the action(s) in question. To take a frequently cited example, in Shakespeare's *Julius Caesar*, Marc Antony's funeral oration is understood (and intended by the speaker to be so understood) as much more than a lament for Caesar's death. It is received as a particularly dramatic and partially ironic[29] form of indirect encouragement to the Roman citizens to take up the fight against Caesar's assassins.[30] What makes the speaker criminally culpable, on this view, is the fact that, in the particular circumstances where the words are spoken, it can be forseen that some members of the audience will be moved to commit a criminal offence. English law however makes the inciter liable regardless of whether a member of the audience does so act, treating the incitement as a wrong in itself. The strictness of English law in this regard is problematic in the context of political expression, failing as it does to recognize the (potentially) considerable free expression interests of speakers and listeners that are at stake in such cases.

A further, though less obviously satisfactory, justification for restrictions on indirect encouragement is located in the idea that some expressions may amount to an affront to democracy and liberal democratic values. As was noted earlier in relation to PM Blair's reaction to the websites of Al Massari after the July 2005 bus and tube bombings, politicians may urge a symbolic strike against anti-democratic speakers in the aftermath of a terrorist atrocity in which citizens have been killed and injured or even in situations where fears of such an attack in the future have become heightened. A symbolic strike against those who limit themselves to expressive support is considered to be needed in order to assuage feelings of outrage that are reverberating around the targeted community.[31] Consider California's 1930s criminal ban on the display of a red flag in the United States as 'a sign, symbol or emblem of opposition to organized government.'[32] In *Stromberg* v. *California*, a 7–2 majority struck down the California law on the basis that its apparent width and vagueness might criminalize constitutionally protected activities such as that of peaceful opposition to government.[33] Rather than tackle the anarchists who had acted (or were about to act) upon such beliefs via prosecutions for the breach of pre-existing criminal laws, the California Legislature had unlawfully targeted expression of the sort that the majority of its citizens doubtless considered wholly outrageous advocacy. Two decades on in the Cold War era, US lawmakers were determined to strike a signal blow against persons who would not forswear anti-social/anti-democratic viewpoints, irrespective of the perceived harmful consequences of such viewpoints.[34]

The foregoing discussion has sought to isolate some different strands from arguments for speech restrictions in counter terrorism policy. To evaluate them fully, we need to set out some deeper level arguments about the ordering of state and personal security interests on the one hand and claims to personal liberty on the other. In the next section of materials, I look first at some conceptual arguments for security and liberty before considering specific and pragmatic arguments for the recalibration of liberty in favour of enhanced security and the adequacy of constitutional arrangements for the oversight of security agencies.

## Conceptual arguments from security and liberty

With the exception of the 'affront to democracy' case for restricting inciteful expression, the arguments detailed in the previous section rest upon a common underlying rationale, namely the need to safeguard the security of the state, its institutions, and citizens. This justification can be located in two distinct philosophical traditions. The first takes an essentially Hobbesian approach to the legitimacy of political authority wherein the preservation of security and order is paramount. As has been observed elsewhere,[35] the social contract foundations of this line of argument start with the claim that, in the absence of political authority, humans are naturally prone to acts of violence against each other to acquire others' land or personal possessions, resulting in a state of lawlessness and anarchy. In return for being given the sovereign's protection from an immediate and violent death, citizens agree among themselves to transfer all other rights (and thus confer absolute authority) upon the sovereign. With Hobbes, order is valued intrinsically, i.e. it is a good in itself, to be valued over and above claims to individual liberty. The sovereign power remains legitimate for as long as it is able to guarantee security and the preservation of life from internal and external threats. The sovereign must, therefore, be given untrammelled powers to maintain order. No guarantee of liberty of expression can be enforced as against the sovereign. Only where the sovereign fails to secure the peace and order is the bond between the citizen and the state broken, thereby relieving the citizen from obeying its demands.

Even at times of serious threats to security and public safety, few if any among the current proponents of reduced personal liberty have argued in Hobbesian terms for an absolute priority to security interests and, with it, unlimited executive powers to interfere with personal freedoms to safeguard life. Working within a liberal framework of constitutional rights protected by legislatures and courts, most advocates of enhanced security measures accept the core Lockean idea of a liberal society where all laws (including laws intended to protect the state and personal security) must have as their objective the preservation of liberty. To safeguard the liberal democratic way of life, an incremental move away from more extensive to less extensive personal liberty is urged. What is required is a recalibration of the balance between security and liberty in favour of the former. The argument for recalibration is put thus: Before the last attack we thought we were safe, but the latest atrocity points to a need to revisit criminal law provisions regarding police/security service powers and/or add to the list of existing offences. The proposed diminishment of specific non-absolute rights (e.g. terrorist suspects' rights under questioning, rights to privacy and expression among the population at large) can be defended on the basis that these curtailments are needed to maximize the continued enjoyment of the overall set of liberties enjoyed by citizens in democratic states.

In support, it is noted that leading liberal rights theorists such as Dworkin and Rawls do not claim in their respective accounts that individual rights may *never* be overridden by policy goals such as state security. It is rather that rights cannot be sacrificed on the basis simply of *any* incremental gain to the common good. In Dworkin, for example, this is famously expressed in the idea as 'rights as trumps'. To be meaningful, a right must possess a threshold level which immunizes it against certain cost/benefit type appeals to competing policy/welfare concerns. The deontological 'bite' of a particular rights claim will determine the nature of the threshold that has to be overcome. For example, the more vital a right is to the attainment of liberal values such as personal fulfilment and informed citizen participation in democratic structures, the more compelling the policy arguments for restriction of the right would have to be. Nonetheless if, as Tesón maintains, we treat the goal of preserving the total system of liberties as a valid policy objective, then non-absolute rights may conceivably be set aside in certain circumstances.[36] In Tesón's view this would require the state to show that the rights reduction were both necessary to preserve the total system of liberties and a proportionate means of doing so – a formulation that human rights courts are experienced in interpreting.

A number of aspects of this structured recalibration exercise are worthy of closer examination, specifically as they relate to curtailments of expressive freedom.[37] There is at the outset the formal notion that the rights-reduction is applied under the rule of law *equally* in respect of each citizen. In practice, the lived experience of rights-reductions is often felt unevenly and more keenly in certain sections of society than others. In the immediate aftermath of 9/11, for example, the extension of powers of indefinite detention in Part IV of the Blair government's Anti-terrorism, Crime and Security Act 2001 was confined to foreign terror suspects. UK nationals who were terror suspects were not subject to these draconian provisions. In the face of parliamentary acquiescence, it required judicial intervention by the House of Lords in the *Belmarsh* ruling to condemn the discriminatory and irrational basis of the legislation.[38] More recently, a body of evidence has emerged to support claims that the operationalization of the Prevent policy in Muslim communities is regarded as alienating.[39] Conversely, most non-Muslims experience little or no tangible curtailment of our freedoms under Prevent. Alongside a recalibrated security vs liberty balance (and unacknowledged by the Home Office), there is also a 'most vs few' citizens dimension to the trade-off. In relation to the glorification and indirect incitement provisions of UK domestic law, it can be seen that the main impact of these laws is most keenly felt by the critics of UK foreign/military policy in the Middle East. At the same time, supporters of the UK's armed intervention and regime change policies remain free to celebrate the implementation of successive governments' efforts.

A second noteworthy feature of the recalibration argument is the seeming rational pragmatism of its proponents. Arguments for greater security measures tend to be presented in terms of a hard-headed, objective calculation about nuanced, downward adjustments to personal liberty that have become vital in the fight against the enemies of the state.[40] What is curious however in this presentation is the failure to come clean on how precisely the rights reduction will in practical terms make us safer from our violent enemies. How does the additional security measure being proposed actually make us safer? In a liberal democracy, where security serves the end goal of preserving a free society, the burden falls upon those proposing such measures to make good their claims of enhanced protection. In truth, executive arguments regularly rely on vague and speculative claims that, when pared back, rely upon the idea of public trust in the expert assessment of security agencies and the politicians who formulate policy in the light of such agencies' work.[41] The damning assessment of the Chilcot Inquiry into the Iraq War shows that senior UK politicians and members of the UK intelligence community have not always been worthy of such trust in the past. PM Blair was found to have made claims to parliament about Iraq's nuclear weapon programme that were simply not borne out by the evidence he was supplied with by the security agencies, nor did these agencies review properly the flawed intelligence claiming the existence of weapons of mass destruction.[42] Public trust has been further eroded by suggestions that UK security agencies were complicit in the rendering and alleged torturing of terror suspects by foreign powers in the post 9/11 era.[43]

To compound matters, parliamentary oversight of the executive in these matters has been found wanting. In the view of the highly respected Joint Committee on Human Rights, the Intelligence and Security Committee has lacked expert and independent staff and is considered not to have operated in a transparent way with regard to appointment and reporting procedures.[44] To this day, it is the Prime Minister who vets parliamentarians nominated by their colleagues to serve on the Committee. The importance of critical, informed, and independent parliamentary oversight is made all the more vital on account of the natural and self-interested tendency that security agencies have in talking up the threats to national security. The greater the threat, so it is said the greater the nation's need for well-resourced bodies tasked with keeping us safe.

Some of the general weaknesses in enhanced security claims identified above carry through into more particularized arguments for curtailing freedom of expression. Consider, for example the support given in 2005 by Lord Carlile the Independent Reviewer of Terrorism Legislation for a new offence of indirect encouragement of terrorism:

> In my view this proposal in its revised form is a proportionate response to the real and present danger of young radically minded people being persuaded towards terrorism by apparently authoritative tracts wrapped in a religious or quasi-religious context. The balance between the greater public good and the limitation on the freedom to publish is no more offended by this proposal than it would be by, say, an instruction manual for credit card fraud were such to be published.[45]

These remarks fail entirely to engage with the value or deontological bite of the free speech interests at stake. Instead, Lord Carlile invokes somewhat formulaically the balance metaphor and rounds things off with a wholly unconvincing analogy with speech-enabling credit card fraud. The terse and uncritical analysis from the *independent* reviewer of terrorism legislation is disappointing, especially as it occurred at a time when the executive was seeking a serious erosion of freedom of political communication. Lord Carlile was apparently untroubled by the extremely broad definition of 'terrorism' in UK law, which extends to any threats of 'action' against totalitarian, rights-violating regimes.[46] It is this definition that serves as the foundation for a vast panoply of liberty-reducing measures in counter-terrorism law. Neither did he confront the lesson of experience. As Emerson had earlier remarked, the repression of unorthodox opinion is 'difficult to keep in hand'.[47] In the next section of materials, an effort is made to put right this omission. The nature and force of core free speech arguments in the context of direct and indirect forms of encouragement to engage in terrorist activity are explored in some detail.

## Free speech interests engaged by incitement to terrorism laws

Speech urging citizens to break the law made by freely elected representatives would seem instinctively to be undeserving of constitutional protection.[48] After all, democracies offer up the possibility of campaigning for legal reforms that can culminate in the repeal of the law in question. A critic of indirect incitement to terrorism laws might thus be advised to focus his or her energies on making the case for repeal of Part 1 of the Terrorism Act 2006. This response is unsatisfactory for a number of reasons. First, as Jaconelli observes, it is possible that even the mere campaigning for legal reform might be interpreted as conveying to listeners an implicit (and thus criminally liable) normative claim that the current law ought not to be complied with.[49] Second, the practical constraints that attend campaigns for law reform mean that, whether successful or not, there is usually a considerable time lag before any proposals for law reform come to be debated in parliament.[50] In the meantime, critics of UK foreign policy are expected to remain silent on the topic.

More fundamentally however, the outlawing of all speech that advocates any form of civil disobedience ignores the fact that particular instances of advocacy may be deserving of *some* degree of constitutional protection. Consider this (most unpromising) example of direct encouragement published online on social media platforms as a public tweet or as a public post:

> Kill the racist mayor of Barset City Council

Arguments may be made under each of the principled justifications for freedom of expression to include this statement as treatable *ab initio* within the ambit of constitutionally protected speech, even if, upon closer analysis, countervailing arguments for suppression in particular scenarios are ultimately judged to be stronger. Take first, Mill's argument from truth in *On Liberty* which rules out restrictions on both: (i) possibly true claims; and (ii) definitely false claims, unless the speech in fact constitutes an 'action' where the circumstances in which the speech occurs makes violence a likely outcome of the speaker's words.[51]

At the outset the argument from truth looks to be an unpromising basis upon which to found constitutional protection. What sort of truth claims are involved when someone urges others to break the law? If I tell followers on my open Facebook group, 'You should kill Kevin' there is no obvious truth claim here. If, by contrast, I tell them 'You should kill Kevin, the racist Mayor' it is clear that my urging contains an assertion about the actual conduct of the mayor that may or may not be grounded in fact.[52] Indeed two disputable truth claims are being made. First, that Kevin has been acting in a racially discriminatory way and, second, that it would be better for the city and its inhabitants if Kevin was removed from office by force and a non-racist be elected/appointed as his successor. My post about Kevin could well lead to a debate about the moral justifications for political assassination. Those wishing to condemn my position would doubtless respond and a broader debate around the idea of justified killing would occur. Moreover, if we could be sure that no one was actually inclined on the basis of my post to kill or attempt to kill Kevin,[53] the greater understanding of the ethics surrounding political assassination would seem to offer a fairly sound basis for affording some degree of constitutional protection for my inciteful remark.[54] In a variation of the original scenario, what if my original post had been more oblique and rhetorical asking, 'will no-one among us rid the city of its racist politics?'[55] without expressly mentioning Kevin or the Mayor. Ought this ambivalent statement command even greater constitutional protection than more direct forms of encouragement? Here, without contextual information that points in a particular direction, the incitement cannot be given an exclusively murderous reading. That is, it is capable of being read in different ways by different readers. Is the fact that at least one reader understands the post to be an incitement to murder Kevin sufficient to ground the criminal liability of the speaker, notwithstanding the ensuing debate about racism in city politics and how best to tackle it (and assuming, *ex post facto,* that no unlawful action against Kevin occurs). In the absence of direct and immediate physical harm to Kevin, Millian arguments for freedom of expression would probably come to my aid on this occasion, even if this entailed damage to intra-community relations.

The interest that each member of my Facebook group has as a recipient of my speech would separately ground an initial claim to constitutional protection. As a claim based on the intrinsic value to each person, it need not be shown that publication of my words works to the benefit of the community or general welfare. Rather, it is the fact that each person in the development of their own personality and intellectual maturation has the right to form and express his/her own beliefs and to hear others' opinions as a basis for reflection upon their own beliefs.[56] Suppressing the inciteful speaker denies the rest of us an opportunity to reflect on the speaker's views and come to a fuller understanding of why political violence is advocated. The opposing case for interfering with audience interests rests on at least two possible objections. First, that an autonomous citizen might choose to forgo a degree of autonomy since members of the audience are, as Amdur suggests in the case of many incitements of political violence, the potential victims of that speech.[57] Alternatively it might be thought that members of the audience are not to be trusted to evaluate claims made by the proponents of political violence. Some, perhaps the more gullible among the audience, might be tempted to engage in terrorist acts in the future.[58] This latter objection looks like a version of the UK government's arguments in 2005 for the kind of suppression detailed at the beginning of this chapter.

Amdur's argument of a voluntary waiver of listener autonomy does not, of course, deal with the person who refuses to waive their autonomy interest and insists upon hearing the inciter's message. Moreover, the condition of waiver – that a listener might be a potential victim of a subsequent terrorist act at some point in the future – is such a loosely constructed criterion for permitting interference with political expression as to offer no protection to listener autonomy at all.[59] The alternative argument, premised for its part upon the possible reaction of a gullible member of the audience, would curtail all sorts of literature, art, cinema, and theatre where an act of violence proposed by one of the characters or otherwise is depicted. From the paintings of Caravaggio to the films of Stanley Kubrick[60] and Quentin Tarantino, much in the way of human creativity would be lost to us. More generally, to formulate the boundaries of freedom of expression for adults by reference to the *possible* reactions of the most sensitive or uncritical among us is to apply a standard that is not replicated elsewhere in law on account of its disproportionate impact on the law-abiding majority.[61] It is when the 'gullible' audience member begins actively to prepare an act of terrorism that the law properly steps in. The foregoing distinction between speech and preparation for acts of terrorism offers robust protection for valuable anti-government expression and is explored further below.

Arguments for listener autonomy of the sort considered above do not place particular weight on the value of political expression to self-fulfilment. Listener interests in receiving information and opinions about the merits of rival brands of washing powder, toothpaste, and motor vehicles all have an equal claim to be protected alongside political advocacy. As we readily permit governmental regulation of misleading advertising claims because audience members are simply unable to assess whether the veracity of specific statements about a product might be true, might not similar patrician arguments be made for the regulation of political expression in general, and incitements to political violence in particular? If so, listener autonomy would not seem to offer a workable basis for protecting much inciteful expression. What then of alternative arguments that declare freedom of expression to be central to the proper functioning of a democratic polity?

If, as is commonly maintained, representative democracy rests upon the idea of popular sovereignty, then freedom of expression and open discussion of societal questions are vital to the securing of meaningful consent to laws. There is a rich body of scholarship in this tradition, which defends broad rights to political expression that most certainly includes public ideological expression of an inciteful kind.[62] Citing the Declaration of Independence, the US First Amendment scholar, Thomas Emerson, maintains that once we accept that governmental authority derives in that founding document's words 'from the consent of the governed', the people 'must, in order to exercise their right of consent, have full freedom of expression both in forming individual judgments and in forming the common judgment'.[63] Eric Heinze, in *Hate Speech and Democratic Citizenship*, makes a broader claim – spanning across both those jurisdictions with formally enacted and entrenched 'Bills of Rights' and those where the extent of personal freedom is determined by the latest laws emanating from the legislature – where democracy is longstanding, stable, and prosperous. In such societies, he argues for the citizens' prerogative of participation in public discourse without fear of being closed down by the state on the basis of viewpoint discrimination. Citizen participation in the democratic life of their communities is what makes the polity truly democratic. Freedom of expression is thus both an individual right and 'an essential attribute of democratic citizenship'.[64] In examining a specific act of indirectly inciteful speech,[65] Heinze concludes that what prompts restriction is the 'ugliness' of the expression and its 'disfiguring' effect on society.[66] He rightly perceives that, in the absence of proof of actual or attempted material harms traceable to the expressive content, the speaker is being penalized (and likely imprisoned) by the state for an instance of discourteous, uncouth speech. The coarsening of public expression by marginal groups and dissenting individuals must be met with the full force of the criminal law to satisfy the majority's sense of disgust, and to dissuade other like-minded citizens from causing similar affronts in future. Yet, to deploy civility norms in this way is to offer up, at best, a caricature of democratic self-government that excludes the passionate and forceful speaker.[67]

Another theorist, Robert Post, focuses on the question, 'what makes law-making democratically legitimate?' Starting from a definition of democracy as active and mediated self-rule by the citizens, Post argues that, for citizens to experience government as their own government, each 'must have the warranted conviction that they are engaged in the process of governing themselves'.[68] This conviction rests upon the perception that the state is responsive to the values of each citizen and, moreover, that every individual might influence the outcomes of public discourse through their own contributions. The opportunity to participate in public discourse promotes individual identification with the state and its decision-making processes even if the actual outcomes of public discourse are at odds (as they must be from time to time) with our own preferences. To enable this identification with the state, each person must, within the realm of public discourse, be treated equally with other citizens and as an autonomous, self-determining individual. If, to the contrary, the state were to exclude an individual from participating in the speech by which public opinion is formed, those so excluded will experience a loss of 'democratic legitimacy' and feel alienated from the process of self-government.[69]

Before moving on to look at some constitutional standards and distinctions that are applied to inciteful speech, a further principled objection to protecting inciteful expression must be briefly considered. This is the claim that urging a violation of the law breaks a commitment on the part of the speaker to the orderly resolution of disputes. We should be careful not to place undue or conclusive weight on this point. A number of constitutional democracies today trace their origins to the non-peaceful overthrow of governmental authority and, prior to that, emboldened forms of advocacy that urged the overthrow of oppressive regimes.[70] To outlaw calls for the overthrow of the government may, therefore, be seen as lacking fidelity to an important facet of the original constitutional settlement.

## The constitutional reception of advocacy/incitement laws

If, as I have argued, inciteful political expression engages substantial free speech interests that command degrees of constitutional recognition, the manner in which liberal democratic states manage the difficult exercise in line-drawing must now be examined. For the purposes of this section of analysis, and given constraints of word space, attention is concentrated here on contrasting: (i) broad; and (ii) narrow (and more typical) constitutional protections found respectively in two jurisdictions across the speech/security spectrum (US and UK). To defend in methodological terms this choice of comparator regimes, several points may be briefly adduced.[71] First, the outlier US jurisdiction has a rich body of judicial and academic literature from which to draw that reaches well beyond cases and statutes to engage with ideas in political philosophy concerning the relationship between the citizen and the state. Second, the US holds out the most extensive liberty for inciteful and anti-democratic expression among liberal democracies. At the same time, the US could hardly be described as a 'soft touch' on homeland security matters. As Edward Snowden revealed, state security agencies have spied unlawfully on US citizens for many years.[72] Moreover, a heightened emphasis upon security after 9/11 witnessed a considerable increase in formal surveillance powers under the Patriot Act.[73]

Taking Tesón's principled preservation of overall liberty approach, this section asks whether the reduction of expressive freedoms is both necessary to preserve the total system of liberties and a proportionate means of doing so. The latter inquiry allows a focus on the purpose, rationality, and extent of any rights reduction. It will be seen that UK law fails both tests, permitting pre-emptive strikes against implied support for political violence. To begin with, an account of constitutional freedom for inciteful expression under the outlier First Amendment is considered.

## *The road to* Brandenburg *v.* Ohio – *protecting inciteful advocacy*

The First Amendment hasn't always been interpreted to give extensive protection to speech urging others to use force or to otherwise break the law. There was no constitutional challenge to the Sedition Act passed by a Federalist-dominated Congress in 1798 to silence the critics of President Adams until 1964.[74] In the First World War era and the immediate aftermath, the attacks of socialists and pacifists on US involvement in the conflict and the conscription of working men were held to fall outside of constitutional protection. A Supreme Court that included Justice Oliver Wendell Holmes devised and applied a 'clear and present danger' test to uphold disloyalty convictions under espionage legislation in the 1919 trilogy of *Schenck*,[75] *Frohwerk*,[76] and *Debs*.[77] Switching attention away from the actual words used by the speaker,[78] this test focuses on the consequences of the expression at issue by asking whether there is a sufficient degree of likelihood of bad consequences. In the case of Eugene Debs, leader of the US Socialist Party, his offence had been to criticize of the war, the burden it placed on the working class, and to predict the ultimate triumph of socialism.[79] The 'dangerous' consequences of obstructing the recruitment among working men were sufficiently likely as to uphold the speaker's conviction under the espionage laws.

Later prosecutions under the Smith Act 1940, during the Cold War with the Communist Bloc, for the 'knowing or wilful advocacy of the necessity, desirability or propriety of overthrowing or destroying any government in the United States…' showed the Court's supine approach towards both the review of legislative line drawing and the evidence needed to support a conviction in individual cases.[80] The defendants in *Dennis* were convicted for teaching Marxism to others. The convictions were held not to violate the First Amendment since the 'gravity of the evil discounted by its improbability, justifies such invasion of free speech as is necessary to avoid the danger'.[81] This formulation has been understood to mean that speech with a low probability level of actually causing harm may still be restricted constitutionally if the gravity of the danger it poses is sufficiently serious. So, a slight risk that a publication may cause the overthrow of the democratically elected government is sufficient to deny constitutional protection. In the converse case of a high probability of trivial harm, suppression of such speech would presumably not be First Amendment-compliant – as Justices Douglas and Black were later to comment in *Brandenburg* v. *Ohio* when explaining their 'great misgivings' about the application of the clear and present danger test

> First, the threats were often loud, but always puny, and made serious by judges so wedded to the status quo that critical analysis made them nervous. Second, the test was so twisted and perverted in *Dennis* as to make the trial of those teachers of Marxism an all out political trial which was part and parcel of the cold war that has eroded substantial parts of the First Amendment.[82]

They might have added that allowing jury members to make predictions about the consequences of dissenting speech during wartime or other national security crisis was unlikely to yield significant protections for expression.[83] Emerson, for his part, further has doubted the institutional capacity of courts and legal procedures in cases such as *Dennis* to acquire and process the factual information that is needed under the clear and present danger test. An informed baseline of historical, political, economic, psychological, and social facts about the US Communist Party's ability to influence others is clearly needed before pronouncing whether the teaching of a particular doctrine causes a clear and present danger of substantial harm.[84] Such a set of factual inquiries is well beyond the competencies of the courts and legal procedure.

*Brandenburg* v. *Ohio* represents a sea change in judicial attitudes towards inciteful political agitation away from the pure consequentialism of 'clear and present danger' and the deferential stance in *Dennis*. It continues to this day to offer a high threshold of constitutional protection for political advocacy at odds with majoritarian sentiment.[85] State or federal laws that regulate speech urging the use of force or violation of the law will pass First Amendment scrutiny only if the prohibited advocacy is: (i) directed at inciting or producing imminent lawless action; and (ii) is likely to produce such action. The strategic importance of the ruling is, as Weinstein remarks, the breathing space it affords to a range of political dissent.[86] The extent of the protection can be gauged from the fact that in all of scenarios involving a physical meeting of persons, outlined in (a)–(d) below, the speech in question is constitutionally protected:[87]

(a) The speaker uses ambivalent words that stops short of directly inciting the use of force or violation of the law, in respect of which, he/she is unaware that others might hear the words as an encouragement to commit an act of terrorism.

(b) The speaker defends the idea of a theocratic state based on sharia law to an audience, some of whom will, in the next few hours, carry out assaults on persons considered to be non-believers.

(c) The speaker's words in fact immediately inspire others to start planning a terrorist act. However that plan is never carried out.

(d) The speaker intends to produce imminent lawless action and uses highly inflammatory language declaiming to the audience, 'Annihilate all those who slander Islam', but his/her words do not produce any obvious immediate effect upon those who hear the words, nor are they considered likely to do so in the future.

### *The UK position*

By contrast with the position pertaining in the US, UK law as set out in the 2006 Terrorism Act criminalizes the speaker in each of the scenarios (a)–(d) for the following reasons: In (a) this indirect encouragement of others' use of violence for political ends is caught under the 2006 legislation where it is reasonably understood by the audience (though not actually appreciated by the speaker) to amount to an encouragement to commit an act of terrorism. The speaker in (b) is unable to invoke a pure advocacy defence in UK law in the way that he/she would have been able under the *Brandenburg* standard. Again, the speaker's liability hinges upon whether the words spoken would be reasonably understood as amounting to an encouragement to engage in terrorist action. The speaker's liability in (c) does not depend on the incited persons acting at *any point in the future*. It does not even need to be shown that the words had the *effect* of encouraging someone to engage in terrorist activity. All that needs be shown is that was said/published would be likely to be understood as an encouragement to engage in terrorism (that is regardless of whether any addressee was in fact encouraged so to act).[88] The imminence requirement in *Brandenburg* rests on a view about the possible de-escalatory effects of responsive, counter-inciteful expression by the state. Under the First Amendment, incitement is lawful where the inciter does not urge imminent unlawful action. This stance is based on the view that, in cases of an unlawful action that is likely to result sometime after the inciteful speech, the state has an opportunity for (and is able to resource) counter speech to undo/minimize the inciteful effect. Aside from its narrowing of criminal liability for speech, the lawfulness of non-imminent incitement may mean that would-be terrorists will be less guarded and secretive in their communications. This could facilitate focused surveillance of those planning a terrorist atrocity. For (d) no evidence needs to be presented by the prosecution that anyone was actually moved to plan, prepare or commit a terrorist act. That is to say that no actual danger of a terrorist act is needed to be shown by the state before liability is incurred. Here though, the speaker is likely to be charged under other laws such as incitement to religious hatred and/or murder.[89]

Thus analysed, it seems beyond doubt that the provisions of ss.1 and 2 of the Terrorism Act 2006 spectacularly fail the tests of permissible interference with liberty set out by Tesón. UK law is concerned with neither the necessity of the measures in terms of safeguarding the total set of liberties of citizens, nor their commensurability with the actual dangers posed by the prohibited speech. These aspects of domestic counter-terrorism law are pre-emptive, speculative, and disproportionate. They deploy the criminal law to penalize expression long before any evidence linking the expressive act to a subsequent harmful action is shown. At the time of writing, the government is seeking to criminalize yet further instances of pure expression in its Counter-Terrorism and Border Security Bill 2018. The bill explicitly aims to allow for earlier prosecutorial interventions with speech that is 'supportive' of proscribed terrorist organizations and thus considered to be a precursor to terrorist actions. Clause 1 responds to the Court of Appeal ruling in *R* v. *Choudhary and another* on the interpretation of the offence of 'inviting support for a proscribed organisation' in s.12 of the Terrorism Act 2000.[90] In *Choudhary*, the Court of Appeal ruled that the *actus reus* of the offence could consist in the invitation by the speaker of encouragement or moral support.[91] It need not be shown that the speaker invited listeners to provide practical help to the proscribed organization. As for the *mens rea* element, the prosecution need not show that the defendant speaker knew that the organization had been proscribed, merely that he/she knew that he was inviting support for that organization.[92] At the same time, the Court of Appeal was careful to add that 'the (mere) expression of personal beliefs, or an invitation to someone else to share an opinion or belief' did not fall within the s.12 offence.[93] What is being suggested here, perhaps, is that a speaker would not commit a s.12 offence if all that he/she does is express to another moral/intellectual agreement with a list of ideological objectives that corresponds closely (or even possibly exactly) with those of the proscribed organization or invites others to share those ideological positions. If the speaker stops short of referring to the proscribed organization, criminal liability might not be incurred, at least under s.12 of the 2000 Act.[94]

Whatever its actual worth in protecting speakers who are critical of UK foreign policy, the residual degree of protection for freedom of political speech set out in *Choudhary* clearly troubled the government. It moved to close the gap identified there by proposing to make it a new criminal offence to 'express an opinion or belief that is supportive of a proscribed organisation' and to lower the *mens rea* requirement from an intentional invitation to support a proscribed organization in s.12 of the Terrorism Act 2000 to mere recklessness as whether the listener will be encouraged to support a proscribed organization. The Joint Committee on Human Rights has since reported its concern about the 'inherent ambiguity' of Clause 1.[95] It might, for example, catch academic debates in which speakers argue for the de-proscription of a particular group. The Committee concluded by stating that 'there is a very clear risk that it would catch speech that is neither necessary nor proportionate to criminalize....' and, as such, be in breach of Article 10 of the ECHR. *Liberty* was also critical of Clause 1, suggesting that it shifts the law's focus away from 'actual terrorism into the realms of pure speech and opinion'.[96]

## The dynamics of governmental limitations on speech

Mill observed in *On Liberty* that individuals were impelled by powerful forces 'towards the elimination of unorthodox expression....'[97] The disposition towards censorship, shared by rulers and citizens alike, to impose their own views on others was difficult to restrain, being as it was 'energetically supported by some of the best and by some of the worst feelings incident to human nature....'[98] Indeed, even those that we have come to associate with a strong defence of unorthodox opinion have been more amenable to arguments for restriction upon gaining office.[99] In the case of their less principled counterparts, the suppression of unpopular opinion has always been attractive as a means of securing the affection of mainstream voters.

Given human ingenuity and literary creativity via such devices as allegory and metaphor, the official tasked with crafting incitement laws (or laws limiting political expression more broadly) is likely to opt for an over-inclusive rather than an under-inclusive strategy. Far better to fall back on generalized words of limitation that offer prosecutorial flexibility and hence discretionary freedom to the administration to decide which cases of inappropriate expression to clamp down upon. The empirical evidence in the UK and elsewhere bears out this claim of over-inclusivity, including restrictions on the disclosure of purely factual information. Section 2 of the UK's Official Secrets Act 1911, for example, was justly criticized for criminalising a broad swathe of innocuous disclosures of government-held information.[100] It was also used to clamp down on whistleblowing activities by civil servants.[101] The successor legislation contains no public interest for journalists who reveal officially-held information about security/intelligence matters.[102] The provisions on indirect encouragement in the Terrorism Act 2006 fit this pattern, building as they do upon an already expansive definition of 'terrorism' in earlier legislation.[103] In prosecutions under the 2006 Act, the Crown is not required to show that the indirect encouragement caused *any degree of danger* of a terrorist attack whatsoever. Across the Atlantic in the United States, from the Alien and Sedition Act 1798[104] through to the espionage legislation deployed against socialist and pacifist politicians in the First World War[105] and, later in the Cold War era, the Smith Act against communists and socialists,[106] the pattern of overbroad legislation that inhibits minority and unpopular speech is well established. Notwithstanding the Bill of Rights and judicial review of primary legislation asserted in *Marbury* v. *Madison*[107] excessive judicial deference towards executive and legislative judgments has helped sustain disproportionate assaults by the political branches upon minority opinion at times of crisis. The non-interventionist attitude of the US Supreme Court at this time was rightly lamented by one of its members, Associate Justice William Brennan, in an extra-judicial lecture.[108]

Once on the statute books, there is little desire on the part of legislators in subsequent years to initiate the repeal of laws targeting allegedly subversive speech. Linde accurately described the repeal process as a 'quixotic undertaking, thankless and very likely futile'.[109] What possible motivation would a legislator have to seek the repeal of laws that criminalize subversive advocacy. Instead, as Linde perceived in the case of the US, it has fallen to the courts to 'clean out' albeit sporadically the statute book.[110] In majoritarian systems of parliamentary government, by contrast, where a judicial 'clean out' is not on offer, a wholly outmoded statute may remain in force for centuries. What is more concerning, arguably, is that the statute may subsequently be used by the executive against different dangers posed by wholly different groups or individuals whom parliament did not have in mind in its contemplation at the time of the original enactment.[111] The longevity of the UK's Incitement to Mutiny Act 1797 offers a pertinent example that was touched upon earlier in this chapter. Parliament only got round to repealing the legislation in 1998.

## Conclusion

> Suppressing advocates of overthrow inevitably will silence critics who do not advocate overthrow but fear their criticism may be so construed … it is a sobering thought that in sustaining the convictions before us we can hardly escape the restriction on the interchange of ideas.
>
> (Justice Frankfurter, concurrence in *Dennis* v. *US* 341 US 494, 549)

For those looking for algorithmic constructions of bright constitutional lines between protected advocacy of anti-government speech and unprotected incitement, this chapter will have disappointed. The task I set myself here was to understand and then critique the United Kingdom's indirect encouragement of terrorism laws. I have sought to show that Part 1 of the Terrorism Act 2006 impacts adversely on possibly inciteful, anti-government expression. Liability for speech is grounded on the merest possibility that an oblique encouragement to act/threaten to act against governmental authority anywhere in the world might result in that action/threat of action at some point in the future. The 2006 Act thus states a weaker level of protection for anti-government expression than that offered by the supine US Supreme Court in *Dennis*, where at least the *gravity* of the evil connected to the speech had to be deemed sufficiently serious. In contrast, UK law on the indirect encouragement of terrorism fails to require that speech restrictions: (i) preserve the overall system of liberties enjoyed by citizens in the UK; or (ii) constitute a proportionate curtailment of expressive liberty. Instead, the provisions operate pre-emptively to catch expression that is so very far removed from the commission and preparation of acts of political violence. As such, criticism can rightly be levelled at the design of UK laws. The democratic costs may be counted principally in terms of an impoverished political discourse as public ideological communications are brought within the grasp of prosecuting authorities. Whether one chooses to invoke ideas of a loss of democratic legitimacy or, alternatively, an infringement of citizens' prerogative to participate in the shaping and re-shaping of laws and norms by which they consent to be governed, the qualitative narrowing of viewpoint sanctioned by law (aided and abetted by more recent policy initiatives against 'non-violent extremism'), provides much to be concerned about. Properly understood within the recent context of communities' lived experiences of unequally distributed recalibrations of liberty and weaknesses in systems of parliamentary and extra-parliamentary oversight of executive agencies, an informed onlooker would be hard-pressed to adopt a sanguine outlook. The interchange of ideas matters in a functioning democracy, especially those ideas that are troubling to existing power holders. Broadly drafted incitement laws will always threaten the people's authorship of laws. Future law reform in this area that does not appreciate this point will continue to constrain controversial speech forms excessively.

## Notes

1 (2005–6) HC Debs 26 October, col.334.
2 (2005–6) HC Debs 9 November, col. 392.
3 CETS 196 Council of Europe Warsaw 16 May 2005 accessible at https://rm.coe.int/168008371c
4 M Peck, *The Terrorism Bill 2005–06* House of Commons Library Research Paper 05/66.
5 The full speech is available at http://webarchive.nationalarchives.gov.uk/+/www.number10.gov.uk/Page8041
6 Prior to being taken down in 2005, Al-Massari's website contained material that celebrated the deaths of British and US soldiers in Iraq and praised suicide bombers in Iraq.
7 M Phillips, *Londonistan* (New York, Encounter Books, 2006), 6; R Pantucci, '*We Love Death As You Love Life – Britain's Suburban Terrorists*' (London, Hurst Publishers, 2015), 47–8.
8 D Leppard and J Ungoed-Thomas, 'Masari pulls plug on his hate website' *Sunday Times* (2005) 28 August.
9 Besides Prevent, other strands of the CONTEST policy comprise Pursue (gathering intelligence to understand the terrorist threat, detecting and disrupting terrorist networks, working with partners abroad); Protect (improving border security, reducing vulnerability of key sites such as utilities and transport) and Prepare (focusing on the capacity to deal with the consequences of terrorist attacks and the continuous testing and evaluation of preparedness): Countering International Terrorism: The United Kingdom's Strategy (2006) Cm 6888.
10 Ibid., at p. 1.
11 The private sector is not subject to these duties, but it is not clear why the government believes that no risk is posed by firms.
12 The impact of the Prevent strategy in schools is considered in detail by Helen Fenwick and Daniel Fenwick, 'Prevent in Schools after the *Trojan Horse Affair*' in this volume of essays.
13 Part 5 Counter Terrorism and Security Act 2015 (hereafter 'CTSA'). For various critical perspectives of developments in the university context see, inter alia, the chapter by Andrew Neal 'University free speech as a space of exception in Prevent?' in this collection and also I Cram and H Fenwick, 'Protecting free speech and academic freedom in universities' (2018) 81 *MLR* 825. By contrast, S Greer and L Bell, 'Counter-terrorist law in British universities: a review of the "*Prevent*" debate' (2018) *PL* 84 takes a more sanguine line, believing the 2015 legislation to need nothing more than 'fine-tuning'.

14 This chapter does not address the speech restrictive policies of some student bodies in the UK. 'No Platform' and 'safe spaces' have played a part in reducing the range of views to which students are exposed, although the picture across the UK is varied. See further the previous endnote and also the Joint Committee on Human Rights, Freedom of Speech in Universities (4th Report of Session 2017–19) at: https://publications.parliament.uk/pa/jt201719/jtselect/jtrights/589/589.pdf

15 S.31 of CTSA 2015.

16 *Butt* v. *Secretary of State for the Home Department* [2017] EWHC 1930 (Admin). The court stated that expression-restricting aspects of the *Prevent* Guidance might be ignored by universities and the statutory safeguarding duties disregarded where they do not comply with the overriding s.31 duty to pay 'particular regard' to the values of free speech.

17 Prevent Strategy (2011) Cm 8092, para. 3.10.

18 See for criticism, the Parliamentary Joint Committee on Human Rights 2nd Report Counter-Extremism (2016–17) HL Paper 39, HC 105, at para. 108:

> The Government gave us no impression of having a coherent or sufficiently precise definition of either 'non-violent extremism' or 'British values'. There needs to be certainty in the law so that those who are asked to comply with and enforce the law know what behaviour is and is not lawful.

19 I refer here to laws which criminalize speech without requiring the state to show that the advocacy incited anyone to harm another.

20 See thus former US Attorney General John Ashcroft at www.justice.gov/archive/ag/speeches/2002/100702chiefsofpolicemn1.htm where he stated,

> Today, America confronts a war against liberty like no other that we have ever seen – it is a conflict that endangers not just our soldiers abroad but also imperils our citizens at home; a war against an enemy that lives among us, attempting to turn our freedoms into the means of freedom's destruction.

21 T Emerson, 'Toward a General Theory of the First Amendment' (1963) 72 *Yale L.J.* 877, 887.

22 See further, M Head, *Crimes Against the State: From Treason to Terrorism* (Oxford, Routledge, 2016), 108–15; K Ewing and C Gearty, *The Struggle for Civil Liberties – Political Freedom and the Rule of Law in Britain 1914–1945* (Oxford, OUP, 2000), 237 *et seq.*

23 Statute Law (Repeals) Act 1998, s.1(1) and Sch.1 Part 1.

24 M Head, *Crimes Against the State: From Treason to Terrorism* (London, Routledge, 2011), 118.

25 See *Citizen Journalists: Newer media, republican moments and the constitution* (Gloucester, Edward Elgar, 2016).

26 L Alexander, 'Incitement and Freedom of Speech' in *Freedom of Speech and Incitement against Democracy*, eds. D Kretzmer and F Kershman Hazan (The Hague, Martinus Nijhoff, 2000).

27 A separate basis for retributive punishment could be the affront to democratic values, see further below.

28 M Kremnitzer and K Ghanayim, 'Incitement not Sedition' in *Freedom of Speech and Incitement against Democracy* at n. 26 above, at 147, 164.

29 Antony makes much of the honourable status of the conspirators to suggest, if only initially at least, that the 'ambitious' Caesar's death is justified.

30 In producing the draped body of Caesar, Marc Antony tells the people, 'Look, in this place ran Cassius' dagger through. See what a rent the envious Casca made. Through this the well-belovèd Brutus stabbed.' Act 3 Scene 2.

31 H Linde, '"Clear and Present Danger" Reexamined: Dissonance in the *Brandenburg* Concerto' (1970) 22 *Stan. L. Rev.* 1163, at 1179–80. The 'symbolic' nature of the

legislation may be evidenced subsequently by its relative disregard by prosecuting authorities in favour of other preferred offences, a feature perhaps of the UK's glorification and indirect encouragement of terrorism laws.

32 California Penal Code s.403(a).

33 283 US 359 (1931).

34 See n. 26 ibid.

35 See thus F Tesón, 'Liberal Security', in *Human Rights and the 'War on Terror'*, ed. R Ashby Wilson (Cambridge, CUP, 2005).

36 Ibid.

37 For general discussion see J Waldron, 'Security and Liberty: the Image of Balance.' *Journal of Political Philosophy* 11, no. 2 (May 2003): 191.

38 *A* v. *Secretary of State for the Home Department* [2004] UKHL 56.

39 See, inter alia, I Awan, 'I am a Muslim Not an Extremist': How the Prevent Strategy Has Created A Suspect Community. Politics and Policy 40, no. 6 (2012): 1158; P Thomas, 'Between Two Stools? The Government's Preventing Violent Extremism Agenda'. The *Political Quarterly* 80, no. 2 (2009): 282–91; B Spasek and L McDonald, 'Terror Crime Prevention: Constructing Muslim Practices and Beliefs as 'Anti-Social' and 'Extreme' through CONTEST 2'. *Social Policy and Society* 9, no. 1 (January 2010): 123–32; see further the written comments of David Anderson QC Independent Reviewer of Terrorism Legislation at: http://data.parliament.uk/written evidence/committeeevidence.svc/evidencedocument/home-affairs-committee/countering-extremism/written/27920.pdf (29 January, 2016.)

40 J Waldron, 'Security and Liberty – the image of balance'. *Journal of Political Philosophy* 11, no. 2 (May 2003): 191–210.

41 Acknowledging damaged levels of public trust in the agencies, the former Independent Reviewer of Terrorism Lord Carlile called in November 2015 for an end to 'the demonisation of the security services'. At the time of making this comment, Lord Carlile was a joint partner with former head of MI6 Sir John Scarlett of *SC Strategy Ltd* a consultancy offering strategic advice on UK security policy and regulation. The firm's clients included among others the Qatari government, see: www.theguardian.com/world/2015/nov/03/former-reviewer-of-anti-terror-laws-co-owns-consultancy-with-ex-mi6-chief

42 *Report of the Iraq Inquiry* Executive Summary (2016) HC 264 at paras. 538–51, 567; see also J Kampfner, *Blair's Wars* (London, Simon & Schuster, 2004), ch. 13.

43 www.theguardian.com/world/2013/feb/05/cia-rendition-countries-covert-support noting the report of the *Open Society Justice Initiative* in 2013 and published at www.opensocietyfoundations.org/reports/globalizing-torture-cia-secret-detention-and-extraordinary-rendition

44 A point made by the Joint Committee on Human Rights *Counter-Terrorism – Seventeenth Report of Session 2013–14* HC 231 (July 2014) at pp. 78–85; see also A Horne and C Walker, *'Parliament and National Security' in A Le Sueur, Parliament: Legislation and Accountability* (Oxford, Hart Publishing, 2016).

45 Lord Carlile, *Proposals by Her Majesty's Government for Changes to the Laws Against Terrorism* (2005) DEP 05/1221 paragraph 23.

46 The breadth of the statutory definition was noted in negative terms by both the Supreme Court in *R* v. *Gul* [2013] UKSC 64 at paras. 26 and 38 (where it was described as 'concerningly wide') and the Court of Appeal in *R* v. *F* [2007] EWCA Crim 243. Carlile's successor as Independent Reviewer of Terrorism Legislation, David Anderson QC, did comment in 2013 that s.1 was 'absurdly' broad, *The Terrorism Acts in 2012* at 4.3. See: https://terrorismlegislationreviewer.independent.gov.uk/wp-content/uploads/2013/07/Report-on-the-Terrorism-Acts-in-2012-FINAL_WEB1.pdf

47 'Toward a General Theory of the First Amendment' (1963) 72 *Yale L.J.* 877, 893.

48 I am not concerned here with private communications between two individuals, such as direct messaging on a service such as a text message on the phone or direct

messaging on *Twitter* where A encourages B to break the law since this lacks the vital element of an intended contribution to public discourse.

49 J Jaconelli, 'Incitement: A Study in Language Crime' *Criminal Law & Philosophy* 12 (2018): 245, 262.

50 In the case of a proposal to allow speech advocating an unpopular/minority viewpoint, it is in any event unlikely that MPs/Lords would rush to support such a proposal.

51 John Stuart Mill, *On Liberty* (London: Penguin, 1985), 119.

52 For a contrasting approach see J Jaconelli, 'Incitement: A Study in Language Crime' see above at n. 49, who claims that 'sentences that express commands lack truth conditions….' I disagree and think it is entirely possible for a sentence expressing a command to contain in ordinary usage an explicit/implicit claim to truth.

53 Consider also the situation where Kevin is murdered on account of his racist conduct as Mayor, but that the murderer would have murdered him even in the absence of my words.

54 As will be known, incitement law in England and Wales does not work in this way. The liability of the inciter in criminal law does not depend upon the carrying out of the crime proposed, see in the terrorism context Terrorism Act 2006, s.1(5)(b); and outside of terrorism cases the Serious Crime Act 2007, s.49(1). For earlier common law on the point see *The King* v. *Higgins* [1801] EngR 444 (1801) 2 East 5, cited by Jaconelli.

55 A variation of Shakespeare's Henry II's 'Will no one rid me of this turbulent priest?'

56 Here, there is also the speaker's interest in self-fulfilment that is advanced by the act of communicating with others. For dismissal of this interest see Barendt n. 58 below at 452.

57 R Amdur, 'Scanlon on Freedom of Expression' (1980) 9 *Philosophy and Public Affairs* 9, no. 3 (1980): 287–300 (and cited in Barendt below).

58 E Barendt, 'Incitement to, and Glorification of, Terrorism', in *Extreme Speech and Democracy* eds. I Hare and J Weinstein (Oxford, OUP, 2009), 445 and 451.

59 It also falsely ascribes moral equivalence between the government's failure to censor speech and the active physical and mental harms caused by the terrorist's violent act.

60 Kubrick's *A Clockwork Orange* and the original novel of the same name by Anthony Burgess were both said by critics to constitute an incitement to violence, see Blake Morrison's *Introduction* to the 1996 Penguin edition of the book.

61 Even UK obscenity laws which allow expression to be restricted on the ground of a tendency to deprave or corrupt is generally understood to refer to a 'significant proportion' of those likely to come across the publication, see *R* v. *Calder and Boyars Ltd* [1969] 1 QB 151. In the US, the criterion is offensiveness and is required to be shown by reference to community standards. For discussion in the US context see B Boyce, 'Obscenity and Community Standards' *Yale Journal of International Law* 33 (2008): 299.

62 Greenawalt, for example, considers public ideological expression to have substantial value and only punishable where it severely threatens the public interest, *Speech, Crime and the Uses of Language* (New York, OUP,1989), 268.

63 T Emerson 'Toward a General Theory of the First Amendment' *Yale Law Journal* 72 (1963): 877 and 883.

64 E Heinze, *Hate Speech and Democratic Citizenship* (Oxford, OUP 2016), 4.

65 'Imagine … (a) local bearded imam, eyes fiery, fist raised, preach(ing) to a crowd of young, agitated followers, with a heavy foreign accent: "Being unarmed makes you despised…. It is much safer to be feared than to be loved!"' from E Heinze, *Hate Speech and Democratic Citizenship* (Oxford, OUP, 2016), 173. Heinze's imagined imam is of course quoting from Machiavelli's *The Prince.*

66 E Heinze ibid. at p. 175 (referring here to J Waldron, *The Harm in Hate Speech* (Boston, Harvard University Press, 2012).

67 The unfortunate emphasis upon civilized, rational, and empathetic interchanges between citizens in contested political matters may be traced to theories of deliberative democracy that enjoyed a resurgence in late 1980s and 1990s scholarship. For a useful critical overview see M Wenham, *Agonistic Democracy* (Cambridge, CUP, 2013), 83–6.

68 'Democracy and Equality' *ANNALS of the American Academy* 603, no. 1 (January 2006): 24, 26.

69 This alienation of the censored, however, could be justified on Post's terms where the consequence of allowing the censored expression is to 'alienate *all other citizens* from participating in public discourse.' (Emphasis added).

70 K Greenawalt, *Speech, Crime and the Uses of Language* (New York, OUP, 1989), 233. Even the so-called 'Glorious Revolution' of 1688 in England, which is treated as the founding moment of the UK's system of parliamentary rule, the victory over the incumbent Stuart dynasty was secured through military success and encouraged by Protestant pamphleteers. For more details see: R Dolan, 'Buttressing a Monarchy: Literary Representations of William III and the Glorious Revolution', Georgia State University 2005, and available electronically at https://scholarworks.gsu.edu/cgi/viewcontent.cgi?referer=www.google.com/&httpsredir=1&article=1000&context=english_diss

71 See thus R Hirschl, *Comparative Matters* (Oxford, OUP, 2014) who is critical of the lack of methodological rigour in comparative constitutional scholarship.

72 G Greenwald, *No Place to Hide – Edward Snowden, the NSA and the Surveillance* State (London and New York, Penguin Books/Random House, 2014).

73 D Cole and X Dempsey, *Terrorism and the Constitution* (New York, First Amendment Foundation, 2006).

74 See the remarks of Justice Brennan in *New York Times* v. *Sullivan* 'Although the Sedition Act was never tested in this Court, the attack upon its validity has carried the day in the court of history – 376 US 254 (1964) at 276'. The other statutes dealing with aliens were variously amended and repealed soon after the Federalists left office.

75 249 US 47 (1919). Robert Cover described the criminalisation of speech merely on account of it posing some future risk of harm as 'an apology for repression.' in 'The Left, the Right and the First Amendment: 1918–28' (1981) 40 *Md. L. Rev*. 349 and 372.

76 249 US 204 (1919).

77 249 US 211 (1919).

78 An emphasis on the actual words used by the speaker rather than a prediction about their consequences was preferred by Justice Learned Hand in *The Masses* 244 F.535 (S.D.N.Y.) (later reversed by the 2nd Circuit Court of Appeals at 246 F.24 (1917) where an alternative reading of the Espionage Act 1917 was preferred, by which a speaker who was opposed to US involvement in the First World War would only fall foul of the Act if he/she urged others directly to break the law. If a speaker merely argued that the policy of recruitment was unjust and immoral then, in Hand's view, no liability should arise under the Act.

79 The shift on Justice Holmes' part towards greater protection for dissenting speech may be traced to *Abrams* v. *US* 250 US 616 (1919). For insights into the evolution of Holmes' thinking on this point and the role played by Justice Learned Hand in correspondence with Holmes, see G Gunther, 'Learned Hand and the Origins of Modern First Amendment Doctrine: Some Fragments of History.' 27 *Stanford Law Review* 27, no. 3 (1976): 719–73. To appreciate just how Justice Learned Hand's approach represented a radically different test of unconstitutional advocacy, see J Weinstein, 'Lessons from *The Masses*' in *Extreme Speech and Democracy* eds. I Hare and J Weinstein (Oxford, OUP, 2009).

80 341 US 494 (1951).

81 This is of course a reformulation of the clear and present danger test.
82 *Brandenburg* v. *Ohio* 395 US 444, 454 (1969).
83 A point made by Gunther at n. 79 at p. 725.
84 'Toward a General Theory of the First Amendment.' *Yale Law Journal* 72, no. 877 (January 1963): 877 and 910.
85 Prior to *Brandenburg*, there had been some stepping back from *Dennis* in cases such as *Yates* v. *US* 354 US 298 (1957) where the advocacy in abstract terms of forcible overthrow of government authority was held to be protected under the First Amendment.
86 J Weinstein, 'Lessons from *The Masses*' in *Extreme Speech and Democracy* eds. I Hare and J Weinstein (Oxford, OUP, 2009), 23 and 53–5.
87 I don't consider here the public communication of the speaker's words virtually via Twitter, Facebook, You Tube or other social media platforms. Where this does occur, it would seemingly be harder (though not impossible) for the state to show that the speaker intended to produce *imminent* unlawful action.
88 A Hunt, 'Criminal prohibitions on direct and indirect encouragement of terrorism' [2007] *Crim. L. Rev.* 441, 453.
89 As occurred in the case of Mizanur Rahman who was convicted of these offences in November 2006 for his part in the London protests against the publication in a Danish newspaper of cartoons linking Islam with terrorism, see 'Cartoon protester found guilty' at: http://news.bbc.co.uk/1/hi/uk/6133516.stm
90 [2016] EWCA Crim 61.
91 Thus overlapping with the ss.1–2 offences of the Terrorism Act 2006.
92 [2016] EWCA Crim 61, para. 48.
93 Ibid., para. 49.
94 The same expression might well be liable under the indirect encouragement provisions of the Terrorism Act 2006.
95 *Legislative Scrutiny: Counter-Terrorism and Security Bill* (9th Report of Session 2017–19) HC 1208; HL Paper 167 (July 2018) para.17. See the full report for separate criticisms of new offences of publication of images of clothing or other articles (clause 2) and obtaining or viewing material over the Internet (clause 3 – amending s.58(1)(a) Terrorism Act 2000.
96 *Liberty's Second Reading Briefing on the Counter-Terrorism and Border Security Bill 2018* (June 2018) para. 11.
97 John Stuart Mill, *On Liberty and Other Essays* (Oxford, OUP, 1998, OUP), 18.
98 Ibid.
99 T Emerson, 'Toward a General Theory of the First Amendment.' *Yale L.J.* 72 (1963), 877 and 888 – citing the example of Thomas Jefferson who complained of the 'licentiousness and lying of the Federalist press and proposed the prosecution of a few prominent critics in order to restore the integrity of the press', see *Letter to Governor McKean* (February 19, 1803) in Vol. 8 *The Writings of Thomas Jefferson* 216, 218.
100 See thus the Franks Report's comment that s.2

> catches all official documents and information. It makes no distinction of kind, and no distinctions of degree. All information which a Crown servant learns in the course of his duty is "official" for the purposes of section 2, whatever its nature, whatever its importance, whatever its original source [...] nothing escapes. The section catches all Crown servants as well as all official information.
>
> Home Office, Departmental Committee on Section 2 of the Official Secrets Act 1911, Cmnd. 5104 (1972) at para 17. Section 2 was repealed by the Official Secrets Act 1989

101 Consider most notoriously the case of Clive Ponting who was prosecuted under s.2 of the 1911 Act for disclosing to an MP information concerning the movements of

the Argentine warship *The General Belgrano* during the Falklands War which was at odds with the official account issued by Mrs Thatcher's government. The jury acquitted Mr Ponting despite an unambiguous instruction from the judge to convict. See further Ponting's own account *The Right to Know* (London, Sphere Books, 1985).

102 Official Secrets Act 1989, s.1. See also *R* v. *Shayler* [2002] UKHL 11.

103 The reassurance that no prosecution for certain offences (including indirect encouragement) can occur without the Attorney General's consent is weakened in cases of politically controversial conduct/expression by the fact that the Attorney General is party politician and MP who sits in Cabinet.

104 See for a magisterial overview of the entire history of speech restrictions in the US G Stone, *Perilous Times: Free Speech in Wartime from the Sedition Act 1798 to the War on Terrorism* (New York, WW Norton & Co, 2004). Emerson states that the Alien and Sedition laws 'became a major weapon in the Federalist effort to wipe out all political opposition and suppress the egalitarian ideas of the French Revolution.' in 'Toward a General Theory of the First Amendment' (1963) 72 *Yale L J* 877, 892.

105 Z Chafee, 'Free Speech in War Time' (1919) 32 *Harv. L Rev.* 932 noting that the publications in question reached much wider audiences after being banned by officials at the Department of Justice and the Post Office. See further E Freund, 'The Debs Case and Freedom of Speech' *New Republic* May 3, 1919 who commented 'As in the case of all political persecution, the cause of the government has gained nothing while the forces of discontent have been strengthened.' at p. 13.

106 See H Linde, '"Clear and Present Danger" Reexamined: Dissonance in the *Brandenburg* Concerto.' *Stan. L. Rev.* 22 (1970): 1163 for criticism of Congress in failing to subject *proposed* laws to rigorous First Amendment scrutiny

107 5 US (1 Cranch) 137 (1803).

108 W Brennan, 'The Quest to Develop a Jurisprudence of Civil Liberties in Times of Security Crises.' *Israeli Yearbook on Human Rights* 11 (1988).

109 H Linde, '"Clear and Present Danger" Reexamined: Dissonance in the *Brandenburg* Concerto' (1970) 22 *Stan. L. Rev.* 22 (1970): 1163 and 1181. Nonetheless for this to happen a legal dispute must first reach the court.

110 Ibid.

111 Obviously this happens in counter-majoritarian systems as well but there at least the statute may be struck down. Thus Ohio's Criminal Syndicalism Act 1919 which was used to convict a speaker at a meeting of the Ku Klux Klan in 1967 was declared unconstitutional by the US Supreme Court in *Brandenburg* v. *Ohio* 395 US 444 (1969).

# 3 Legal vs. non-legal responses to hateful expression

*Nadine Strossen*

We must recognize the limits of legislation to combat hate speech.[1]

– Adama Dieng, United Nations Special Adviser on the Prevention of Genocide (from Senegal)

Legal scholars are dedicated to the theoretical interpretation of hate speech legislation … but do not examine its actual impact.… [I]t is time to verify whether the theoretical expectations stand the test of reality.[2]

– Andrea Scheffler, Friedrich-Ebert-Stiftung (German foundation)

## Punishable and protected 'hate speech' under US law

The laws of many countries, including developed democracies, outlaw so-called hate speech. Along with other commentators, I use quotation marks to underscore that the term has no specific agreed-upon meaning, and has been defined by laws in other countries to encompass a wide range of expressions that convey hateful, discriminatory views on the basis of personal characteristics such as race, religion, gender, and sexual orientation. The U.S. Supreme Court has long held that the free speech guarantee in the U.S. Constitution's First Amendment bars the government from restricting any speech based solely upon its hateful or hated message. The court has stressed that such expression should be countered not by suppression, but rather, by more speech – what is often called 'counter-speech'. Notably, pertinent decisions have been unanimously endorsed by Justices all across the court's ideological spectrum.

The Justices' consensus in these hate speech cases flows from the 'viewpoint neutrality' principle, which the court has hailed as the 'bedrock' principle underlying the freedom of speech guarantee: i.e. that the government may never regulate speech solely due to the disfavoured, distressing or generally feared nature of its viewpoint or message. Rather, the government may restrict speech in light of factors that go beyond its *content*, to encompass its *context*. Regulation is permissible – indeed, warranted – if, in a particular context, speech (including hate speech) directly causes certain imminent, specific, serious harms that cannot be averted through other means. The Supreme Court has laid out particular criteria for several types of speech that satisfy this general standard, including 'true threats', intentional incitement of imminent violence, and targeted harassment. This demanding general standard, which is often called the 'emergency' test, replaced the earlier 'bad tendency' or 'harmful tendency' test, which the court invoked until the second half of the twentieth century. Under that more lenient standard, which is still reflected in the hate speech laws in other countries, the government many punish speech because of a more indirect, speculative, potential connection between the speech and some feared harm it might cause.

In many situations, hate speech is conveyed in contexts that satisfy the emergency principle, and hence it may be restricted. For example, if someone targets hateful expression at another with the intent of instilling a reasonable fear that s/he will be subject to violence, that constitutes a punishable 'true threat'. However, in contrast with most other comparable countries, the US does not permit punishment of hate speech that does not satisfy such appropriately demanding contextual standards. To underscore the important point that even under the speech-protective US approach, significant instances of hate speech may be punished, I use the term 'constitutionally protected hate speech' to signify the subset of hate speech that may *not* be punished. Correspondingly, I use the term 'hate speech law' to signify any law that punishes constitutionally protected hate speech.

My 2018 book *HATE: Why We Should Resist It with Free Speech, Not Censorship* lays out the reasons why censoring constitutionally protected hate speech is at best ineffective, and at worst counterproductive, for advancing the important goals that its proponents seek to promote, which I wholeheartedly support: equality, dignity, diversity, inclusivity, individual well-being, and societal harmony. Accordingly, the anti-censorship case is not dependent on First Amendment tenets, but is also independently justified by universal human rights principles, as well as policy concerns.

## Universal concerns about the problematic impact of hate speech laws

I hope that the general principles and policy considerations I discuss in this chapter will contribute to the understanding of all who seek to advance both free speech and equality anywhere in the world. Indeed, it is noteworthy that the American approach to these issues has been championed by human rights advocates, lawyers, and other experts in international agencies and in many other countries. These international supporters of the American approach have witnessed first-hand the actual impact of hate speech laws in other countries, concluding that, no matter how well intentioned, these laws have been detrimental in practice. Here are just a few recent examples of pertinent statements from these many worldwide 'hate speech' law critics:

- In 2017, the European Centre for Press and Media Freedom, based in Germany, opposed German legislation requiring social media to remove hate speech, explaining: 'Combating illegal incitement to violence, hatred, … and discrimination is … crucial.… But … censoring speech has never

[been] shown to be effective: it is rather by more speech … that our societies will be helped'.[3]

- In 2017, a racially diverse coalition of prominent South African comedians and satirists called for limiting that country's hate speech laws to essentially track the American approach. The coalition members expressed concern about the laws' censorial impact on humour, including political humour.
- In 2015, the European Commission Against Racism and Intolerance issued a report critiquing European hate speech laws as potentially even counterproductive; the report urged European countries to prioritize non-censorial alternative measures, including counterspeech, concluding that they were 'much more likely' than censorship 'to prove effective in ultimately eradicating' hate speech and its potential harmful effects.[4]
- In 2015, UNESCO (United Nations Educational, Scientific and Cultural Organization) issued a report on 'Countering Online Hate Speech', which stressed that 'Counter-speech is generally preferable to suppression of speech'.[5]
- In 2017, British human rights barristers Amal Clooney and Philippa Webb wrote:

> [I]nternational law on insulting speech should be applied in a manner that is … more protective of speech, in line with the approach espoused by the U.S. Supreme Court under the First Amendment.… Intent to incite hatred, hostility or discrimination should be insufficient to justify criminal sanctions.[6]

- In 2017, Anna Sauerbrey, editor of the German newspaper *Der Tagesspiegel*, wrote:

> [T]he American way of dealing with Nazism … always seemed to me the more mature way of handling threats to liberal democracy. Germany's [outlawing of hate speech] seems like a permanent declaration of distrust in … argument and … education.… I have faith in a democratic public's ability to police itself. I wish Germany did.[7]

- In 2017, Auckland University of Technology History Professor Paul Moon stated:

> What we need is open debate, which will change racist and intolerant views, not censorship.… If what they say is racist or promoting hate, then we should expose and ridicule it, not just shut it down.[8]

## Why hate speech laws are at best ineffective and at worst counterproductive

*HATE: Why we Should Resist It With Free Speech, Not Censorship* quotes many experts who raise serious questions about whether constitutionally protected hate speech materially contributes to its feared harms: discrimination, violence, and psychic injury. Even if we assumed that these harms were markedly fuelled by constitutionally protected hate speech – as distinguished from hate speech that is punishable even under US law – censorship would not significantly reduce the problematic speech or the feared harms. Moreover, in several important respects, hate speech laws can actually exacerbate rather than reduce the feared harms. In sum, wholly apart from their First Amendment flaws, hate speech laws are bad public policy no matter where they are enforced.

## *No correlation between hate speech laws and reduced hateful speech or violence*

### *No inter-country correlation*

Many countries with hate speech laws have experienced no positive impact in terms of reducing discrimination; in fact, some governments that have enforced criminal hate speech laws have brutally discriminated on the bases of race, ethnicity, and religion. For instance, Canadian Professors Louis Greenspan and Cyril Levitt noted that '[t]he rise of France's National Front party, which under the leadership of Jean-Marie Le Pen was overtly racist, … occurred in a country that had supposedly immunized itself' through hate speech laws.[9] They concluded further that 'respectable' racists' have gained political power in Germany, even though it 'has some of the toughest anti-hate legislation in the world'. In 2017, a German journalist observed that 'Germans have long argued over whether' this legislation 'has worked', citing Germany's 'severe problem with right-wing extremist violence', and the strength of the right-wing Alternative for Germany party, whose 'ideas … might be construed as racist', and which received 12.6 per cent of the vote in the September 2017 national elections.[10]

Based on extensive experience in countries around the world, the respected international human rights organization, Human Rights Watch, repeatedly concluded that suppressing hate speech does not effectively promote equality. For example, in 1992, in response to the push for hate speech codes on US college campuses to remedy discrimination, Human Rights Watch endorsed the US opposition to such regulations, explaining: '[A] careful review of the experience of many other countries … has made clear that there is little connection in practice between draconian hate speech laws and the lessening of ethnic and racial violence or tension'.[11] In 2016, Human Rights Watch reached the same conclusion concerning India's hate speech laws, noting that they 'are used to stifle political dissent, harass journalists, restrict activities by non-governmental organizations, arbitrarily block Internet sites or take down content, and target religious minorities and marginalized communities, such as Dalits'.

Other experts have concurred. In 2013, the European Parliament acknowledged that hate speech and bias crimes were increasing in European Union countries despite their strong hate speech laws.[12] A 2011 study of hate speech laws that was prepared for the UN High Commissioner for Human Rights concluded that 'massive ... criminal regulations' of hateful speech did 'not seem to have made a meaningful contribution to reducing racism or ... discriminatory conduct'.[13] Likewise, in his 2016 book, which surveyed the experience of many mature democracies with hate speech laws, Oxford University professor, Timothy Garton Ash, concluded that there is no correlation between the existence of such laws and any reduction in the amount of either hateful speech or discriminatory conduct.

This general pattern is illustrated by anti-Semitic expression and violence. In 2013, the European Union Fundamental Rights Agency conducted a survey of European Jews – 76 per cent said that anti-Semitism had become worse in their countries within the last five years, despite the prevalence of European hate speech laws.[14] Similarly, recent surveys by the Anti-Defamation League showed that France had twice the level of anti-Semitism as the United States, despite France's vigorous enforcement of its strict hate speech laws against anti-Semitic expression.[15] Jacob Mchangama, founder and director of Justitia, a Copenhagen-based think tank, commented that these laws 'may have actually increased' anti-Semitism, and that 'laws against denying the Holocaust ... may have even encouraged Holocaust denial by endowing it with a veneer of ... intellectual martyrdom'.[16]

### *No intra-country correlation*

There is no evidence that countries that enact hate speech laws experience a decline in the amount of either hateful speech or discriminatory behaviour. Of the many illustrations of this non-correlation, I will cite just a few. Britain adopted its first hate speech law in 1965.[17] Recalling his own personal experience of racist attacks, as someone who had been born in India, British writer Kenan Malik has noted that the ensuing decade 'was probably the most racist in British history', involving not only 'Paki-bashing', when racist thugs would seek out Asians to 'beat up', but also openly racist public institutions that included the police [and] immigration officials.[18] Focusing on the current European situation, Agnès Callamard, who is Director of Columbia Global Freedom of Expression, noted that although 'European governments have produced more laws ... prohibit[ing] "Hate Speech" than any other region, with the possible exception of the Middle East', European countries 'are ravaged by intolerance and ... increasing inequality', citing 'rising levels of violence and hate, anti-immigrant, anti-Roma and anti-Semitic rhetoric.'[19]

Another pertinent study was conducted by two Australian professors who examined the impact of that country's multiple hate speech laws from 1989, when the first such law was enacted, through to 2010. The authors concluded that after the laws were enacted, minority communities in Australia continued to experience 'high levels of verbal abuse' and in some cases even an increase in such abuse.[20] As one final example, I will cite a UNESCO research project that tracked hate speech in Kenya leading up to its 2013 elections. Kenya had adopted a hate speech law in 2008 in an effort to stem the type of rampant inter-group violence that had occurred during the 2007 to 2008 post-election period. Notwithstanding this law, the study concluded that hate speech, including calls for discriminatory violence, was 'still … serious [and] extensive.'[21]

### *The rise of Nazism in Germany despite hate speech laws*

Given the horrors of the Holocaust, even diehard free speech stalwarts would support hate speech laws if they would have averted that atrocity. That is certainly the case for me, as the daughter of a German-born Holocaust survivor, who nearly died at Buchenwald. That also is true for international human rights champion Aryeh Neier, who escaped from Nazi Germany as a child with his immediate family, while the Nazis slaughtered his extended family. Neier was the ACLU's executive director between 1977 and 1978, when the ACLU successfully – but controversially – defended the First Amendment rights of neo-Nazis to hold a demonstration in Skokie, Illinois,[22] a town that had a large Jewish population, many of whom were Holocaust survivors. He declared:

> I am unwilling to put anything, even love of free speech, ahead of detestation of the Nazis…. I could not bring myself to advocate freedom of speech in Skokie if I did not believe that the chances are best for preventing a repetition of the Holocaust in a society where every incursion on freedom is resisted. Freedom has its risks. Suppression of freedom, I believe, is a sure prescription for disaster.[23]

Proponents of hate speech laws assume that the enforcement of such laws might have prevented the spread of Nazi ideology in Germany, but the historical record belies this assumption. Throughout the Nazis' rise to power, there were laws on the books criminalizing hateful, discriminatory speech, which were similar to contemporary hate speech laws. As noted by Alan Borovoy, general counsel of the Canadian Civil Liberties Association, when he opposed Canada's current hate speech legislation:

> Remarkably, pre-Hitler Germany had laws very much like the Canadian anti-hate law. Moreover, those laws were enforced with some vigour. During the fifteen years before Hitler came to power, there were more than two hundred prosecutions based on anti-Semitic speech.[24] And, in the opinion of the leading Jewish organization of that era, no more than 10% of the cases were mishandled by the authorities.

The German hate speech laws were enforced even against leading Nazis, some of whom served substantial prison terms. But rather than suppressing the Nazis' anti-Semitic ideology, these prosecutions helped the Nazis gain attention and support. For example, Danish journalist Flemming Rose reports that between 1923 and 1933, the virulently anti-Semitic newspaper *Der Stürmer*, published by Julius Streicher, 'was either confiscated or [its] editors [were] taken to court on

… thirty-six occasions.' Yet, '[t]he more charges Streicher faced, the greater became the admiration of his supporters. The courts became an important platform for Streicher's campaign against the Jews'.[25]

The major problem with Germany's response to rising Nazism was not that the Nazis enjoyed too much free speech, but that the Nazis literally got away with murder. In effect, they stole free speech from everyone else, including anti-Nazis, Jews, and other minorities.

### *Factors contributing to hate speech laws' ineffectiveness*

The lack of correlation between hate speech laws and reduced discrimination or violence is not surprising in light of several features of such laws, which make them ineffective in reducing hateful speech and thus in reducing the harms that such speech is feared to cause.

#### *Inevitable under enforcement*

To begin with, hate speech regulations are invariably unduly vague, so that those charged with enforcing them must make discretionary judgments. Some judgments are inevitably overinclusive, penalizing speech that is important for individual freedom, as well as for democratic self-government. Let me cite just two examples of such expressions that have recently been punished under European hate speech laws: a French LGBT rights leader's use of the term 'homophobe' to describe the leader of an opposition group; and a British politician's quotation of a critical statement about Islam from a book by Winston Churchill, during a campaign speech.

The sweeping discretion with which hate speech laws inherently invest enforcers is also inevitably exercised in ways that are underinclusive, immunizing politically powerful hatemongers. The underenforcement problem is especially acute in countries that lack longstanding democratic structures or traditions, where powerful political figures routinely engage in speech that violates their countries' hate speech laws, but are not held legally accountable for doing so. This is true, for example, in Poland, where popular politicians target gays, Jews, Roma, and other ethnic minorities;[26] in Hungary, where powerful political groups target Roma and Gypsy minorities;[27] in Zimbabwe, where former President Robert Mugabe's loyalists targeted his political opponents;[28] in India, where powerful politicians, including Prime Minister Narendra Modi, target marginalized minority castes, religions, and sects;[29] and in Rwanda and Kenya, where government officials target ethnic minorities.[30] Likewise, Singaporean LGBT rights activists have complained that 'the LGBT community in Singapore … experience[s] hate speech … in public statements by influential newsmakers, such as politicians or religious leaders,' but receives 'no … protection' under that country's hate speech laws.[31] Hong Kong Baptist University professor Cherian George has concluded that hate speech laws are less effective than 'US political culture' in constraining 'politicians who indulge in hate speech,' with the result that 'hate speech appears more flagrant and prevalent in elections in India than in the United States, despite the wider latitude that the First Amendment offers American politicians.'[32]

Ironically but predictably, it is precisely in those countries where there is the most discrimination, and the most hate speech, that authorities are least likely to enforce hate speech laws designed to prevent or redress such discrimination. This point was stressed in a study of such laws in Latin America by Fordham Law School professor Tanya Hernandez, an internationally recognized comparative race law expert, who concluded:

> Entrusting the enforcement of … [a] criminal [hate speech] law to public authorities risks having the law undermined by the complacent inaction of public officials who may harbor the same racial bias as the agents of hate speech. This is a particular danger in Latin America, where police officers are consistently found to discourage Afro-descendants from filing racial discrimination complaints, and are often the perpetrators of discrimination and violence themselves.[33]

### *Driving some expression underground*

> [A]s my grandmother used to tell me, every time a fool speaks, they are just advertising their own ignorance. Let them talk. If you don't, you just make them a victim, and then they can avoid accountability.[34]
>
> (President Barack Obama, 2016 Howard University Commencement address)

Censorship drives some discriminatory expression underground, with important negative consequences. First, because some people who harbour hateful, discriminatory ideas are deterred from expressing them, we don't realize who they are. We therefore lose the opportunity to dissuade them and to monitor their conduct to ensure it is not discriminatory. Second, we lose the opportunity for people to listen to these ideas and to realize their flaws. Third, those of us who deplore such ideas are deprived of the opportunity to formulate and communicate responses, and everyone else is deprived of the opportunity to hear such exchanges. In the long run, an open airing of discriminatory ideas, and an ensuing debate about them, may well be more effective in curbing them than censorship would be. Fourth, as a 2015 UNESCO report observed: '[H]ate speech is … a window into deeply-rooted tensions and inequalities, which … do need addressing'.[35] Hate speech thus has the positive impact of energizing citizens to engage in social justice activism in an effort to address the discrimination and hatred that plague our society. As the old saying puts it, 'Sunlight is the best disinfectant.'[36]

### *Incentivizing more palatable and thus more potent hateful speech*

Hate speech laws induce some speakers with hateful ideas to 'sugarcoat' them, with the perverse result that they are more widely circulated and accepted. Based on their study of the hate speech laws in six European nations, professors Louis Greenspan and Cyril Levitt concluded that these laws had forced politicians with racist agendas to adopt 'carefully worded racist programs,' making them 'more potent'. They drew a telling contrast between the sanitized racist expression in Europe and the American Nazi Party's uncensored speech: 'With slogans such as "Hitler was right – he gassed the Jews," ... the [U.S.] racist right could make no headway in the general population.'[37]

### *Increasing attention and support*

Censoring any material increases an audience's desire to obtain it and disposes the audience to be more receptive to it. By casting the silenced speaker as a free speech martyr, censorship also ousts critics from the moral high ground. Not surprisingly, then, many hatemongers welcome hate speech laws and prosecutions under them. Consider an early major prosecution under Canada's federal criminal hate speech law against James Keegstra, a virulently anti-Semitic public school teacher. He was charged under the law in 1984, two years after he had been dismissed from his teaching job because of his anti-Semitic indoctrination of students.[38] The ensuing protracted legal proceedings ultimately resulted, in 1996, in a one-year suspended sentence, one year of probation, and 200 hours of community service. As University of Calgary law professor Peter Bowal summed up the case:

> [Fourteen] years from the time Keegstra was dismissed from his teaching job, after [legal proceedings] ... costing an estimated million dollars, an unrepentant Keegstra was sentenced to the equivalent of a tap on the wrist.... Ironically, that public stage granted him 14 more years to publicize his opinions. The extensive media coverage of the cumbersome legal saga may even have garnered Keegstra more sympathy.

This outcome, Bowal commented, 'may explain why there have been few successful prosecutions' under Canada's criminal hate speech law in the years since.[39]

### *The technological impossibility of silencing hate speech*

Given the recent explosion of decentralized communications technologies, including the internet and mobile phones, today it is practically impossible to block any type of expression completely. Even after online hatemongers have been imprisoned under hate speech laws, their websites remain active. For example, Ernst Zundel, a purveyor of neo-Nazi propaganda, was prosecuted and convicted for engaging in hate speech in both Canada and Germany, in litigation that dragged out for 11 years, from 1996 to 2007. But as one expert noted in 2010, 'Even now, Zundel's website is still running and regularly updated with his "letters from prison" despite his incarceration.'[40]

*Enforcement frustrations*

As illustrated by the Canadian *Keegstra* case, an additional drawback of hate speech laws from the perspective of the people the speech disparages is that their eventual remedy, and the perpetrator's eventual penalty, if any, often comes too late and at too high a transaction cost to afford meaningful relief. The most thorough study of the enforcement problems in these cases was undertaken by Australian professors Katharine Gelber and Luke McNamara, who reviewed the enforcement of their country's hate speech laws. Because the Australian laws are typical, there is no reason to believe that the problems Gelber and McNamara documented are in any way out of the ordinary. They concluded that 'pursuing a remedy under Australia's hate speech laws is arduous, stressful, time-consuming, and possibly expensive.' Individuals who were targets of such speech, as well as their lawyers and the organizations that supported them, consistently complained that 'you might win in the end, but it's going to take so much out of you.' Too often, the complainants end up winning what they dismiss as merely 'a pyrrhic victory'.[41]

### *How effective are hate speech laws at reducing … intergroup hostility?*

Far from reducing intergroup violence, hostility, and tensions, hate speech laws often tend to fuel them. This problem is so prevalent that the Singaporean communications scholar, Cherian George, who has studied these laws in various countries, coined a term to describe it: 'hate spin'. Politicians 'spin' expression by rival groups as hate speech, thus bringing charges under their countries' laws, thereby stirring up hostilities, to their political advantage.[42]

Even in developed democracies, enforcement of hate speech laws is likely to increase, not decrease, intergroup tensions. Experience teaches that the most effective way to reduce or resolve intergroup conflicts is through cooperative, conciliatory approaches, rather than through 'lawfare'.

Hate speech laws curb the sort of intergroup dialogue about bias that experts consider a precondition for reducing intergroup hatred and discrimination. As Pierre Bierre of Stanford University's Neuropsychology Laboratory has observed, '[T]he first step to resolve conflicts is to get people to open up and share unedited gut feelings, … and the second step is to remove the listening blocks that prevent the other side from hearing those feelings.' For that reason, he criticizes hate speech laws, which have a chilling impact on both open expression and open-minded listening.[43]

*... Retaliatory violence?*

Another potential harm to which constitutionally protected hate speech is feared to contribute to is retaliatory violence against the speaker or the speaker's allies by those who despise the message. If a government capitulated to such threats of retaliatory violence by suppressing the speech, that would only encourage further threats and violence rather than curbing them. This was a recurrent theme throughout the US civil rights movement, when courts refused to halt speeches and demonstrations by civil rights advocates because of threatened and even actual violence by opponents of their cause.

In 2012, the then President, Barack Obama, flagged this concern (among others) in explaining to the UN General Assembly why the United States did not censor the anti-Islamic video that was then (erroneously) believed to have spurred the murderous attacks on the U.S. Embassy in Benghazi, Libya: '[F]or us to respond in that way to hateful speech empowers any individual who engages in such speech.... We [would] empower the worst of us.'

### *The costs of hate speech laws outweigh their benefits*

The case for censoring constitutionally protected hate speech is often based largely on reciting the potential harms to which such speech is feared to contribute, with no rigorous analysis of other factors that we logically must consider in evaluating whether such laws are warranted. As I have shown, though, hate speech laws do not effectively suppress constitutionally protected hate speech or its feared harmful impact, and might even aggravate at least some feared harms. These considerations provide an independent basis for rejecting hate speech laws, even beyond the grave damage they do to freedom of speech, equality, and democracy. Further, as I discuss in more detail below, experts concur that non-censorial alternative measures, including counterspeech, are much more effective than hate speech laws in reducing both the incidence and potential harmful impact of constitutionally protected hate speech.

## How non-censorial methods effectively curb the potential harms of constitutionally protected hate speech

In 2015, the European Commission against Racism and Intolerance (ECRI) issued a report strongly urging European nations to pursue non-censorial responses to hate speech. This is especially note-worthy because in recent decades many European nations have enacted hate speech laws with the encouragement of regional bodies, including ECRI. But, as a result of its monitoring of the efforts of European nations to curb hate speech and discrimination, ECRI concluded that alternative, non-censorial measures are '*much more likely* to prove effective in ultimately eradicating hate speech' and its potential harmful effects [44] than laws forbidding hate speech.

### *Counterspeech*

> [T]he strongest weapon against hateful speech is not repression; it is more speech – the voices of tolerance that rally against bigotry … and lift up … mutual respect.[45]
>
> (President Barack Obama)

> In the end, we will remember not the words of our enemies, but the silence of our friends.
>
> (Martin Luther King, Jr.)

> [H]ardly any of the voices that should have been raised in moral protest against Nazism were to be heard in Germany or the territories conquered by the Reich. Where political and religious leaders did speak out against the Nazis, notably in … Denmark, most Jews were saved. Those Jews who died … were victims of the silence of Europe's moral leadership as they were victims of the Nazis.[46]
>
> (Aryeh Neier, international human rights leader, and a Holocaust survivor)

Speech that counters the potentially harmful impact of hate speech comprises a broad range of expression, including information and ideas that directly refute the hateful message; broader, proactive educational initiatives; and expressions of remorse by discriminatory speakers. The internet not only makes it easier than ever to convey hateful messages; it also makes it easier than ever to rebut them. What's more, the internet makes it easier to measure the extent and impact of counterspeech. Although the field is still young, there have been promising online counterspeech initiatives and studies of their efficacy. For example:

- Google has added to its website a disclaimer about sites containing hateful messages. If any such site shows up prominently in response to a search request, the user will see an explanation of how search results are ranked, as well as an apology, to dispel any impression that Google endorses such messages.[47]
- YouTube has developed videos to counter hateful messages.[48]
- Facebook has created tools that enable users to privately notify authors of content they find objectionable before formally asking Facebook to remove it.[49]

Facebook engaged the US public policy organization, Demos, to undertake research about the extent to which counterspeech is produced and shared on its platform. Demos' initial report, issued in 2015, found that hateful online speech is 'often met with disagreement, derision, and counter-campaigns,' and that this 'crowd-sourced response' has significant advantages over suppression: '[I]t is faster, more flexible and responsive, [and] capable of dealing with [problematic expression] from anywhere and in any language'. Some Facebook users actively search out hate speech for the express purpose of challenging it. Some counter-speech is shared publicly, and some is conveyed via private communications with the speaker. The report concluded that some types of content and format were especially effective at countering hate speech: photos and videos; 'constructive' comments; and comments about specific policy issues.[50]

In 2016, a report was issued about counterspeech on Twitter, co-authored by a group of scholars from the United States and Canada. The report concluded that hateful and other extremist speech was most effectively undermined by counterspeech rather than by removing it. Echoing the Demos report about Facebook, the Twitter report concluded that images are more persuasive than text alone, and that humour, including satire, is especially powerful. The report indicated that by combining these two approaches, humour and images, 'people who do not share a language,' can effectively 'counterspeak together, often in large numbers and across cultural and national boundaries.'[51] Among the examples the report cited was the following:

> Dani Alves, a [black] Brazilian soccer player, was subjected to a humiliating racist gesture when a spectator threw a banana at him on the field.... Another player ... quickly posted an image of himself eating a banana, on the hashtag #Somostodosmacacos, meaning 'we are all monkeys'. That hashtag ... spread quickly.... [T]housands of people posted banana-eating selfies in spontaneous support.[52]

Impressively, the Twitter report noted situations in which counterspeech was able to accomplish 'lasting changes in beliefs' even when the speaker seemed 'firmly committed ... to hateful ideology' and 'to declaring it publicly.'[53] The report identified the strategies that were successful in these situations, including the use of an empathic or kind tone in response to the speaker rather than targeting the speaker as hateful or racist (although identifying the speech as such).[54]

Paradoxically, experts concur that in some circumstances the most effective form of counterspeech can be silence. By deliberately choosing to ignore provocative, hateful speakers, silence can powerfully convey implicit messages of disdain, while at the same time denying hateful speakers the attention they seek and often get from sparking controversy. Those engaged in counterspeech should be careful not to act in ways that are ultimately counterproductive, including efforts to silence hateful speakers through aggressive counter-demonstrations. Although such tactics might seem morally justified, they almost always backfire.

### *Empowering disparaged people to engage in counterspeech*

> I believe deeply that minority group members who are discriminated against ... have the ... responsibility [to] speak on their own behalf.
>
> (Theodore Shaw, former director-counsel and president, NAACP Legal Defense and Educational Fund)

> We have to teach [our young people] how to deal with adversarial situations. They have to learn how to survive with offensive speech they find wounding and hurtful.
>
> (Gwen Thomas, U.S. civil rights activist)

> The … protection [of a 'hate speech' law] incapacitates.… To … be told that white folks have the moral character to shrug off insults, and that I do not.… That is … the most racist statement of all![55]
>
> (Conservative political activist, Alan Keyes)

While all of the activists quoted above are African-American, they are ideologically diverse, spanning the left-right spectrum. They all agree, though, that hate speech laws that aim to promote equal rights in fact do the opposite, through paternalism and protectionism. Accordingly, these activists urge those who are disparaged by hate speech to confront it directly. Admittedly, this is often easier said than done, for such speech can have both the intent and the effect of silencing those it disparages.

We have seen increasing social justice advocacy in the United States in recent years, with members of minority groups actively leading and engaging in such efforts, including on campus. Surveys indicate that this trend promises to continue. It is essential for the well-being of both individuals and society that we encourage and facilitate such counterspeech rather than adopting the disempowering, anti-democratic censorial approach.

As I acknowledged above, in some instances the adverse psychic and emotional impact of hate speech might be so incapacitating for some people that they are unable to engage in effective counter-speech, at least in the moment, and other people who are exposed to such speech might lack the education or access to means of communication that would make their counterspeech effective. These are serious concerns, which can and must be addressed through a range of measures, including: proactive counselling and training about engaging constructively with hate speech; education about utilizing social media and other communications vehicles for drawing attention and responding to hate speech; and providing access to helpful technology, organizations, and other resources. Fortunately, there is a rapidly expanding treasure trove of easily accessible online resources.

A related problem with advocating counterspeech by those who are targeted by hate speech – as the above-quoted African-American activists do – is that it is arguably unfair to expect the targeted persons to shoulder this burden. While this is a significant issue, there are countervailing considerations. First, such individuals of course have no *duty* to engage in counterspeech. Second, others in our society who are committed to equality and individual dignity have a moral responsibility to condemn hate speech and to express support for people whom it targets. Third, the time, effort, and energy that disparaged people expend to engage in counterspeech can be viewed as a sound investment that will yield benefits for them personally, as well as for all concerned. Barack Obama has repeatedly articulated this view. Having exhorted minority students to engage in counterspeech in response to racist speech, he acknowledged that this 'may not seem fair, but … if you want to make life fair, then you've got to start with the world as it is.' As he told the 2017 Howard University graduating class: '[Y]ou have the responsibility to speak up in the face of injustice.… And you might as well start practicing now, because … you will have to deal with ignorance, hatred, racism … at every stage of your life.'[56]

*Education*

> No one is born hating another person because of the colour of his skin or his background or his religion.… People must learn to hate, and if they can learn to hate, they can be taught to love.[57]
>
> (Nelson Mandela)

Education is a vital form of counterspeech. One key educational strategy is to convey accurate, positive information about traditionally marginalized groups. This proactive approach can be pursued in myriad ways, including through the school system, mass media, social media, and entertainment. Social science studies have shown that positive media depictions reduce prejudice and promote a more tolerant and integrated society.[58] These studies parallel the famous 'inter-group contact theory' that psychologist Gordon Allport pioneered in the mid-twentieth century about the positive impact of actual contact with people from other groups. In 1956, sociology professors Donald Horton and Richard Wohl coined the term 'para-social interaction' to refer to the illusion of face-to-face relationships that audience members sensed with mass media characters.[59] Since then, social scientists have continued to document that media exposure generates the same prejudice-reducing impact as real-world intergroup contact.

Initiatives to counter discrimination through media depictions began in the immediate aftermath of the Holocaust. In 1947, for example, Hollywood released two films that exposed the anti-Semitism that was still pervasive in North America: *Gentleman's Agreement* and *Crossfire*. Although both films were artistically acclaimed, they were controversial – and almost not made – because of the very anti-Semitism they were created to counteract.[60] Today's ongoing controversies about '#Oscarsowhite' and '#Emmysowhite' make clear that, for all the progress the US entertainment industry has made since 1947, much remains to be done.[61]

Many other educational initiatives can curb the potential negative effects of hate speech. For members of minority groups who are disparaged by hate speech, it is especially important to develop the skills and outlooks that can help them to avert or minimize the potentially adverse psychic and emotional impact of such speech, and to refute its message. Some psychologists endorse teaching college students and others general cognitive-behavioural therapy techniques for reducing anxiety and other negative reactions that might result from stressful situations, including exposure to hate speech.[62] Psychologists also endorse educational approaches for developing people's resilience in the face of such situations – their ability to maintain their sense of self-esteem and to carry on effectively with their work and personal activities.

### *Apologies*

> 'I'm sorry' are the two most healing words in the English language.[63]
>
> (Psychologist, Harriet Lerner)

A specific 'more speech' measure that experts have hailed as mutually beneficial, both for those who engage in hate speech and for those whom they disparage, is a refreshingly simple one: a sincere apology. Proponents of hate speech laws stress that targeted speech can contribute to adverse psychological and physiological effects. It therefore should not be surprising that healing words, in the form of sincere apologies, can have positive psychological and physiological benefits. Psychotherapist Beverly Engel cites research showing that 'receiving an apology has a noticeable positive physical effect on the body.... [I]t actually affects the bodily functions of the person receiving it – blood pressure decreases, heart rate slows and breathing becomes steadier.'[64]

Experts warn, however, that the benefits of sincere apologies do not flow if they are coerced. According to Engel, an apology that you make because someone else tells you it is the right thing to do will lack healing power.[65] This is yet another reason why we should address discriminatory speech through a constructive educational approach rather than an adversarial, punitive one.

The actual experience under hate speech laws confirms the psychologists' teachings. Australian Professors Katharine Gelber and Luke McNamara concluded that one reason why their country's hate speech laws are counterproductive is that they undermine the constructive remedy that a sincere apology can afford. People who are disparaged by hateful, discriminatory speech initially tend to seek only genuine apologies. However, when the protracted legal proceedings finally do culminate with a court-ordered apology, this frustrates complainants who seek a genuine acknowledgement of wrongdoing.[66]

### *Counterspeech by government and campus officials*

Social scientists have confirmed that counterspeech by leaders in the pertinent community is especially persuasive in rebutting hateful speech and in countering its potential harmful effects. Government officials may engage in counterspeech as long as their counterspeech does not, in practical effect, have such a deterrent effect on the ideas at issue as to become the functional equivalent of censorship. If it is difficult to draw the line between censuring and censoring in a specific situation, the official should refrain from comment. To reduce the danger of de facto suppression, officials who are engaging in counterspeech should stress that they are not seeking to punish the speaker.

Likewise, in a university setting, where intellectual freedom is especially important, campus officials should not convert their 'bully pulpit' into a pulpit for bullying speakers whose views they oppose. A university should avoid creating even the appearance of ideological orthodoxy. If university officials specifically criticize particular hateful messages, they should also emphasize their support for the freedom of all members of the university community to express contrary views, to minimize the risk that the officials' statements will chill discussion and dissent.

### *Developing thicker and thinner skin*

> No one can make you feel inferior without your consent.[67]
>
> (Eleanor Roosevelt)

For our own well-being, we should develop relatively thick skins, so that our sense of self-confidence is not threatened by hateful words. This is how I understand that old nursery rhyme, 'Sticks and stones may break my bones, but words will never hurt me'. It is not a statement of fact; all of us have been hurt by words in myriad ways. Given words' indisputable power to hurt us, the old nursery rhyme is not a descriptive statement, but rather an exhortation; it encourages us to respond to words in a way that empowers us and disempowers those who seek to hurt us.

To be sure, some of us are less able than others to withstand the hurtful impact of particular wounding words, including hate speech. A member of a marginalized minority group will likely find it harder than others to face down discriminatory words with the attitude that they 'will never hurt me'. Moreover, each of us has our own unique degree of (in)sensitivity to hurtful words; we range across the spectrum from the most thin-skinned to the most thick-skinned. But no matter who we are as individuals, and no matter which societal groups we belong to, we can, and must, increase our capacity to resist the hurtful potential of hateful, discriminatory words that target us, while also becoming more sensitive to such words that target others. In short, we should develop a thicker skin on behalf of ourselves and a thinner skin on behalf of others. Behavioural psychologists and other experts attest to having successfully taught methods for doing so.

### *Outreach and interaction*

Social science studies have confirmed what everyday experience suggests: that the most effective way to decrease people's negative attitudes toward members of any societal group is to give them an opportunity to get to know one another.[68] The 'inter-group contact theory' was first formulated by Harvard professor Gordon Allport in his trailblazing 1954 book *The Nature of Prejudice*. Allport posited that interaction is especially constructive in settings such as school, work, and community groups, where people collaborate on common endeavours. Allport's findings have been corroborated by a vast social science literature, which documents that inter-group contact plays a vital role in reducing prejudice and promoting a more tolerant, integrated, and harmonious society. The evidence demonstrates that contact overcomes prejudice and forges positive relationships among people from many different groups, including racial and ethnic groups, the elderly, LGBT persons, mentally ill people, persons with disabilities, and AIDS victims. A 1993 study of heterosexuals' attitudes toward gay men, for example, found that the extent of contact predicted these attitudes better than any other variable, including political ideology.[69]

### *Self-restraint*

> In Europe, we have more legal limitations on speech but less social pressure, while in the U.S. you have very few legal limits but far more social pressure.[70]
>
> (Flemming Rose, Danish journalist)

Just because one has the right to say something does not mean that it is right to do so. So when critics tell us that some things we say are unnecessarily hurtful or insensitive, even unintentionally, we should rephrase our message whenever we can do so without undermining its substance or viewpoint. When we choose to do that, we are exercising our free speech rights – thoughtfully.

In addition to voluntarily chosen sensitive and respectful language, another type of voluntary self-restraint involves 'trigger warnings', alerting an audience that one is going to use language or discuss a topic that might upset some audience members. Such warnings should not be mandated by government or by university officials. As the Supreme Court has long recognized, forcing people to say something they do not choose to say violates the principles of free speech and academic freedom as fully as forcing people *not* to say something they want to say.[71] But if a teacher or other speaker chooses to issue such a warning, that is an exercise of free speech. Moreover, if it is offered with the intent and effect of facilitating certain audience members' engagement with the subject, it could foster free speech, rather than suppressing it.

In addition to individual self-restraint, public- and private-sector entities may discourage the use of hate speech, and in some contexts may even penalize such speech. Many organizations have restricted hate speech as a matter of business practice and professional ethics. Such self-regulation is one of the non-censorial alternatives to hate speech laws that the ECRI (the European Commission against Racism and Intolerance) has endorsed. Indeed, the ECRI concluded that it 'can be the most appropriate and most effective approach to tackling hate speech'.[72]

## Conclusion

The evidence that this chapter discussed supports the conclusions of many expert individuals and organizations around the world – that counterspeech and other non-censorial alternatives are much more likely than hate speech laws to prove effective in limiting hate speech and its possible harmful effects. This constitutes an independently sufficient and universally relevant basis for rejecting hate speech laws, even beyond their damage to freedom of speech, democracy, equality, and societal harmony.

## Notes

1 Michelle Eberhard, 'When Hateful Speech Is Transformed Into Hateful Deeds: Examining Freedom of Speech, Hate Speech, and Incitement to Genocide,' *The Auschwitz Institute for Peace and Reconciliation* (March 2013). www.auschwitzinstitute.org/blog/genprev-in-the-news-26-march-2013
2 Andrea Scheffler, The Inherent Danger of Hate Speech Legislation – A Case Study from Rwanda and Kenya on the Failure of a Preventative Measure (2015) (Fesmedia Africa Series, 2015) http://library.fes.de/pdf-files/bueros/africa-media/12462.pdf
3 ECPMF Staff, 'Why the So Called "Facebook Law" Is the Wrong Tool Against Hate Speech.' European Centre for Press and Media Freedom (6 February 2017) https://ecpmf.eu/news/ecpmf/why-the-so-called-facebook-law-is-the-wrong-tool-against-hate-speech
4 European Commission Against Racism and Intolerance, 'ECRI General Policy Recommendation No. 15' (2015) On Combating Hate Speech 13 https://rm.coe.int/ecri-general-policy-recommendation-no-15-on-combating-hate-speech/16808b5b01
5 Iginio Gagliardone, 'Countering Online Hate Speech' (2015) UNESCO Series on Internet Freedom 5 http://unesdoc.unesco.org/images/0023/002332/233231e.pdf
6 Amal Clooney and Philippa Webb, 'The Right to Insult in International Law' *Columbia Human Rights Law Review* 48, no. 2 (2017): 1, 52.
7 Anna Sauerbrey, 'How Germany Deals With Neo-Nazis' (*New York Times*, 23 August 2017) www.nytimes.com/2017/08/23/opinion/germany-neo-nazis-charlottesville.html
8 New Zealand Herald Staff, 'High-profile Kiwis: Free speech under threat in NZ Universities' (New Zealand Herald, 4 April 2017). www.nzherald.co.nz/nz/news/article.cfm?c_id=1&objectid=11831306
9 Louis Greenspan and Cyril Levitt, *Under the Shadow of Weimar: Democracy, Law, and Racial Incitement in Six Countries* (Westport, Praeger Publishers, 1993).
10 Sauerbrey (n.7).
11 Fund for Free Expression, '"Hate Speech" and Freedom of Expression: A Human Rights Policy Paper 4' (1992).
12 'Resolution on Strengthening the Fight against Racism, Xenophobia, and Hate Crime' (European Parliament, 3 June 2013). www.europarl.europa.eu/sides/getDoc.do?type=MOTION&reference=B7-2013-0123&language=EN
13 Eduardo Bertoni, 'A Study on the Prohibition of Incitement to Hatred in the Americas' (2011) Office of the High Commissioner, Human Rights www.ohchr.org/Documents/Issues/Expression/ICCPR/Santiago/SantiagoStudy_en.pdf
14 'Discrimination and hate crime against Jews in EU Member States: experiences and perceptions of antisemitism' (2013) European Union Agency for Fundamental Rights 12. http://fra.europa.eu/en/publication/2013/discrimination-and-hate-crime-against-jews-eu-member-states-experiences-and
15 'ADL Global 100: A Survey of Attitudes Toward Jews in Over 100 Countries Around the World' (2014) Anti-Defamation League: 16–17. http://global100.adl.org/public/ADL-Global-100-Executive-Summary.pdf
16 Jacob Mchangama, 'How (Not) to Fight Racism and Anti-Semitism' (The Daily Beast, 2 February 2014) www.thedailybeast.com/how-not-to-fight-racism-and-anti-semitism

17 'Race Relations Act 1965' (1965) Parliament www.parliament.uk/about/living-heritage/transformingsociety/private-lives/relationships/collections1/race-relations-act-1965/race-relations-act-1965 (accessed 1 April 2018).
18 Kenan Malik, 'How Did the Left Radicalism of My Manchester Youth Give Way to Islamism?' (*Guardian*, 28 May, 2017). www.theguardian.com/commentisfree/2017/may/28/islamism-separation-other-peoples-even-muslims
19 Agnes Callamard, 'Comments and Recommendations on ECRI General Policy Recommendation No. 15 on Combating Hate Speech' (2015) Global Freedom of Expression @ Columbia University 3 https://globalfreedomofexpression.columbia.edu/wp-content/uploads/2015/06/ECRI-CONSULTATION-A-Callamard.pdf
20 Katherine Gelber and Luke J. McNamara, 'The Effects of Civil Hate Speech Laws: Lessons from Australia' *Law and Society Review* 49, no. 3 (2015): 631.
21 Iginio Gagliardone *et al.*, 'Countering Online Hate Speech' (2013) UNESCO Series on Internet Freedom 37 http://unesdoc.unesco.org/images/0023/002332/233231e.pdf
22 See 'Neier, Aryeh 1937-' Encyclopedia www.encyclopedia.com/arts/educational-magazines/neier-aryeh-1937 (accessed 31 March 2018).
23 Aryeh Neier, *Defending My Enemy: American Nazis, the Skokie Case, and the Risks of Freedom* (International Debate Education Association, 2012).
24 A. Alan Borovoy, *When Freedoms Collide: The Case for Our Civil Liberties* (Toronto, Lester and Orpen Dennys, 1988).
25 The New Yorker Staff, 'Copenhagen, Speech, and Violence' (*The New Yorker*, 14 February, 2015). www.newyorker.com/news/news-desk/copenhagen-speech-violence
26 Leonid Bershidsky, 'Why Polish Jews Are Growing Uneasy' (Bloomberg, 27 February 2018) www.bloomberg.com/view/articles/2018-02-27/polish-jews-are-growing-worried-about-anti-semitism
27 Chuck Sudetic, 'Roma in Political Life: Hungary—From Transition to Hate Politics' (Open Society Foundations, 10 September 2013) www.opensocietyfoundations.org/voices/roma-political-life-hungary-transition-hate-politics; Barbora Černušáková, 'The Roma People's Hungarian Hell' (Politico, 27 January 2017) www.politico.eu/article/the-roma-peoples-hungarian-hell
28 Andrew Meldrum, 'Mugabe's Thugs Kill Five More Opponents' (*Guardian*, 29 April 2000) www.theguardian.com/world/2000/apr/30/zimbabwe.andrewmeldrum
29 Siddhant Mohan, 'India targets Western, Christian Groups at Odds with Hinduism' (*Washington Times*, 27 January 2016) www.washingtontimes.com/news/2016/jan/27/narendra-modi-selectively-targeting-western-christ; 'Actions of the Indian Government with Respect to Minority Communities – Universal Periodic Review 27th Session (May 2017)' (Minority Rights Group, 24 April 2017) http://minorityrights.org/advocacy-statements/actions-indian-government-respect-minority-communities-universal-periodic-review-27th-session-may-2017
30 'Report On Minority Issues In Rwanda Presented At Human Rights Council' (Unrepresented Nations & Peoples Organization, 30 March 2012) http://unpo.org/article/14097; Zipporah Nyambura, 'In Kenya, Politics Split on Ethnic Divide' (Deutsche Welle, 26 October 2017) www.dw.com/en/in-kenya-politics-split-on-ethnic-divide/a-37442394
31 Kirsten Han, 'How Singapore Is Abusing Its Laws on "Hate Speech"' (Southeast Asia Globe, 24 May 2017) http://sea-globe.com/singapore-hate-speech
32 Cherian George, *Hate Spin: The Manufacture of Religious Offense and Its Threat to Democracy* (Cambridge MA, MIT Press, 2016).
33 Tanya Katerí Hernández, 'Hate Speech And The Language Of Racism In Latin America: A Lens For Reconsidering Global Hate Speech Restrictions And Legislation Models' *University of Pennsylvania Journal of International Law*, no. 32 (2011): 805, 829.
34 Politico Staff, 'Obama's Full Remarks at Howard University Commencement Ceremony' (Politico, 7 May 2016) www.politico.com/story/2016/05/obamas-howard-commencement-transcript-222931

35 Iginio Gagliardone *et al.*, 'Countering Online Hate Speech' (2015) United Nations Educational, Scientific and Cultural Organization 16 http://unesdoc.unesco.org/images/0023/002332/233231e.pdf
36 Louis D. Brandeis, *Other People's Money and How Bankers Use It* (CreateSpace Independent Publishing Platform, 2009).
37 Greenspan (n. 9).
38 *R* v. *Keegstra* 3 S.C.R. (1990): 697, 698.
39 Peter Bowal, 'What Ever Happened to … Jim Keegstra' (Law Now, 1 July 2012) www.lawnow.org/what-ever-happened-to-jim-keegstra
40 Yaman Akdeniz, 'Governing Racist Content on the Internet: National and International Responses' *University of New Brunswick Law Journal* 56 (2007): 103, 123.
41 Luke McNamara and Katharine Gelber, 'The Impact of Section 18C and Other Civil Anti-Vilification Laws in Australia' (40 Years of the Racial Discrimination Act 1975 (CTH) Conference, Sydney, February 2015).
42 George (n. 32).
43 'Letter from Pierre Bierre' *Stanford Report* (Stanford, 22 March 1989): 20.
44 ECRI (n. 4).
45 Barack Obama, 'President Obama's speech to the UN general assembly – full transcript' (*Guardian*, 25 September 2012) www.theguardian.com/world/2012/sep/25/obama-un-general-assembly-transcript
46 Neier (n. 23).
47 Jeff John Roberts, 'Google's Big Changes to Search: What You Need to Know' (Fortune, 25 April 2017) http://fortune.com/2017/04/25/google-search-update
48 Alex Hern, 'YouTube to Fund Videos That 'Counter Hate' as Pressure over Extremism Grows' (*Guardian*, 25 January 2018) www.theguardian.com/technology/2018/jan/25/youtubefund-videos-counter-hate-extremism-google-creators-for-changeprogramme
49 Iginio Gagliardone *et al.*, 'Countering Online Hate Speech' (2015) United Nations Educational, Scientific and Cultural Organization 31 http://unesdoc.unesco.org/images/0023/002332/233231e.pdf
50 Jamie Bartlett and Alex Krasodomski-Jones, 'Counterspeech on Facebook' (2015) Demos www.demos.co.uk/wpcontent/uploads/2016/09/Counter-speech-on-facebook-report.pdf
51 Susan Benesch *et al.*, 'Counterspeech on Twitter: A Field Study' (2016) Dangerous Speech Project https://dangerousspeech.org/counterspeech-on-twitter-a-field-study
52 Ibid.
53 Ibid.
54 Ibid.
55 'Press Release' *Stanford News* (Stanford, 19 March 1990).
56 Politico Staff (n. 34).
57 Nelson Mandela, *Long Walk to Freedom: The Autobiography of Nelson Mandela* (Great Britain, Little Brown & Co, 2008), 542.
58 Adam Rutland and Melanie Killen, 'A Developmental Science Approach to Reducing Prejudice and Social Exclusion: Intergroup Processes, Social-Cognitive Development, and Moral Reasoning', *Social Issues and Policy Review* 9, no. 1 (2015): 121.
59 Donald Horton and Richard R. Wohl, 'Mass Communication and Para-social Interaction: Observations on Intimacy at a Distance', *Psychiatry* 19, no. 3 (1956): 215.
60 Saul Austerlitz, 'When Hollywood Was Scared to Depict Anti-Semitism, It Made 'Gentleman's Agreement'' (Tablet, 15 May 2015) www.tabletmag.com/jewish-arts-andculture/172526/gentlemans-agreement-tcm
61 Chi Chi Izundu, 'Oscars So White: What People Are Saying About Diversity in Hollywood' (BBC, 19 January 2016) www.bbc.co.uk/newsbeat/rticle/35349772/oscars-sowhite-what-people-are-saying-about-diversity-in-hollywood
62 Greg Lukianoff and Jonathan Haidt, 'The Coddling of the American Mind' (The Atlantic, September 2015) www.theatlantic.com/magazine/archive/2015/09/the-coddling-of-the-Americanmind/399356

63 Harrier Lerner, *Why Won't You Apologize? Healing Big Betrayals and Everyday Hurts* (Simon & Schuster, 2017), 175.
64 Beverly Engel, 'The Power of Apology' (Psychology Today, 1 July 2002) www.psychologytoday.com/articles/200207/thepower-apology
65 Ibid.
66 Gelber (n. 20): 647–648
67 Eleanor Roosevelt, 'This Is My Story' (1940) 37 Reader's Digest 84.
68 Dr Charles Stranger, 'Stereotypes, Prejudice, and Discrimination' in *Principles of Social Psychology* (Flat World Knowledge Inc., 2011).
69 GW Dowsett, 'I'll Show You Mine, If You'll Show Me Yours: Gay Men, Masculinity Research, Men's Studies, and Sex', *Theory & Society* 22, no. 5 (1993): 697, 703.
70 The New Yorker Staff (n. 25).
71 *West Virginia State Bd. of Educ.* v. *Barnette* 319 U.S. 624, 644 (1943).
72 ECRI (n. 4).

# 4 Counter-terrorism policies and freedom of association – international and comparative perspectives

*Ashutosh Bhagwat*

## Introduction

In light of the steady spate of terrorist attacks on western targets in recent years, it is no surprise that counter-terrorism investigations and prosecutions have become a staple of modern law enforcement and intelligence. Most such prosecutions, when they target actual violence or plans or conspiracies to engage in violence, of course raise no serious civil liberties issues themselves (though the surveillance methods used to gather evidence may well raise concerns). Often, however, the subject of counter-terrorism prosecutions goes beyond targeting actual violence to targeting speech or groups that advocate or incite violence, targeting the act of joining with terrorist groups, or targeting the provision of 'material support' to such groups. In such instances, there is an inevitable tension between counter-terrorism policy and civil liberties, particularly rights of free speech and free association. How have courts resolved these tensions? The answer, in short, is rather poorly.

In the United States, the Supreme Court has meaningfully addressed the conflict between terrorism prosecutions and the First Amendment in only one case: its 2010 decision in *Holder* v. *Humanitarian Law Project*.[1] In this case the court rejected a First Amendment challenge to 18 U.S.C. §2339B(a)(1), the so-called material support statute, which bans the provision of material support to designated foreign terrorist organizations (FTOs).[2] As discussed in detail in Chapter 8, however, the *Humanitarian Law Project* decision did very little to clarify the law regarding the interaction between First Amendment rights and antiterrorism measures; indeed, the decision, if anything, increased the already high levels of confusion and uncertainty. And when we turn to the lower federal courts, as this chapter does, we find opinion after opinion that rejects First Amendment defences to terrorism charges as insubstantial, with barely any sustained discussion. As in *Humanitarian Law Project,* the pattern is one of assertion and obfuscation rather than careful analysis.

This chapter begins by summarizing cases from the lower U.S. federal courts where First Amendment defences were raised in terrorism prosecutions. I then examine a few decisions from the European Court of Human Rights, which also involved conflicts between counter-terrorism policies, on the one hand, and the rights of association and speech protected under the European Convention on Human Rights on the other hand. What emerges is a pattern of failing to take seriously the free speech and association issues implicated by counter-terrorism policies in both lower federal courts and the European court. The chapter concludes by suggesting that this pattern of judicial incoherence might be explained by a failure of courts to systematically consider both the importance of, but also the important limitations on, speech and association rights in this most fraught area, where politics, religion, and potential violence collide.

## I Terrorism and the First Amendment in the lower courts

This section summarizes a number of cases in the lower federal courts of the United States in which defendants raised non-frivolous First Amendment defences to counter-terrorism prosecutions. These cases tend to fall into one of two groups. The first is made up of anti-terrorism prosecutions, generally brought pursuant to either 18 U.S.C. §2339B, the material support statute upheld in *Humanitarian Law Project*; or its sibling, 18 U.S.C. §2339A, which prohibits the provision of material support or resources 'knowing or intending that they are to be used in preparation for, or in carrying out' various violations (the latter statute prohibits material support intended to aid actual acts of terrorism, as opposed to material support to FTOs). The second set of cases involves organizations seeking to challenge their designations as terrorist organizations.

### *Material support prosecutions based on speech*

#### *Tarek Mehanna*

Tarek Mehanna is a native-born US citizen with a doctorate in pharmacology who lived with his parents in the upscale suburb of Sudbury, Massachusetts.[3] In December 2011, Mehanna was convicted following a jury trial on multiple counts of providing material support to terrorism (as well as counts involving lying to the FBI).[4] Mehanna's prosecution was based in part on his translation from Arabic, and distribution on the Internet, of jihadi literature (in particular, a text titled *39 Ways to Serve and Participate in Jihad* and a video depicting Al Qaeda activities and propaganda involving Iraq).[5] The prosecution also introduced evidence that Mehanna flew to Yemen in 2004 seeking to obtain weapons training at a terrorist training camp, but conceded that he did not succeed in locating a camp (Mehanna denied that he was seeking weapons training).[6] The main thrust of the government's case at trial court level, however, was clearly the translation and distribution of jihadi materials.[7] Importantly, the government provided no proof that Mehanna coordinated his propaganda with any members of Al Qaeda or any other FTO.[8] Indeed, it is unclear whether Mehanna had any direct contact at all with Al Qaeda members.[9] Instead, the government's case relied on evidence that Mehanna described himself as Al Qaeda's 'English Wing'[10] and on other statements Mehanna made expressing support for Osama bin Laden and Al Qaeda.[11]

Mehanna's attorneys unsurprisingly sought to have the material support charges against Mehanna dismissed on First Amendment grounds.[12] The primary thrust of Mehanna's argument was that the *Humanitarian Law Project* decision required proof of coordination with an FTO (or in the case of §2339A, with known terrorists) and that the overt acts for which Mehanna had been indicted constituted protected, independent advocacy.[13] The government's response was to deny that coordination was a required element of a §2339A violation and that, in any event, coordination did not require direct contact between the defendant and an FTO – it was sufficient for a defendant to respond to an FTO's call for assistance, and to believe that he was assisting the organization.[14] The district court denied Mehanna's motion to dismiss, and ultimately Mehanna was convicted by a jury and sentenced to seventeen-and-a-half years in prison.[15]

### *Javed Iqbal and Saleh Elahwal*

Javed Iqbal is a Pakistani national who has resided in the United States since he was a teenager.[16] Iqbal lived on Staten Island, New York and ran a business providing specialized satellite programming.[17] In 2006, Iqbal was arrested and charged with material support for terrorism.[18] The gravamen of the charge was that, as part of his business, Iqbal retransmitted the signal of Al Manar, a television station associated with the Lebanese Shia organization, Hezbollah (sometimes spelled Hizballah).[19] Hezbollah is a complex organization that conducts charitable activities and is a political party within Lebanon, but it also uses terrorism to achieve its political goals.[20] It has been a designated FTO since 1997.[21] Eventually, after his First Amendment defence was denied by the trial judge on the grounds that Iqbal was being prosecuted for conduct, not speech, Iqbal pled guilty to one count of providing material support.[22] In pleading guilty, Iqbal confessed to receiving money for providing services to Al Manar, a fact that the court emphasized in rejecting Iqbal's First Amendment defense.[23] Iqbal was sentenced to 69 months in prison.[24]

Saleh Elahwal was Iqbal's business associate.[25] He too eventually pled guilty to a material support charge and was sentenced to 17 months in prison.[26]

### *Jubair Ahmad*

Jubair Ahmad is a young Pakistani-American (he was 24 at the time of his conviction) living in Woodbridge, Virginia.[27] When he was a teenager, before moving to the United States, Ahmad attended a training camp run by Lashkar-e-Tayyiba (LeT), a Pakistani militant group that conducts attacks against India because of the ongoing dispute between India and Pakistan over the state of Kashmir. (LeT is believed to be behind the November 2008 terrorist attack on Mumbai).[28] LeT has been a designated FTO since 2001.[29] In 2010, at the behest of the son of LeT's leader, Ahmad prepared a video glorifying LeT's activities and calling for fighters to wage jihad.[30] He then posted the video to YouTube.[31] These actions were the sole basis of his conviction for providing material support to terrorism, resulting in a 12-year sentence.[32]

### *Material support prosecutions based on money*

#### *Mohamad Hammoud*

Mohamad Hammoud is a Lebanese citizen who came to the United States in 1992.[33] While in the United States, he became involved in various illegal activities, including cigarette smuggling.[34] In addition, he assisted in raising money for Hezbollah and he personally donated $3,500 to that organization.[35] On the basis of these actions, Hammoud was tried and convicted of providing material support to a terrorist organization (along with a number of other offenses).[36]

On appeal, Hammoud argued that his material support conviction violated his First Amendment right to freedom of association.[37] The *en banc* Fourth Circuit rejected this view.[38] The primary grounds for its ruling was that the material support statute 'does not prohibit mere association; it prohibits the *conduct* of providing material support to a designated FTO. Therefore, cases regarding mere association with an organization do not control.'[39] Because it found that the statute did not directly target First Amendment protected activity, the court applied the more lenient O'Brien test that courts apply to facially neutral statutes that incidentally restrict expressive conduct. Under this standard, it easily upheld the statute.[40]

#### *Hossein Afshari, Roya Rahmani* et al.

Between 1997 and 2001, a group of individuals, including Hossein Afshari and Roya Rahmani, is alleged to have solicited funds at the Los Angeles International Airport, purportedly on behalf of an organization named Committee for Human Rights.[41] The collected funds were then allegedly forwarded to an organization called Mujahedin-e Khalq (MEK).[42] The MEK is an Iranian Marxist group which was designated as an FTO in 1997 (that designation was lifted in September of 2012).[43] As a consequence, Afshari, Rahmani, and their confederates were indicted for violating the material support statute.[44] The district court dismissed the indictment on the grounds that the procedures used to designate MEK as an FTO were unconstitutional.[45] On appeal, the Ninth Circuit reinstated the indictment.[46] In addition to rejecting the district court's analysis, the Ninth Circuit also considered, and rejected, a First Amendment claim brought by the defendants.[47] Specifically, the court rejected the argument that the First Amendment protected the defendants' activities by noting that '[t]hough contributions of money given to fund speech receive some First Amendment protection, it does not follow that all contributions of money are entitled to protection as though they were speech.'[48] The defendants' contributions were not entitled to First Amendment protections because '[i]n this context, the donation of money could properly be viewed by the government as more like the donation of bombs and ammunition than speech.'[49] The court concluded by quoting its own earlier decision in the *Humanitarian Law Project* v. *Reno* case (which later went before the Supreme Court) for the oft-quoted proposition that '[t]here is no First Amendment right to facilitate terrorism.'[50]

## Groups challenging terrorist designations

### *The Holy Land Foundation for Relief and Development*

The Holy Land Foundation for Relief and Development was an Islamic charitable foundation that operated in the United States, beginning in 1989.[51] It described itself as 'the largest Muslim charity in the United States'.[52] In December 2001, the Holy Land Foundation (HLF) was designated as a 'Specially Designated Global Terrorist' and all of its assets were frozen by the Department of the Treasury pursuant to an Executive Order issued by President Bush following the September 11, 2001 attacks.[53] The Executive Order was, in turn, issued under the authority of the International Emergency Economic Powers Act, passed by Congress in 1995.[54] The primary basis for the Holy Land Foundation's designation was evidence indicating that the Foundation had financial connections to Hamas, and had provided funding to Hamas as well as to charitable organizations and individuals linked to Hamas.[55] Hamas is the well-known Palestinian group engaged in armed struggle against the Israeli occupation of the Occupied Territories.[56] Hamas has been designated as a Specially Designated Terrorist (SDT) group since 1995 and a Specially Designated Global Terrorist (SDGT) since 2001.[57] It has also been an FTO for the purposes of the material support statute since 1997.[58]

The Foundation challenged its designation as a terrorist organization on a number of grounds, including a claim that 'the government had violated its First Amendment rights [including freedom of association] by prohibiting it from making any humanitarian contributions by blocking its assets.'[59] The D.C. Circuit offhandedly rejected this claim, stating that the law is established and that 'there is no constitutional right to facilitate terrorism'.[60] The lower court had rejected the Foundation's First Amendment claims on the same grounds,[61] noting as well that designating the Foundation a Specially Designated Global Terrorist organization and blocking its assets was permissible because these actions 'do not prohibit membership in Hamas or endorsement of its views, and therefore do not implicate HLF's associational rights.'[62] In the course of holding that 'there is no First Amendment right nor any other constitutional right to support terrorists', the D.C. Circuit cited the Ninth Circuit's opinion in *Humanitarian Law Project* v. *Reno*.[63]

### *Islamic American Relief Agency*

The Islamic American Relief Agency was, like the Holy Land Foundation, an Islamic charity, founded by a Sudanese immigrant in 1985.[64] In 2004, it, too, was designated as a Specially Designated Global Terrorist by the Bush Administration.[65] The factual basis for the Agency's designation was a bit more complicated than with the Holy Land Foundation but, in short, came down to allegations that the Agency had provided funding to another entity, which was itself acknowledged to be a terrorist organization.[66] Like the Holy Land Foundation, the Islamic

American Relief Agency raised a freedom of association challenge to its designation.[67] The D.C. Circuit predictably rejected this claim on the same grounds as before, citing its decision in Holy Land Foundation as well as the Ninth Circuit's decision in *Humanitarian Law Project*.[68] The court went on to reject the argument that the Supreme Court's First Amendment case law required proof of a specific intent to advance the terrorist organization's illegal ends, concluding that this requirement was limited to instances of pure association, not funding.[69]

## II Terrorism and association in the European Court of Human Rights

Article 11(1) of the European Convention on Human Rights states that '[e]veryone has the right to freedom of peaceful assembly and to freedom of association with others, including the right to form and to join trade unions for the protection of his interests'.[70] However, Article 11(2) of the Convention then goes on to qualify that protection by stating that

> [n]o restriction shall be placed on the exercise of these rights other than such as are prescribed by law and are necessary in a democratic society in the interests of national security or public safety, for the prevention of disorder or crime, for the protection of health or morals or for the protection of the rights and freedoms of others.[71]

In other words, the European Convention provides explicit protections for rights of assembly and association, unlike the First Amendment which does not mention association. But at the same time, the European Convention also (and also unlike the First Amendment) explicitly limits these rights by authorizing proportionate restrictions necessary to advance such vague goals as 'public safety' and 'morals'. Does this textual divergence result in differences in how courts resolve conflicts between associational rights and counter-terrorism policy? As it turns out, in practice it makes almost no difference, albeit the routes taken by the courts to reach similar results are a bit different.

Consider in this regard two cases decided by the European Court of Human Rights (ECHR), about a decade apart. The first was *United Communist Party of Turkey and Others* v. *Turkey*.[72] In that case, the United Communist Party of Turkey (going by its Turkish initials TBKP) challenged a decision by the Turkish Constitutional Court to dissolve the party.[73] The ECHR began by rejecting the Turkish government's (somewhat astonishing) claims that Article 11 did not even apply to political parties,[74] and that even if Article 11 protected the formation of protected associations it did not prevent their dissolution.[75] The ECHR then concluded that the dissolution of the TBKP was indeed intended to advance one of the 'legitimate aims' set forth in Article 11 – national security – because the TBKP's platform might be understood to advocate the creation of a separate Kurdish nation and so undermine the territorial integrity of the Turkish state.[76] Ultimately, however, the ECHR concluded that suppressing the TBKP for national security purposes was not 'necessary in a democratic society' (quoting the limiting language of Article 11(2)). It noted the importance of political parties in a democratic system and concluded that, for that reason, restrictions on the freedom of association of political parties required 'convincing and compelling reasons'.[77] Here, it was critical to the ECHR that the TBKP had neither engaged in, nor advocated, any form of violence or terrorism. For that reason, and because the TBKP's views on the Kurdish question were a part of democratic debate, the ECHR concluded that its suppression could not be reconciled with Article 11.[78]

The result in the TBKP litigation can be contrasted with the very different result in *Herri Batasuna and Batasuna* v. *Spain.*[79] The *Batasuna* litigation also involved a challenge to a judicial order dissolving political parties – in this case, an order by the Spanish Supreme Court dissolving two Basque parties, Herri Batasuna and Batasuna, because of their alleged affiliation with, and subservience to, the Basque terrorist organization ETA.[80] As with the TBKP, the ECHR agreed that the decision to dissolve these parties was intended to advance the legitimate aims, recognized in Article 11(2), of 'public safety, the prevention of disorder and the protection of the rights and freedoms of others'.[81] Next, the ECHR turned to the crucial question of whether the dissolution of the Batasuna parties was 'necessary in a democratic society'. It began by reiterating the point made in the TBKP litigation (indeed, citing that case) that political parties are an essential component of a democratic society and so may be restricted only for 'convincing and compelling reasons'.[82] But then the ECHR shifted tack by emphasizing that because political parties must comply with democratic norms, protection for such associations are not unlimited.[83] Therefore,

> a political party whose leaders incite violence or put forward a policy which fails to respect democracy or which is aimed at the destruction of democracy and the flouting of the rights and freedoms recognized in a democracy cannot lay claim to the convention's protection against penalties imposed on those grounds.[84]

Applying this principle, the ECHR concluded that because the banned parties had actively supported the ETA's terrorist strategies through a number of means, including holding pro-ETA demonstrations and naming ETA terrorists as honorary citizens of towns controlled by the parties, the Batasuna parties' dissolution did not violate Article 11.[85] In a particularly striking (at least to American eyes) passage, the ECHR stated that 'the refusal to condemn violence against a backdrop of terrorism that had been in place for more than thirty years and condemned by all the other political parties amounted to tacit support for terrorism.' It thus treated the Batasuna parties' failure to condemn ETA as a legitimate factor in their dissolution.[86]

The *United Communist Party of Turkey* and the *Batasuna* cases together established important principles underlying the freedom of association protected by Article 11, but they also identified important limitations on that freedom when claimed by allegedly violent or terrorist organizations. One notable point was that, in the *Batasuna* case, the petitioning political parties raised freedom of expression claims under Article 10 of the Convention as well as association claims under Article 11. The ECHR, however, dismissed the Article 10 claims summarily on the grounds that the discussion of the Article 11 claims effectively resolved the Article 10 claims – the obverse, it should be noted, of the U.S. Supreme Court's approach in *Humanitarian Law Project*, which subsumed the plaintiffs' association claim into the court's free speech analysis.[87] Ultimately, however, the bottom line is that that the European Court of Human Rights and the U.S. Supreme Court agreed that when a group is actually associated with violence or terrorism, it sheds both its speech and its associational rights.

## III Lessons and conundrums

### *Violence and associations*

That both the European and the United States courts have restricted associational protections to peaceful groups or, more accurately, have excluded violent groups from its protection is entirely sensible, at least at first blush. First of all, the association right is undoubtedly closely related to the right of assembly, and both the First Amendment to the United States Constitution and Article 11 of the European Convention on Human Rights explicitly state that they protect only *peaceable* assemblies.[88] Moreover, as a historical matter, the right to freedom of association that the United States Supreme Court has read into the First Amendment (because the text of the First Amendment does not mention association) was derived from the 'Assembly' clause. In particular, in the cases from the early- to mid-twentieth century, in which the Supreme Court first recognized an association right, the court generally used the terms 'assembly' and 'association' interchangeably, clearly implying that the textual right of assembly also protected a right to form groups.[89] This history, and the deep overlap it reveals between the non-textual association and textual assembly rights, makes it entirely reasonable to limit protection to peaceable associations just as the text protects only peaceable assemblies.[90] And while Article 11 of the European Convention on Human Rights does *not* explicitly limit association rights to peaceful groups, Article 11(2) recognizes the power of states to restrict association in order to protect both national security and public safety, and to prevent disorder. This effectively accomplishes the same result of restricting protection to peaceful associations. At first cut, therefore, the transatlantic rule that emerges is clear: associations are generally protected, but violent ones are not. And terrorist groups are, of course, violent in that they actively plan and engage in violent activities.[91]

It must be acknowledged, however, that while this simple statement fairly describes the reasoning of the European courts (albeit not without some complications, as we shall see), it is *not* in fact consistent with how American courts justify the results they reach. In *Humanitarian Law Project*, for example, the court engaged in extremely fact-specific (and unconvincing) free speech analysis, and did not even consider seriously the question of what sorts of associations receive constitutional protection. Moreover, in the leading Supreme Court case addressing violent associations, *Scales* v. *United States*, the court had held that association, even with purportedly violent groups (there, the Communist Party), was protected unless the individual's membership was an 'active and purposive membership, purposive that is as to the organization's criminal ends'.[92] It is obviously difficult to reconcile this approach with the result in *Humanitarian Law Project*, leaving a puzzle about how the court truly views the association right.

The truth is, however, that the *Scales* formulation is simply incorrect if understood as a *constitutional* holding. (The caveat is necessary because, while the *Scales* court purported to be engaging only in statutory interpretation,[93] later Supreme Court opinions seem to treat *Scales* as a constitutional decision.[94]) The discussion above makes it quite clear that the right of association, properly understood, does not extend to violent groups at all. Therefore any individual who seeks to associate with such groups is *a fortiori* acting outside the First Amendment, whatever his or her intentions regarding the group's unlawful ends and whatever the nature of his or her contributions to the group. That is why the D.C. Circuit was correct to reject the Islamic American Relief Agency's claim, relying on *Scales*, that its lack of specific intent to advance terrorism meant that its association rights were being violated, though *not* as the D.C. Circuit reasoned, because the association in that case involved funding. And once one recognizes that the First Amendment provides absolutely no protection to individuals seeking association with violent groups such as FTOs, the *result* in *Humanitarian Law Project* is clearly correct (as is the court's dictum suggesting that independent advocacy on behalf of FTOs would receive constitutional protection, because in that situation the key unprotected element of violent association is missing).[95] However, the reasoning of the Supreme Court, based as it is on an utterly unconvincing interpretation of free speech doctrine, cannot support the result it reached for the reasons discussed in Chapter 8 (though, as also explained in that chapter, the court was probably correct to reject the free speech claims in that case *in light of the correct association analysis*, which the court failed to engage in).

When we come to the lower federal courts in the United States, the problems with the judiciary's reasoning become even more severe. Recall that in many of the key terrorism cases discussed in Part I, both involving individuals who made financial contributions to FTOs and involving groups challenging their designation as terrorist groups, lower courts rejected associational claims on the theory that donating money to terrorist groups constitutes 'conduct' rather than protected speech or association and that, therefore, the First Amendment gives no protection to 'facilitating terrorism'. The difficult with this analysis is that it is clearly wrong. The ability to pool resources is, and must be, a central aspect of association, since it is through such pooling that associations effectuate their members' participation in the democratic process. It is surely no coincidence that *all* significant democratically engaged associations, including most clearly political parties, spend much of their time and effort raising money from members – i.e.

soliciting and accepting contributions. Without such financial contributions it is no exaggeration to say that most politically engaged associations would simply collapse. And, indeed, when we look beyond the terrorism context, it comes as no surprise to learn that the United States Supreme Court and other courts have *repeatedly* held (notably in cases involving campaign finance reform) that restrictions on financial contributions burden the right of association.[96] The lower courts' assertion that financial contributions have no relationship to the association right is thus patently wrong.

Nonetheless, in light of the limitations to the association right recognized above, the results in these cases are surely correct. The reason is *not*, as the courts said, that financial contributions do not constitute association. The reason is, rather, that such association is unprotected when directed at violent groups such as FTOs, because violent associations are unprotected. It is the nature of the groups at issue, not the nature of the defendants' actions, that permits prosecution – which makes perfect sense because, given the fungibility of money and many other resources, *any* support to a violent group can be said to support violence itself, whatever the theoretical aims of that support.

It would seem, therefore, that the terrorism/association conundrum is not a conundrum after all. It is merely (another) example of sloppy judicial reasoning leading to instinctively correct results. Unfortunately, the truth is somewhat more complicated. The simple statement that violent associations are unprotected may be true, but it hides a multitude of sins. Let us close by considering some of those sins, beginning with the problem of speech on behalf of associations.

### *Kinks in the armour*

One question that must be considered is how the principle of non-protection for violent associations is relevant to those terrorism prosecutions – such as those of Tarek Mehanna, Javed Iqbal, Saleh Elahwal, and Jubair Ahmad – which are based primarily on the defendants' speech. Can such purely speech-based prosecutions be reconciled with the First Amendment?

The critical legal background here is that the United States Supreme Court has long interpreted the First Amendment to provide *extremely* strong protection, even for speech that explicitly calls for violence (as the speech in all the lower court cases did). Under the leading decision in *Brandenberg* v. *Ohio*, speech that incites violence falls outside the First Amendment only if it is 'directed to inciting or producing imminent lawless action and is likely to incite or produce such action'.[97] Under this standard, which the court has consistently interpreted to require a very high degree of both likelihood and imminence of violence to permit prosecution,[98] none of the speech in these cases constituted unprotected incitement since in none of the cases did the government prove that violence was likely and imminent. As such, these cases would seem to be inconsistent with *Brandenburg*. Moreover, none of the lower court decisions even attempted to explain how their results did not punish protected speech, aside from advancing the abstruse argument that giving material support to an FTO constitutes 'conduct', even when the 'support' constituted only speech, as was true in all four of the prosecutions at issue. The *Humanitarian Law Project* court at least had the good grace to reject the government's argument that the speech at issue there constituted mere 'conduct'.[99]

Nonetheless, the *results* in these cases may well be correct. We will see in Chapter 8 why that is so with *Humanitarian Law Project*: the material support statute is best read as not criminalizing speech in favour of FTOs, but rather criminalizing association with FTOs either through speech or conduct (such as providing funds) and association with violent groups is unprotected. Furthermore, any independent free speech interest in that case (if such an interest even existed) was, at best, moderate. The same principles might also be invoked to rationalize the other cases. In the Iqbal and Elahwal cases, for example, the defendants were actually paid by the FTO Hezbollah to retransmit Hezbollah's television station. While the transmission of a television station's signal is surely 'speech', and so presumptively protected absent proof of imminent and likely violence, doing so on behalf of Hezbollah is just as surely punishable as unprotected association. Similarly, the propaganda video that Jubair Ahmad created for the LeT was also speech that did not meet the *Brandenburg* threshold, but the fact that he created the video at the specific request of and under the direction of the LeT left his actions unprotected by the First Amendment. And in both cases, any independent speech interest the defendants had was surely outweighed by the government's interest in combatting terrorism, given that in these cases (unlike the *Humanitarian Law Project*), the defendants' actions were advancing the violent goals of FTOs.

But there is a problem, and his name is Tarek Mehanna. The gravamen of the government's theory at Mehanna's trial was that his distribution of Jihadi propaganda on behalf of Al Qaeda constituted material support of terrorism. But the government provided no evidence that Mehanna had actually been in contact with *anyone* associated with Al Qaeda, and at trial went so far as to argue that coordination was not a necessary element of a material support prosecution under 18 U.S.C. §2339A. As such, the government sought largely to break down the distinction drawn in *Humanitarian Law Project* between protected independent advocacy and unprotected association. And it is worth noting in this regard that Mehanna's trial occurred in December of 2011, well after the Supreme Court issued its *Humanitarian Law Project* decision in June of 2010. The lesson of the *Mehanna* case is that if the law is to draw a key distinction between speech and association, it *must* also clearly define the contours and limits of the concept of association. In other words, the law must clearly define when there is sufficient contact and coordination between a speaker and a violent group to be able to say that the speaker is no longer engaged in protected advocacy, but rather has crossed the line into unprotected association. The *Humanitarian Law Project* decision provides little guidance on this issue because of its dismissive treatment of the association claim in that case; the Mehanna prosecution neatly illustrates how, absent clear guidelines, prosecutors (and courts) are likely to push hard to find association with the barest of evidence. It was the trial court's failure to provide a clear definition of coordination – a failure which was upheld by the Court of Appeals on convoluted and unconvincing grounds[100] that makes the Mehanna prosecution so problematic.

Furthermore, this problem is obviously not limited to the United States. Consider, in this respect, the ECHR's decision in the *Batasuna* litigation. There was no doubt in that case that the actual terrorist group at issue, the ETA, was an unprotected association, membership of which could be freely criminalized. But in *Batasuna* the Spanish government was seeking to suppress two political parties, not the ETA, on the grounds that there were too closely associated with the ETA. And the ECHR agreed. But why? At times, the opinion seems to suggest that the mere fact that elected members of Batasuna had expressed sympathy with the ETA's goals, and (more importantly) violent methods, was enough. It also emphasized Batasuna's failure to condemn ETA violence. Such an approach, however, is chillingly reminiscent of the worst excesses of the Espionage Act prosecutions in the United States during the First World War, when mere expressions of sympathy with or support for individuals resisting the draft were sufficient to create criminal liability.[101] And it is entirely irreconcilable with the principle of American law that independent expressions of support for violence remain protected unless they rise to the level of incitement.[102] This is not to say that the ECHR was wrong to uphold the dissolution of the Batasuna parties. Perhaps there was enough historical coordination between ETA and Batasuna, or enough overlap in leadership, to treat them as effectively one umbrella association. But the ECHR's decision is distressingly free of detailed analysis of *when* common goals, and even political sympathies, transform into association subject to legal sanction. And the court's seeming indifference is accentuated by the fact that it dismissed the Batasuna parties' Article 10 freedom of expression claims with the throwaway comment that 'the Court considers that the questions raised by the applicant parties under this Article concern the same facts as those raised under Article 11 of the Convention. Consequently, it does not find it necessary to examine them separately'.[103] If the ECHR is serious in this statement, then it effectively is saying that speech becomes unprotected if it merely expresses sympathy with, or even fails to condemn, the independent violent actions of others.[104] That surely cannot be correct, even if not all jurisdictions wish to adopt the extremely speech-protective definition of incitement under the First Amendment, as interpreted in *Brandenburg*.

None of this is to say that the correct answer here, as to how to define the limits of association, is an easy one. Difficult questions remain about when an association can be characterized as non-peaceable and therefore unprotected – surely isolated acts of violence by members of the group, so long as not controlled by the group itself, cannot be enough. The United States Supreme Court has so held, stating that

> liability may not be imposed merely because an individual belonged to a group, some members of which committed acts of violence. For liability to

be imposed by reason of association alone, it is necessary to establish that the group itself possessed unlawful goals.[105]

There is also the question of when an organization that was once violent can be said to have sufficiently disavowed violence to attain protected status. And, of course, sometimes groups have complex organizational structures that make it difficult to determine when particular associations should or should not be considered sufficiently 'affiliated' with other violent groups to merit condemnation – that, arguably, is the problem posed by Batasuna and the ETA. These issues are far too complex to resolve in this limited space. The best that can be said is that, as courts confront different factual settings, a jurisprudence of associations can and must be developed which might well come to rival some of the complexity of existing free speech jurisprudence.

## Conclusion

In both Europe and the United States, courts appear to have come to the common sense conclusion that freedom of association cannot and does not extend to groups that plan or engage in violence towards persons or property. Unfortunately, while the actions of American courts support this view of the law, their analysis has never explicitly embraced this principle. As a result, the jurisprudence of freedom of association remains woefully underdeveloped in the United States. In Europe, the ECHR has been more forthright in its embrace of the view that violence alone is enough to condemn associations. Unfortunately, and despite this, the ECHR has failed to fully explain when and why a particular individual or group can be said to have actually associated with a concededly violent group. As a result, European law also has failed to clearly define the contours of association rights. This legal uncertainty has the potential to chill otherwise protected associations. And in the United States, the courts' failure to clearly state that participation in or planning violence ends all constitutional protections for groups might encourage the formation or continuation of some associations which should not be protected. Moving forward, it is to be hoped that courts will rectify these problems.

*I would like to thank Professor James Weinstein for his help. I would also like to acknowledge that portions of this Chapter were previously published in the Emory Law Journal as Ashutosh Bhagwat, Terrorism and Associations, 63 Emory L.J. 581 (2014).

## Notes

1 561 U.S. 1 (2011).
2 *See id.* at 7–8; *see also* 18 U.S.C. §2339B(a)(1) (2006).
3 *See* Innokenty Pyetranker, *Sharing Translations or Supporting Terror? An Analysis of Tarek Mehanna in the Aftermath of* Holder *v.* Humanitarian Law Project, NAT'L SECURITY L. BRIEF, Spring 2012, at 21; Abby Goodnough and Liz Robbins,

*Massachusetts Man Is Held on Charges of Plotting Attacks, Including One at a Mall*, N.Y. TIMES, 22 October 2009, at A21.

4 *See* Pyetranker, *supra* note 3, at 38; Abby Goodnough, *U.S. Citizen Is Convicted in Plot to Support Al Qaeda*, N.Y. TIMES, 21 December 2011, at A26.

5 *See* Pyetranker, *supra* note 3, at 36 (citing Second Superseding Indictment at 1, 8, 15–16, *United States* v. *Mehanna*, No. 09-CR-10017-GAO (D. Mass. 2011), 2010 WL 2516469); *see also* Nikolas Abel, Note, United States *v.* Mehanna*, the First Amendment, and Material Support in the War on Terror*, 54 *B.C. L. REV.* (2013): 711, 732 (citing Government's Proffer and Memorandum in Support of Detention at 64–66, *Mehanna*, No. 09-CR-10017-GAO (D. Mass 2011)).

6 *See* Abel, *supra* note 5, at 731 & n. 169 (citing Second Superseding Indictment, *supra* note 5, at 5).

7 *See id.* at 732 (citing Second Superseding Indictment, *supra* note 56, at 8). The First Circuit later affirmed Mehanna's conviction in full. *See United States* v. *Mehanna*, 735 F.3d 32, 41 (1st Cir. 2013). Interestingly, the appellate court's decision to affirm Mehanna's conviction on the terrorism counts relied entirely on his 2004 trip to Yemen. *See id.* at 46. Indeed, the court came close to conceding that the government's evidence was insufficient to demonstrate that Mehanna's translation and speech activities were coordinated with Al Qaeda. *See id.* at 50–51. The court concluded that the mass of evidence that had been admitted at trial regarding the government's 'translation-as-material support theory' was irrelevant because the jury was properly instructed, and the factual evidence regarding Mehanna's Yemen trip was sufficient to support his conviction. *Id.* at 51. Whatever the merits of this analysis, it remains true that at trial, before the convicting jury, the government heavily emphasized Mehanna's speech, and the district court failed to provide any detailed definition of the "coordination" with an FTO that was required to bring speech within the scope of the material support statute, as interpreted in *Humanitarian Law Project*. *Id.* at 49.

8 *See id.* at 739–40.

9 *Id.*

10 *Id.* at 732 and n. 175 (quoting Government's Proffer and Memorandum in Support of Detention, *supra* note 5, at 11) (internal quotation marks omitted).

11 *See* Pyetranker, *supra* note 3, at 21–2.

12 *Id.* at 36–7 (citing Defendant's Memorandum of Law in Support of His Motion to Dismiss Counts One Through Three Based on Vagueness and Overbreadth, *United States* v. *Mehanna*, No. 09-CR-10017-GAO (D. Mass. 2011), 2011 WL 3740563.

13 *See id.* at 37 (citing Defendant's Memorandum of Law in Support of His Motion to Dismiss, *supra* note 12, at 3, 5, 16–18); Abel, *supra* note 5 at 732–3 (citing Defendant's Memorandum of Law in Support of His Motion to Dismiss, *supra* note 12, at 11–12).

14 *See* Abel, *supra* note 5 at 732–3 (citing Government's Opposition to Defendant's Motion to Dismiss Counts One Through Three of the Second Superseding Indictment Based on Overbreadth and Vagueness at 21–3, *Mehanna*, No. 09-CR-10017-GAO (D. Mass. 2011), 2011 WL 3959520.

15 Pyetranker, *supra* note 3, at 38.

16 Benjamin Weiser, *A Guilty Plea in Providing Satellite TV for Hezbollah*, N.Y. TIMES, 24 December 2008, at A21.

17 *See id.*

18 *See id.*

19 *See* Timothy Williams & William K. Rashbaum, *New York Man Charged with Enabling Hezbollah Television Broadcasts*, N.Y. TIMES, 25 August 2006, www.nytimes.com/2006/08/25/nyregion/25tv.html

20 *See* Nicholas Kulish, *Despite U.S. Fear, Hezbollah Moves Openly in Europe*, N.Y. TIMES, 16 August 2012, at A1.

21 Bureau of Counterterrorism, *Foreign Terrorist Organizations*, U.S. DEP'T ST. (28 September 2012), www.state.gov/j/ct/rls/other/des/123085.htm
22 *See* Weiser, *supra* note 16.
23 *Id.*
24 Press Release, U.S. Attorney's Office, S. Dist. of N.Y., New Jersey Man Sentenced to 17 Months in Prison for Providing Material Support and Resources to Hizballah (23 June 2009), www.fbi.gov/newyork/press-releases/2009/nyfo062309.htm
25 *See id.*
26 *Id.*
27 *See* Rachel Karas, *Woodbridge Man Sentenced to 12 Years for Terrorist Propaganda Video*, POST LOCAL (13 April 2012, 6:40 PM), www.washingtonpost.com/blogs/crime-scene/post/woodbridge-man-sentenced-to-12-years-for-terrorist-propaganda-video/2012/04/13/gIQACI7tFT_blog.html
28 Press Release, U.S. Attorney's Office, E. Dist. of Va., Pakistani National Living in Woodbridge Pleads Guilty to Providing Material Support to Terrorist Organization (2 December 2011), www.justice.gov/usao/vae/news/2011/12/20111202ahmadnr.html; *see* Karas, *supra* note 27.
29 Bureau of Counterterrorism, *supra* note 21.
30 *See* Karas, *supra* note 27.
31 *Id.*
32 *Id.*
33 *United States* v. *Hammoud*, 381 F.3d 316, 325 (4th Cir. 2004) (en banc), *vacated*, 543 U.S. 1097 (2005).
34 See *id.*
35 *Id.* at 326. Hammoud's associates were also found to have provided "dual use" physical equipment to Hezbollah, but Hammoud declined to participate in these activities. *Id.*
36 *Id.*
37 See *id.* at 328.
38 *Id.* at 329.
39 *Id.*
40 *Id.* (citing *United States* v. *O'Brien*, 391 U.S. 367, 377 (1968)). In *O'Brien*, the Supreme Court upheld the conviction of David Paul O'Brien for burning his draft card during an anti-war rally, on the grounds that the statute prohibiting the burning of draft cards was not directed at speech, but was rather a neutral conduct regulation whose purpose was "unrelated to the suppression of free expression." *O'Brien*, 391 U.S. at 369, 377.
41 *United States* v. *Afshari*, 426 F.3d 1150, 1152 (9th Cir. 2005) (internal quotation marks omitted).
42 *Id.*
43 *Id.* at 1152–53; Scott Shane, *Iranian Dissidents Convince U.S. to Drop Terror Label*, N.Y. TIMES, 21 September 2012, www.nytimes.com/2012/09/22/world/middleeast/iranian-opposition-group-mek-wins-removal-from-us-terrorist-list.html?pagewanted=all&_r=0
44 *Afshari*, 426 F.3d at 1152.
45 *See United States* v. *Rahmani*, 209 F. Supp. 2d 1045, 1059 (C.D. Cal. 2002), *rev'd sub nom. United States* v. *Ashfari*, 426 F.3d 1150 (9th Cir. 2005).
46 *See Afshari*, 426 F.3d at 1153.
47 *See id.* at 1160.
48 *Id.* (footnote omitted) (citing *McConnell* v. *FEC*, 540 U.S. 93 (2003); *Buckley* v. *Valeo*, 424 U.S. 1 (1976)).
49 *Id.*
50 *Id.* at 1161 (quoting *Humanitarian Law Project* v. *Reno*, 205 F.3d 1130, 1133 (2000)) (internal quotation mark omitted).

51 *See Holy Land Foundation. for Relief and Development* v. *Ashcroft*, 333 F.3d 156, 160 (D.C. Cir. 2003). The Foundation was originally named the 'Occupied Land Fund' and changed its name to Holy Land Foundation in 1991. *Id.*
52 *Id.* (internal quotation marks omitted).
53 *See id.*; Exec. Order No. 13,224, 3 C.F.R. 786 (2002).
54 50 U.S.C. §1701 (2006); *see* 3 C.F.R. 786.
55 *Holy Land Found.*, 333 F.3d at 161.
56 *See* Clyde Haberman, *Israeli Tensions Rise as an Officer Is Found Slain*, N.Y. TIMES, 16 December 1992, at A1.
57 *Holy Land Found.*, 333 F.3d at 159.
58 Bureau of Counterterrorism, *supra* note 21.
59 *Holy Land Found.*, 333 F.3d at 164 (citing *FEC* v. *Colo. Republican Fed. Campaign Comm.*, 533 U.S. 431 (2001)).
60 *Id.* at 164–5 (quoting *Holy Land Foundation for Relief & Development* v. *Ashcroft*, 219 F. Supp. 2d 57, 81 (D.D.C. 2002), *aff'd*, 333 F.3d 156 (D.C. Cir. 2003)) (internal quotation marks omitted).
61 See *id.* at 164.
62 *Id.* at 161 (quoting *Holy Land Found.*, 219 F. Supp. 2d at 81) (internal quotation marks omitted).
63 *Id.* at 166 (citing *Humanitarian Law Project* v. *Reno*, 205 F.3d 1130, 1133 (9th Cir. 2000)).
64 *Islamic Am. Relief Agency* v. *Gonzales*, 477 F.3d 728, 730–31 (D.C. Cir. 2007).
65 See *id.* at 731.
66 See *id.*
67 See *id.*
68 *Id.* at 736–37 (citing *Holy Land Foundation*, 333 F.3d at 166; *Humanitarian Law Project*, 205 F.3d at 1133).
69 *Id.* at 737.
70 European Convention on Human Rights, available at www.echr.coe.int/Documents/Convention_ENG.pdf
71 *Id.*
72 *United Communist Party of Turkey and Others* v. *Turkey* [GC], no. 19392/92 (30 January 1998), Reports 1998-I, *available at* https://hudoc.echr.coe.int/eng#
73 *Id.* at 9–10.
74 *Id.* at 25.
75 *Id.* at 33.
76 *Id.* at 40–41.
77 *Id.* at 46.
78 *Id.* at 57.
79 *Herri Batasuna and Batasuna* v. *Spain*, numbers 25803/04 and 25817/04 (11 June 2009), *available at* https://hudoc.echr.coe.int/eng#
80 *Id.* at 30–2.
81 *Id.* at 64.
82 *Id.* at 77 (*citing United Communist Party of Turkey and Others* v. *Turkey*, 30 January 1998, §§23, 25, 46, Reports 1998-I).
83 Though the court did not cite it, its conclusion in this regard is consistent with Article 17 of the Convention, which states that '[n]othing in this Convention may be interpreted as implying … any right to engage in any activity or perform any act aimed at the destruction of any of the rights and freedoms set forth therein.'
84 *Herri Batasuna, supra* note 79, at 79.
85 *Id.* at 85.
86 *Id.* at 88. Ian Cram reads the Spanish Supreme Court's decision to ban Herri Batasuna in similar terms, as rooted in part on the party's failure to condemn ETA violence. I. Cram, "Constitutional Responses to Extremist Political Associations:

ETA, Batasuna and Democratic Norms" (2008) 28 *Legal Studies* 68–95. Cram, writing before the ECHR's decision in *Herri Batasuna*, thought that because of previous precedent the ECHR might reject this rationale. His prediction of course turned out to be incorrect – though, as we shall see, his argument had and retains great merit.

87 *Herri Batasuna, supra* note 79, 97; *Humanitarian Law Project*, 561 U.S. at 39–40. In the TBKP litigation the party had also raised an Article 10 claim, but the court concluded it need not address it given its ruling under Article 11. *See United Communist Party of Turkey, supra* n. 85, at 62.

88 European Convention on Human Rights, *supra* note 83, Art. 11(1) ('[e]veryone has the right to freedom of peaceful assembly'); U.S. Const., Amend. I ('Congress shall make no law … abridging … the right of the people peaceably to assemble').

89 See *Whitney* v. *California*, 274 U.S. 357, 371 (1927); *id.* at 372–9 (Brandeis, J., concurring); *DeJonge* v. *Oregon*, 323 U.S. 516, 518 (1937); *American Communications Ass'n* v. *Douds*, 339 U.S. 382, 399–402, 409 (1950); *NAACP* v. *Alabama ex rel. Patterson*, 357 U.S. 449, 460, 462 (1958). For more detailed descriptions of the derivation from of the association right from the First Amendment's Assembly Clause, *see* Ashutosh Bhagwat, *Associational Speech*, 120 Yale L.J. 978, 983–9 (2011); John Inazu, Liberty's Refuge: The Forgotten Freedom of Assembly 61–2, 79–84, 132–5, 141–4 (2012).

90 For a more detailed exposition of this idea, *see* Ashutosh Bhagwat, *Terrorism and Associations*, 63 Emory L.J. 581, 605–7, 615–18 (2014).

91 Under current U.S. law, it is extremely unlikely that a group which merely advocated or even threatened violence in the abstract could be proscribed, since such speech seems clearly protected under the *Brandenburg* standard, discussed in more detail below. *See supra* notes 98–9 and accompanying text. Other jurisdictions such as the United Kingdom can and do adopt less protective approaches to such speech and so such groups. *See supra* note 102.

92 *Scales* v. *United States*, 367 U.S. 203, 209, 229–30 (1961).

93 *Id.* at 221–22.

94 *See, for example*, *Holder* v. *Humanitarian Law Project*, 561 U.S. 1, 44 (2010) (Breyer, J., dissenting); *NAACP* v. *Claiborne Hardware Co.*, 458 U.S. 886, 919 (1982); *Healy* v. *James*, 408 U.S. 169, 186 (1972).

95 *Holder* v. *Humanitarian Law Project*, 561 U.S. 1, 25–6, 39 (2010).

96 *See, for example*, *FEC* v. *Colo. Republican Fed. Campaign Comm.*, 533 U.S. 431, 440 (2001) ('Spending for political ends and contributing to political candidates both fall within the First Amendment's protection of speech and political association.'); *Buckley* v. *Valeo*, 424 U.S. 1, 18 (1976) ('[T]he present Act's contribution and expenditure limitations impose direct quantity restrictions on political communication and association by persons, groups, candidates, and political parties.'); *Wis. Right to Life State Political Action Comm.* v. *Barland*, 664 F.3d 139, 152 (7th Cir. 2011) (quoting *Colo. Republican*, 533 U.S. at 440); *SpeechNow.org* v. *FEC*, 599 F.3d 686, 692 (D.C. Cir. 2010) (quoting *Davis* v. *FEC*, 554 U.S. 724, 740 n. 7 (2008)); *Carver* v. *Nixon*, 72 F.3d 633, 636 (8th Cir. 1995) (quoting *Buckley* v. *Valeo*, 424 U.S. 1, 18 (1976)); *Casino Ass'n of La.* v. *State*, 2002–0265, p. 8 (La. 6/21/02); 820 So. 2d 494, 500.

97 395 U.S. 444, 447 (1969).

98 *See, for example*, *Hess* v. *Indiana*, 414 U.S. 105 (1973); *NAACP* v. *Claiborne Hardware*, 458 U.S. 886 (1982). For a modern description, and defense, of the *Brandenburg* test, *see* Alan K. Chen, *Free Speech and the Confluence of National Security and Internet Exceptionalism*, 86 Fordham L. Rev. 380 (2017).

99 *Holder* v. *Humanitarian Law Project*, 561 U.S. 1, 27 (2010).

100 *United States* v. *Mehanna*, 735 F.3d 32, 49 (1st Cir. 2013).

101 See, for example, *Schenck* v. *United States*, 249 U.S. 47 (1919); *Debs* v. *United States*, 249 U.S. 211 (1919); *cf. Masses Pub. Co.* v. *Patten*, 246 Fed. 24 (2nd Cir.

1917) (upholding denial of postal service to magazine which expressed sympathy with individuals imprisoned for encouraging draft resistance).

102 Other jurisdictions do not provide the same level of protection for independent speech supporting terrorism as the First Amendment. Great Britain, for example, criminalizes speech which "glorifies the commission or preparation" of terrorist acts. Terrorism Act 2006, §1(3)(a), *available at* www.legislation.gov.uk/ukpga/2006/11 (last visited 25 June 2018)

103 *Herri Batasuna and Batasuna, supra* note 79, at 97.

104 Another possible (though to my mind less plausible) reading of this language is that the ECHR was holding that because Batasuna's association with the ETA was sufficiently close to justify dissolution of the Batsuna parties, any free expression claim they had was irrelevant. If that is what the court meant, then its analysis is consistent with the main argument set forth in this chapter; but it still does not excuse the court's failure to define the limits of association.

105 *NAACP* v. *Claiborne Hardware*, 458 U.S. 886, 920 (1982). For reasons discussed above, however, the *Claiborne Hardware* court was incorrect to then assert (citing *Scales*) that for liability to be imposed, it is also necessary that 'the individual held a specific intent to further those illegal aims.' *Id.*

# 5 University free speech as a space of exception in Prevent?

*Andrew W Neal*

There is much disquiet in British universities about the new 'Prevent' duty imposed on various public sector organizations by the Counter-Terrorism and Security Act 2015, which requires staff 'to have due regard to the need to prevent people from being drawn into terrorism'.[1] For example, the position of the main academic trade union, the UCU, is that this 'seriously threatens academic freedom', 'will stifle campus activism', and 'will force our members to spy on our learners'.[2] The National Union of Students has pursued a 'Preventing Prevent' campaign.[3] This is in the context of more general concerns about how Prevent operates in society, and about how the Prevent duty extends security functions and responsibilities that were once exclusive to the state to professionals in sectors such as education, health and social services. Prevent expands and normalizes the practice and experience of 'security' in everyday life, institutionalizing fear and suspicion.

The chapter begins by reviewing the origins of the Prevent policy and the invention of 'radicalization', which is a pseudo-science unsupported by academic literature. It then explores how Prevent affects freedom of speech in universities. Reviewing some of the evidence gathered by a recent Joint Committee on Human Rights inquiry into 'Free Speech in Universities', this section argues that although there is little quantifiable evidence of a downturn in free speech on campus, the Prevent duty is experienced with suspicion and mistrust by Muslim students in particular. It has a chilling effect on political debate and activity. This is despite special legal protections given to freedom of speech and academic freedom in universities.

Then, going beyond the JCHR report, the chapter explores how universities, in effect, became a space of exception in the Prevent regime. Despite the problems experienced in the sector, free speech is, in theory, protected in universities in a way enjoyed by no other sector, such as schools or health services. There is a large network of concern about university free speech, expressed by parliamentarians, ministers, and university leaders. This section looks briefly at the legislative struggle in parliament over the creation of the Prevent duty, which centred almost exclusively on the threat it posed to freedom of expression and to academic freedom in universities, to the exclusion of concerns about other sectors. University free speech under Prevent is thus the exception that proves the rule. In other sectors, professionals who encounter free speech on 'risky' topics are to treat it as suspicious and potentially report it to the authorities.

However, universities are an exception on paper only. The inherent vagueness of 'being drawn into terrorism' through 'radicalization', combined with a disjuncture between the law and government implementation guidelines, mean that although the university exception may formally exist, Prevent nevertheless creates uncertainty, suspicion, and mistrust on campus. The reporting of 'risky' students who have broken no law remains a possibility.

## What is Prevent?

The Prevent policy was first produced by the Labour government under Tony Blair in 2003. It was one of the four 'Ps' of the wider 'CONTEST' counter-terrorism strategy produced after 9/11, the others being 'Pursue', 'Protect', and 'Prepare'. It was expanded and revised in 2006 after the 7/7 bombings, and revised periodically since, most substantially after the change of government in 2010.

The Counter-Terrorism and Security Act 2015 put parts of the policy into law for the first time. Amongst other things, it created a new statutory 'Prevent duty' – 'to have due regard to the need to prevent people being drawn into terrorism' – that applied to many 'specified bodies' including schools, nurseries, health care providers, prisons, colleges, and universities.

The differences between Prevent under different governments are important because they show the different ways that suspicion has been conceptualized, targeted, and experienced. Under Labour, Prevent was led by the Department for Communities and Local Government. This reflected assumptions about the nature of 'home-grown terrorism', which Labour constructed as a problem of community marginalization. As such, its Prevent policy aimed to tackle structural socio-economic problems, 'disadvantage', and 'inequality'. It distributed money to what it deemed to be 'moderate' Islamic community groups in order to 'create strong, prosperous, and empowered communities'.[4] The aim was to foster communities that would be,

> ... better equipped to effectively reject the ideology of violent extremism, to confront and isolate apologists for terrorism, to channel legitimate grievances through democratic means and to provide support to vulnerable individuals.[5]

The Labour Prevent policy received criticism from several directions. The press raised questions about the groups it funded, some of which could be seen as holding relatively 'extreme', if not violent, views.[6] Moreover, the 7/7 bombers did not fit the policy's vision of marginalized and vulnerable individuals, being for most part well-integrated into their multicultural communities around Leeds.[7] A subsequent Intelligence and Security Community report could not say if this version of Prevent would have prevented the London bombings had it been in place earlier.[8]

Aside from effectiveness, the main problem with the Labour Prevent policy was that it created an association between community cohesion work and counterterrorism. Muslim community projects in receipt of government funding came to be seen as vehicles for 'spying' on those communities. It was also problematic that Prevent funding was targeted at Muslims rather than other communities. This created mistrust both ways: the policy seemed to be built upon suspicion of Muslims, and, in turn, Muslims became suspicious of the policy. The House of Commons Communities and Local Government Select Committee summed up these problems following an inquiry:

> [We] believe that this work can be successful only if untainted by the negative association with a counter-terrorism agenda ... The single focus on Muslims in Prevent has been unhelpful. We conclude that any programme which focuses solely on one section of a community is stigmatising.... We remain concerned by the number of our witnesses who felt that Prevent had been used to 'spy' on Muslim communities ... [Despite] rebuttals, the allegations of spying retain widespread credibility within certain sections of the Muslim community.[9]

This committee report bookended the Labour iteration of the Prevent policy. A general election, change of government, and changes to the Prevent policy followed shortly. Yet mistrust around the policy lingers, and has been exacerbated.

In 2011, in a speech to the Munich Security Conference, Conservative Prime Minister David Cameron signalled a change in direction on government counterterrorism policy. This shifted focus from Labour's efforts to encourage 'moderate' forms of Islam to what he called the 'ideology' of 'Islamist extremism'.[10] Cameron criticized the previous policy of 'state multiculturalism' and called instead for a 'much more active, muscular liberalism'.[11] The problem, he argued, was too much 'passive tolerance' and not enough judgment of Muslim groups:

> Do they believe in universal human rights – including for women and people of other faiths? Do they believe in equality of all before the law? Do they believe in democracy and the right of people to elect their own government? Do they encourage integration or separatism?[12]

This more judgmental discourse fed into the revised Prevent policy published in 2011, and then into the new statutory Prevent duty in 2015. Responsibility for Prevent was passed from Communities and Local Government to the Home Office (the interior ministry), which is the lead ministry for the police and the domestic security service, MI5, and also has its own Office for Security and Counter-Terrorism. Whereas Labour's concern had been to steer people away from 'violent extremism', the new government aimed to intervene earlier in an assumed process of radicalization, tackling 'extremist ideology', even if it did not (yet) embrace violence.[13] However, there is little consensus that such a process exists.

## The invention of 'radicalization'

The term 'radicalization' is recent, vague, contested, and subject to political whim. There is little scientific agreement on whether such a socio-political process of 'radicalization' exists or on how to model it if it did.[14]

The term was almost unheard of before the early 2000s. It has no provenance in terrorism studies, which as an academic discipline is decades old. It was not used in relation to Northern Ireland, nor to explain 'recruitment' processes in other campaigns of political violence. Mark Sedgwick argues that 'radicalization' came to public prominence after the '7/7' London bombings in 2005 as effort to explain 'home-grown' terrorism.[15] Prior to this, the assumption in political debate was that Islamist terrorism was an 'international' rather than domestic problem: assumed to be brought to western countries by foreign enemies, not developed at home. Figure 5.1 shows usage of 'radicalization' in the press.

The concept of 'radicalization' raises more questions than it answers. 'Radical' is a relative term. What was once radical, and policed by law and state, can quite quickly become mainstream. For example, support for gay marriage in the 1980s was a minority view to say the least, but today many countries are legalizing it. This makes state-mandated suspicion of radicalism problematic enough.

However, the $64,000 question is why some radicals turn to violence. All terrorists may be radicals, but not all radicals become terrorists.[16] This raises a number of sub-questions. At what point has someone been radicalized? Is it when they start to hold certain beliefs? Is it when their beliefs diverge from wider political values? Or is it when they act on those beliefs? The relativity problem of assessing radical beliefs has prompted scholars such as Randy Borum to suggest that we abandon the problematization of beliefs and focus only on behaviour.[17] Others, such as Peter Neuman, argue that beliefs and ideologies are relevant in explaining terrorism, because terrorism is a form of political violence

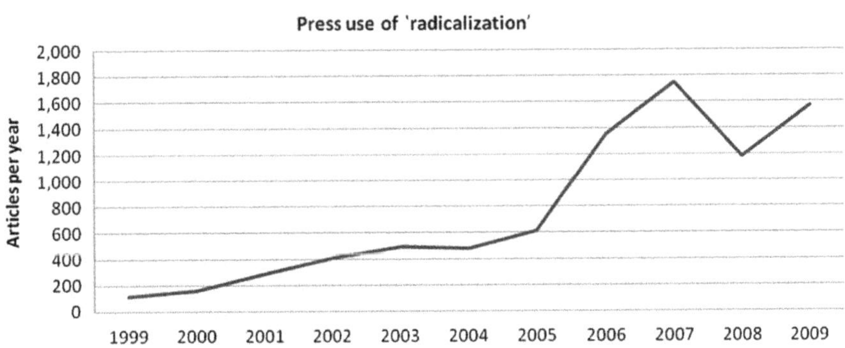


*Figure 5.1* Articles using the term 'radicalization' in the English-language press.

Source: aggregated, time-limited Google News searches.[18]

that makes no sense without its accompanying political belief system.[19] However, even if Neuman is correct, this does nothing to explain why any one particular individual may turn to violence. Scholars have reached similar conclusions against the existence of an unambiguous radicalization process and about why some radicals turn to violence. As Anthony Richards writes, summing up conferences on the issue that were sponsored by the Economic and Social Research Council, Chatham House and the Royal United Services Institute: 'We don't know – nor it appears, are we ever likely to know – why some young men resort to violent extremism and others do not.'[20] The Prevent regime is thus built on a notion of 'radicalization' that has little scholarly support. Its ambiguities feed into the practice of the policy.

## Prevent, free speech and the law

There are many dimensions of the Prevent policy, but this chapter is concerned only with its problematization of free speech in universities. This issue has become politicized of late, not just because of Prevent, but also because of the supposed practice of 'no platforming', whereby student groups deny external speakers a platform at events on campus; 'safe space' policies that restrict topics that may cause some students distress; and disruptive and sometimes violent protests interrupting visiting speakers. Free speech at universities has become a *cause célèbre* across the political spectrum, including some who want to protect egalitarian student debate from the free speech of hate groups; some who want to protect 'suspect communities' from suspicion and surveillance of their free speech and political activity; and some who want to protect free speech from creeping restrictions on libertarian grounds. These issues, practices, and concerns are entangled to an extent.

### *No platforming*

It is worth briefly discussing 'no platforming' for context. The UK National Union of Students (NUS) has a 'no platform' policy, which it created in 1974 to prevent far-right racist groups such as the National Front from speaking on campus. Today, in name of protecting a 'safe environment', 'reducing potential conflict' and 'promoting multiculturalism and equality', the NUS 'no platforms' only six groups, two of which are proscribed (banned) terrorist organizations.[21]

There have been several media stories about high-profile figures supposedly being 'no platformed' by student groups, such as feminist scholar Germaine Greer, human rights activist Peter Tatchell, and United Kingdom Independence Party (UKIP) Member of the European Parliament (MEP) Bill Etheridge. In the first two cases, this was because some students perceived them to be transphobic; the latter, Bill Etheridge, because he had in the past made statements glorifying Hitler and warned against immigration in violent terms.

The reality of apparent 'no platforming' looks rather different when one looks at the detail. These cases are largely a construction of right-wing media.[22] In the cases above, it was true that some students protested their invitation, but in all cases the speakers either ended up giving their talks anyway or withdrawing of their own accord.[23] It was other groups and commentators who called this 'no platforming', and in no case were the speakers 'banned'.[24]

What this shows is the rather murky nature of apparent restrictions on speech. Speech may not be actively restricted, but, nevertheless, speakers may choose not to speak. Furthermore, free speech is not always desirable above all other considerations and is not an absolute right that trumps all other rights, as we will now discuss.

## *Free speech in UK law*

Although Prevent is part of this politicization of university free speech, it is not straightforward to separate the duty 'to have due regard to the need to prevent people being drawn into terrorism' from other considerations and duties that may restrict free speech. One is public order legislation, and the need to mitigate disruption that could threaten the safety of students and staff. This must be a consideration at university events where protest is likely, as was the case with talks given by the Israeli ambassador at SOAS and Edinburgh. Another is the Equality Act 2010, which creates a duty to have 'due regard to the need to promote good relations between different communities',[25] which would be a problem in the case of racially divisive content. A countervailing statutory duty, which we will discuss further, is to 'take such steps as are reasonably practicable to ensure that freedom of speech within the law is secured for members, students, and employees of the establishment, and for visiting speakers'.[26] All of this is in the wider legal context of UK law and European human rights law, which do not offer an absolute guarantee of free speech.

The law does not offer absolute clarity, but it is clear that there is no absolute right to free speech in the UK. As Professor Colin Riordan, President and Vice-Chancellor of Cardiff University, said: 'It is impossible to deny that the laws in this country mean that free speech is not unrestricted. Prevent and the Counter-Terrorism Act are part of that.'[27] On the one hand, there are UK statutes relating to incitement, hate speech, public order, equalities, and Prevent that qualify free speech. On the other hand, free speech is protected as freedom of expression in the Human Rights Act (which incorporates the European Convention on Human Rights into UK law).

Free speech is thus limited in a variety of ways. Some forms of speech are not protected, such as those that may be unlawful or challenge the rights of others.[28] For example, there is no legal protection for a 'deliberate lie', for setting out 'to destroy the rights of other people to speak or to exist' or to advocate violent means to achieve a political end.[29] Incitement to violence and hate speech are illegal in UK law.

There is also evolving case law in the UK and the European Court of Human Rights (ECtHR) relating to the expression of so-called Islamic extremism. The ECtHR has established that the right to say unpopular or politically 'extreme' things, such as calling for Sharia law, is protected under Article 10 of the European

Convention on Human Rights (ECHR), but advocating violent means to pursue it is not.[30] Furthermore, Article 17 prohibits the abuse of rights, and has been used in ECtHR cases to deny freedom of speech to anti-Semitic publications, for example.[31]

The way that laws, rights, and protections interact in the real world means that each instance is different, and lessons from them cannot necessarily be applied universally. Furthermore, there is a difference in strength and status between laws that explicitly make some forms of speech unlawful, and laws that merely call on bodies to have 'due regard' to certain risks relating to speech. Paul Bowen QC told the JCHR inquiry, 'In a nutshell, it is always context-specific: certain forms of speech are given added protection and certain forms of speech are not protected.'[32]

### *Free speech in universities*

Freedom of speech in universities is given special protection in UK law, primarily by the Education (No. 2) Act 1986.[33] Bowen explains that this protection preceded the general protection of freedom of expression in the Human Rights Act 1998, and this gives them special weight.[34] It also uses stronger legal language than the 'due regard' in the Prevent policy:

> [The Education (No. 2) Act 1986] employs the language that 'particular regard' must be given to duty to protect free speech. That is a form of words that we lawyers recognise as having greater weight given to it than, for example, 'due regard'. It is useful in that respect. Even in the light of the Human Rights Act, for Parliament to have legislated specifically to protect a right in a particular context, a judge will give that particular weight, because it comes with the added legitimacy of Parliament's imprimatur, not just from the Human Rights Act but from a specific piece of legislation.... It is difficult to say but generally if Parliament has given something a particular importance, judges tend to give greater importance to it.[35]

Helen Mountfield QC adds that the Education Act is different to the other laws surrounding freedom of speech because it imposes an active duty on universities to promote and secure that freedom.[36] It is a positive duty in contrast to the precautionary duty of Prevent:

> ... the duty under the 1986 Act is a practical requirement to take reasonable steps in relation to freedom of expression. The other duties we have talked about – the Prevent duty, the public sector equality duty and the duty to give due regard to the need to avoid harassment and to foster good relations – are duties to think about the relevant things, not duties to take particular steps.[37]

The key legal passage in the Education (No. 2) Act, protecting freedom of speech in universities, is as follows:

> Every individual and body of persons concerned in the government of any establishment to which this section applies shall take such steps as are reasonably practicable to ensure that freedom of speech within the law is secured for members, students and employees of the establishment and for visiting speakers.[38]

Universities are thus a special site of freedom of speech. This is protected by the law, and by the special attention that parliament has given the issue over several decades. This will become important later in the chapter.

### *Implications of Prevent in universities*

The Prevent duty has implications for university policy in three areas. The first relates to speech and visiting speakers. The Prevent Duty Guidance for Higher Education in England and Wales calls for universities to:

> … consider carefully whether the views being expressed, or likely to be expressed, constitute extremist views that risk drawing people into terrorism or are shared by terrorist groups. In these circumstances the event should not be allowed to proceed except where RHEBs [relevant higher education bodies] are entirely convinced that such risk can be fully mitigated without cancellation of the event.[39]

This has meant new steps in the planning process for organizing such events, and the potential for university and student union officers to deny permission due to risk aversion. 'Fully mitigated' is a high bar that goes beyond the legal duty to have 'due regard'.

The second is academic freedom. Universities are expected to set out 'clear policies and procedures for students and staff working on sensitive or extremism-related research' in order to 'enable the university to identify and address issues where online materials are accessed for non-research purposes';[40] in other words, to be able to distinguish between researchers legitimately accessing 'extremist' material and others for whom this might be a sign of 'radicalization'.

Third, universities must have policies, procedures, and training in place for staff to assess 'where and how their students might be at risk of being drawn into terrorism.'[41] This affects academic staff interacting with students through teaching, but also other student-facing roles such as welfare, security, domestic, and sports services.

All three areas have implications for freedom of speech. The first – events and speakers – for the obvious reason that such policies may limit who may speak on campus and what they may say. The second – research – because Prevent-related policies may hinder academic freedom; for example, if extra steps in ethics procedures are used to prevent research on 'extreme' topics. And the third – assessing the risk of students being 'drawn into terrorism' – because in effect it involves creating a system of monitoring and reporting on student activity and expression. While only the first relates directly to free speech, all three may have a chilling effect on what students are willing to say in class discussions, in their academic work, in student societies or in other areas of student life. This may particularly affect Muslim students, for example, who may feel hesitant to explore or express views critical of UK foreign policy in the Middle East in case this puts them under suspicion of 'extremism'.

However, there is agreement among policymakers and university stakeholders that some event-planning procedures are necessary in advance of inviting speakers because universities and students' unions have duties to ensure public order and equality of opportunity, as well as 'due regard' about radicalization. An unregulated free-for-all could pose particular problems to certain groups. For example, Liron Velleman, campaign manager for the Union of Jewish Students, noted problems from protests against Jewish and Israeli speakers on campus:

> Before Prevent and the current external-speaker guidelines system, there were cases … when some universities did not check which speakers were coming on to campus and some groups brought people from Hizb ut-Tahrir, al-Muhajiroun, the National Front and others. I am not claiming that the current system is perfect or even good; I merely suggest that there has to be a system.[42]

The Joint Committee on Human Rights inquiry into 'Free Speech in Universities' asked university vice chancellors and student union officers about their events vetting procedures and whether they had been affected by the Prevent duty. The figures they offered suggested there were few restrictions on speaker events. Professor Sir Timothy O'Shea, outgoing Principal of the University of Edinburgh, said that out of 1,300 proposed events featuring speakers in 2017, only 10 received extra scrutiny, seven of those required no further action, one never took place anyway, and only two required extra staff oversight in case things went awry.[43] Professor Adam Tickell, vice-chancellor of the University of Sussex, said their amount of extra scrutiny was similar for the same period: 14 events with extra attention, 11 of which required no further action, while the remaining three went 'ahead with minor mitigation actions, which included, for example, having an independent chair.'[44] Baroness Amos, director of the School of Oriental and African Studies, said they hosted 50 speaker events a week and had 'no sense that, as a result of the policies that we put in place, people have not been invited to speak at those events'.[45]

Students Unions are legally separate from universities and follow their own processes. Patrick Kilduff, President of the Edinburgh University Students' Association, gave similar figures: it had hosted 5,462 events in the previous year, none of which had been stopped by event notification processes. In the previous two years, they referred 14 events to the university compliance unit, seven of which were given further analysis.[46] All speakers said that they had seen no quantifiable downturn in events since the introduction of the Prevent duty to their speaker event planning processes.

However, despite there being little quantifiable evidence of a negative effect from the Prevent duty on the number of speaker events held or, indeed, blocked, university actors at many levels claim that Prevent is having a chilling effect on speech, particularly among minority groups such as Muslim students and Islamic societies.

The University and College Union, the main academic trade union in the UK, passed a policy at its 2015 congress stating that 'the Prevent duty is discriminatory towards Muslims, and legitimizes Islamophobia and xenophobia.'[47] Similarly, the National Union of Students Black Students group stated:

> Those on our campuses suffering from the sharpest forms of state repression will find their oppression further institutionalised.... [W]hile for Muslim students there truly will be no respite from the storm of Islamophobia that greets them in every other section of society.[48]

Yusuf Hassan, of the Federation of Student Islamic Societies (FOSIS), told the JCHR inquiry: 'people no longer feel comfortable with holding these discussions, knowing that the amount of bureaucracy required to hold them is not worth it.'[49] Similarly, written evidence from the Student Union of Herriot Watt University, which has taken a strong position against the Prevent policy, said:

> There is a limited amount of concrete evidence that free speech is suppressed by the Prevent agenda; however ... the impact on the student population impacted is great. We have seen the self-censorship from those from Muslim or Middle Eastern backgrounds [and] a demonstrable lack of visibility of cultural or religious events on campus due to fear.[50]

Witnesses giving evidence to the JCHR inquiry complained that the complexity of events planning procedures, combined with lengthy university free speech policies, have an off-putting effect for students and staff who want to invite external speakers.[51] Although there is diversity among universities in their approaches to free speech (their free speech policies can run from two to 47 pages), events planning paperwork has become more arduous with the addition of Prevent-related steps.[52]

Even so, the bureaucratic side of inviting speakers is relatively minor compared to the symbolic negative effects of Prevent on free speech. Even though, in theory, event planning procedures apply to all invited-speaker events, there is a perception that they apply more to Islamic societies. Amos told the JCHR inquiry:

> ... all these things are having an impact on how young people, particularly young people of colour or who are Muslim, feel in terms of being under additional scrutiny. The chilling effect is more about a perception, but also the reality, of the way in which those young people are living in this society.[53]

Similarly, Hassan said:

> Muslim students [feel that] they are seen as different from other students and put under some form of special magnifying glass that prevents them from making their views clear, due to them being intimidated by the ramifications of the Prevent duty.[54]

This perception is shared not only by Muslim students, but by think tank researchers, students' union officers, and other student societies. Ben Ryan of the religion and society think tank Theos said:

> … in the more extreme cases you have student union officers saying that when speaker forms come in from their Islamic society, they are more likely to say no than yes because they do not want the hassle of accidentally picking the wrong person.[55]

Charlotte Moore, a third-year undergraduate studying theology at Bristol University and a practising Christian, said:

> It is important for different faiths to build bridges, but it is difficult to do this if one of these faiths is under suspicion, which seems to be the case within my university as regards Islam, as you say, with the Prevent strategy.[56]

There could be other unintended consequences of these policies too. The forms of discussion perceived to be under suspicion may simply not happen or may move off campus. Dennis Hayes, a Professor of Education at the University of Derby, who has served on a regional Prevent event vetting panel, told the inquiry: 'I know anecdotally that people are not being invited any more.… To some extent, free speech is moving out of university, and there is evidence of that.… People are self-censoring and not inviting people.'[57] This was echoed by Hassan who said, 'the concern is that debate and discussion are starting to lose their ability to take place on campuses.'[58]

The lawyers giving evidence to the JCHR inquiry agreed that the main problem with the Prevent duty was not, in fact, the legislation which creates the duty 'to have due regard to the need to prevent people from being drawn into terrorism', but the government guidance that accompanies it.[59] As discussed, 'due regard' is a relatively weak legal duty that amounts only to giving the matter consideration. Although the idea of 'being drawn into terrorism' rests on dubious assumptions about the existence of a process of 'radicalization', in its favour it is akin to identifying incitement to violence or other serious crimes that could be prosecuted under criminal law. As the guidance states: 'Encouragement of terrorism and inviting support for a proscribed terrorist organization are both criminal offences. RHEBs should not provide a platform for these offences to be committed.'[60] The lawyers thought this was unproblematic.

However, the Prevent guidance goes beyond this to include 'non-violent extremism'. This is not defined in law and is not a crime. The guidance thus goes beyond asking universities to report potential criminal behaviour. Rather, it 'expects' universities to identify forms of legal speech and behaviour that the government merely deems risky or problematic. As the guidance reads:

> RHEBs will be expected to carry out a risk assessment for their institution which assesses where and how their students might be at risk of being drawn into terrorism. This includes not just violent extremism but also non-violent extremism, which can create an atmosphere conducive to terrorism and can popularise views which terrorists exploit.[61]

The government has tried and failed to legally define non-violent extremism. The government's Prevent Strategy policy document defines extremism as, 'vocal or active opposition to fundamental British values, including democracy, the rule of law, individual liberty and mutual respect and tolerance of different faiths and beliefs', but this policy does not have legal status.[62] However, the government tried to put this into law by announcing an Extremism Bill in the 2015 Queen's Speech, and again in 2016 with a Counter-Extremism and Safeguarding Bill, but these were never published.[63] Attempts to legislate failed (as it emerged in the press) because the government's own lawyers warned it was impossible to define 'non-violent extremism' in a way that would be legally workable.[64] The (then) UK Independent Reviewer of Terrorism Legislation, David Anderson QC, and his predecessor Lord Carlile of Berriew QC, had both warned against this in evidence to a JCHR inquiry on 'counter-extremism' in 2016, as had the JCHR.[65]

Thus, there are two problems with the Prevent guidance: legal and political. The legal problem, as explained by Ailenn McColgan, is that universities – in their efforts to follow the Prevent duty guidance – 'are shutting down speech and association, which is contrary to the statutory objective in the 1986 [Education No. 2)] Act, which is to take all reasonable steps to allow speech unless it is unlawful.'[66] The lawyers in the JCHR inquiry all argued that the Prevent duty ('due regard') is in tension with the stronger duty ('particular regard') to protect and promote free speech.

The political problem was identified by Anderson in his 2015 annual report, as echoed by Mountfield in the JCHR inquiry:[67]

> If it becomes a function of the state to identify which individuals are engaged in, or exposed to, a broad range of 'extremist activity', it will become legitimate for the state to scrutinise (and the citizen to inform upon) the exercise of core democratic freedoms by large numbers of law-abiding people.[68]

In other words, the Prevent guidance calls for universities and their staff to be suspicious of lawful activities and free expression among their students, staff, and visiting speakers. There is evidence that this manifests against Muslim students in particular, who see Prevent as being directed at them. As Mountfield suggests, 'My perception is that ... universities are being far more assiduous in their risk assessments when they look at minority ethnic societies or Muslim-based societies.'[69] The government is encouraging universities to follow the guidance as is if it was their legal duty, but it is not. Amos said:

> One of my concerns, which we have raised with HEFCE and the Department for Education, is that we have legislation but we also have guidance that goes further than the legislation and which we are constantly told is statutory. We have very clear legal advice that it is not, yet we are being judged against what we are told is statutory guidance.[70]

Similarly, Mountfield told the JCHR inquiry:

> What worries me is not so much the law, because the law is quite clear that universities must take appropriate steps to protect lawful speech. What concerns me is that the guidance on that law fuzzes the edges in a way that makes universities unduly anxious and ends up, perversely, in them avoiding having people speaking and saying lawful things for fear of breaching the Prevent duty, for example....
>
> I think the Prevent guidance encourages universities to have an overanxious approach to stopping speech for fear that it might be an indicator of a view that is not unlawful speech. However, universities are taking a precautionary approach, and I think that has a particular adverse effect on members of black minority-ethnic groups and Muslim students' organisations.[71]

In 2017, a High Court case – *Salman Butt* v. *Secretary of State for the Home Department*[72] – affirmed that although the Prevent guidance is legal, it does not have the status of law. Gary Attle told the JCHR inquiry, 'the nub of the judgment is that the Prevent duty guidance on higher education is just that: it is guidance.'[73] Although universities do have to consider their duty to have 'due regard' to the risk of radicalization, this does not apply to 'extreme' views in general, but only to those likely to incite terrorism, which is a crime. Most importantly, 'the free-speech duty should be more important' in the university's decision.[74]

### *University free speech as a space of exception*

The JCHR inquiry on 'Free Speech in Universities' serves a useful purpose in bringing together a wealth of evidence on the operation of the Prevent duty, its perception and effects on campus, and its legal status and ambiguities. The subsequent JCHR report is typically balanced in its conclusions, deflating some of the media hype about 'snowflake' students and 'safe spaces' hindering free speech on campus: 'The extent to which students restrict free speech at universities should not be exaggerated. Where it happens, it is a serious problem and it is wrong. But it is not a pervasive problem.'[75] And while the committee 'strongly endorses the need for Prevent as a strategy for preventing the development of terrorism', it also argues that 'the Prevent programme will be counterproductive if it provokes mistrust.'[76] The main arguments are covered above. However, the special focus of the committee on universities expresses the idea that universities are a space of exception, as we can see here:

> [The] right to free speech is a foundation for democracy. It is important in all settings, but especially in universities, where education and learning are advanced through dialogue and debate. It underpins academic freedom. Universities are places where ideas are developed, a diverse range of interesting – and sometimes controversial – topics should be debated. Students are among those particularly affected.[77]

If we review the passage of the Prevent duty through parliament as part of the bill that became the Counter-Terrorism and Security Act 2015, we can see similar tropes. This reveals an overwhelming concern, in both the Commons and the Lords, for the implications for freedom of speech and academic freedom in universities. While it would take too long to examine every single stage of the bill through parliament, the 'second reading' debates in the Commons and Lords, and the amendments to the bill, are quite revealing ('second readings' are the main plenary debates on the principles of a bill, whereas the other stages, including the committee stages, are about the detail.[78]) The Act covers many different aspects of counterterrorism and security, including restrictions on travel, exclusion from the UK, and Terrorism Prevention and Investigation Measures (TPIMs) for terrorist suspects. Here we are only concerned with Part 5: 'Risk of being drawn into terrorism'. This describes the duties imposed on 'specified authorities', including schools, prisons, local authorities, and universities, to have 'due regard to the need to prevent people from being drawn into terrorism'. Looking at discussion of the 'specified authorities' in these two debates shows discussion of universities to be at least 10 times more extensive than discussion of schools, prisons, local authorities, and so on. The main concern is with how universities are to balance their protection of free speech and academic freedom with their new Prevent duties. For example, in a Commons intervention representative of many others in the same debate, Labour MP Yasmin Qureshi said:

> … in universities and places of education there should be spaces for wide-ranging discussion of religious ideology, identity and foreign policy. Those spaces should not be undercut by the fear that expression of radical views will attract the attention of intelligence agencies or counter-terrorism police.[79]

Here is a representative speech in the Lords from Baroness Helena Kennedy (Labour):

> The idea that an academic will feel in some way obliged to report on a student whom she feels is asking questions or expressing views that seem

> inflammatory is a really worrying thing for academic freedom. It would destroy the trust that is so important between the student and the academic, which is where learning is at its best – the point where people are experimenting and thinking the unthinkable. That is where you beat it down with good argument. The idea that we should not have freedom of expression in our universities and that we will have people reporting each other, or that when we go to speak at a university we will have to declare and send ahead the notes of our speeches, is really not workable. I ask the Government to think again and at least to remove universities from the list. I actually think that the whole Prevent project should be looked at again.[80]

The House of Lords won concessions from the government to the effect that the government and universities must prioritize the protection of freedom of expression and academic freedom above the Prevent duty. They tabled a new clause on 'Freedom of expression in universities etc.',[81] which was accepted by the government and included in the final Counter-Terrorism and Security Act 2015 as section 31.[82] This was already implicit in the law, given the fact that parliament legislated in the 1980s to protect university free speech and academic freedom. But the section reiterates the terminology of having 'particular regard' to free speech and academic freedom in universities. This is significant because, as mentioned earlier, in legal terms, 'particular regard' has greater weight than 'due regard', and so, at least in theory, universities are to give greater to weight to freedom of expression and academic freedom than to the Prevent duty.[83]

However, this does not apply to other 'specific authorities', which of course are not affected by the Education Acts. Baroness Kennedy's speech, while noble in intent, expresses this most clearly: 'I ask the Government to think again and at least to remove universities from the list.'[84]

The university exception expresses the liberal democratic ideal of pluralist rational debate. It is not surprising that parliament – a bastion of exactly that – has sought to defend the higher education sector. While the parliamentary debates do not openly suggest that other sectors should be fair game for the Prevent policy, their almost exclusive focus on universities does raise a question about the status of political debate in other areas of life. Moreover, given limited parliamentary time and resources, this focus may distract from the wider implications of Prevent and what it is doing to public sector organizations, including universities.

### *University free speech as a distraction from the wider implications of Prevent*

The focus on universities by parliament, and the space of exception carved out for them by the law, distracts from the wider implications of Prevent and the way it is experienced by both those duty bound to implement it and those on the receiving end.

Prevent is a system based on generalized suspicions and vague indicators of risk that ostensibly does not explicitly target any specific groups. Despite this, indeed because of this, Prevent is experienced by 'suspect communities' as implicitly directed at them. This dynamic is at work in the way Prevent affects free speech, as we have heard, but this is inseparable from the other aspects of the Prevent duty, such as the requirement to report signs of 'extremism' to the police and other specific Prevent authorities.

Charlotte Heath-Kelly points out that while Prevent is a form of crime prevention, it does not follow the long history of crime prevention techniques that use 'statistical data to allocate risk scores to discrete areas' where crime is most likely to occur.[85] Prevent is not statistically targeted.[86] Note again the lack of empirical evidence or scientific agreement on the existence of a process of radicalization. This means that those duty-bound by Prevent are not tasked with detecting a known and statistically-likely 'violent extremist' profile, because no such profile exists. If Prevent was based on the statistical probabilities of where an agreed process of 'radicalization' occurs, it would not take the form it does.

To put it differently, rolling out a general duty to have 'due regard to the need to prevent people being drawn into terrorism' to all workers in schools, hospitals, prisons, and universities is by definition not evidence-based. Discussing the fact that 90 per cent of Prevent referrals in the National Health Service are rejected with no further action, Heath-Kelly writes, 'if Prevent were ... embedded in a statistical calculative rationality, it would have been discarded as a failure.'[87]

Since there is no established profile of what to look for, workers in these sectors are instead encouraged by government guidance and WRAP (Workshop to Raise Awareness of Prevent) training to look for vague indicators of risk, such as 'changes in behaviour in someone that might give you concern', 'disengagement', 'asking inappropriate questions', and the 'unhealthy use of the internet'.[88] Pupils, patients, prisoners, and students are to be sorted into categories of 'risky' and 'non-risky'. None of this relates to an established statistical likelihood of becoming radical and turning to terrorism.

While the efficacy of such a system is questionable, its effects are nevertheless far reaching. The Prevent duty has, in effect, created an army of data collectors and analysts. These are not security professionals based in the police or intelligence services, but rather what Spiller *et al.* call 'deputized' public sector workers and what Francesco Ragazzi calls the 'unprofessionals of security': staff with non-security roles who are required to exercise suspicion reporting and risk assessment.[89] Given that those deputized do not have adequate training or experience to inform their judgments, this regime has led to uncertain effects. For example, university sector workers are asked by the government Prevent guidance to 'consider carefully whether the views being expressed, or likely to be expressed, constitute extremist views that risk drawing people into terrorism'.[90] Given there is no scientific or experiential basis for such a judgment, this is a judgement that the 'unprofessionals of security' are not equipped to make.

However, judge they must. Spiller *et al.* interviewed university lecturers on the Prevent duty. Many of them expressed unease in exercising the duty, given the 'less than obvious ... evidence-base that informs the guidance'.[91] Some thought there was something dangerous about reporting students on the basis of intuitive suspicions.[92]

Charlotte Heath-Kelly and Erzsébet Strausz conducted a survey on a larger sample of NHS workers and their implementation of the Prevent duty. Worryingly, they found that staff drew their suspicions about Muslims not from the government definition of 'non-violent extremism' (problematic as it is), but, more worryingly, from things not mentioned in any government guidance. Not only were they uncertain about detecting signs of radicalization, they also appeared willing to go beyond even the vague indicators offered in their Prevent training to exercise suspicion 'drawn not from official training but from popular culture representations of ISIS and radicalism'.[93] Most were also willing to refer people to Prevent who possessed radical philosophy literature:

> 70% of respondents were 'somewhat likely' or 'very likely' to make a Prevent referral about someone on the basis of radical philosophy possession. Only 22% were 'unlikely' or 'extremely unlikely' to make such a referral. 8% said that they 'didn't know' if they would make such a referral.

Heath-Kelly and Strausz point out that possession of radical books is nowhere mentioned in the Prevent guidance or training, and there is no established evidence that books of any kind can be a source of radicalization (and perhaps even the contrary).[94]

To reiterate, the impressionistic indicators of radicalization offered by the guidance and training are not based on evidence. At best they are an invitation to report and refer on the basis of generalized suspicion. This is not an accident or methodological flaw; it is there by design. Prevent has no metric of success for the detection and prevention of pre-criminal radicalization because there is no clear picture of what radicalization looks like, let alone whether it leads to terrorism.

The Prevent regime is built upon the pseudo-science of 'radicalization'. Its 'success' is difficult if not impossible to measure. Yet the effects are well documented. It creates an atmosphere of suspicion and mistrust, which not only has a chilling effect on free speech and political activity among Muslim students in particular, but, in effect, institutionalizes a system of monitoring and reporting by non-security professionals who struggle to understand what they are meant to be alert for.

## Conclusion

This chapter has outlined the legal and political context in which the Prevent duty has come to operate in universities. It has focused on free speech in particular. This issue has received a wide range of attention and concern from parliamentarians, universities, student unions, and other university stakeholders, such as religious and political student groups. On paper, at least, freedom of speech in universities is protected because of existing education laws and amendments resulting from the legislative struggle over the creation of the Prevent duty. Furthermore, there is little quantitative evidence that Prevent has resulted in a downturn in university speaker events. However, while in some ways this is encouraging, it misses the wider implications. First of all, the focus on universities has come at the expense of attention on the effects of Prevent on free speech in other sectors. While everyone, including the government, has affirmed the importance of universities as sites of rational debate and the formation of political awareness, there has been little affirmation of the importance free speech and political activity elsewhere. A non-student mental health patient with an interest in the politics of the Middle East may thus experience Prevent differently to a university student with the same interests. Yet, the university space of exception does not mean there is no cause for concern. There is widespread reporting by university stakeholders of a chilling effect on free speech and political activity that is difficult to quantify but nevertheless felt and expressed by Muslim students in particular. It is difficult to put numbers on the debates that were not initiated, the political views that were not expressed, and the speaker invitations that were not sent out. Even less tangible are the effects the existence of Prevent may have on the political subjectivity and social integration of students. Again, the lack of public reporting and statistics on the operation of Prevent means that some of its effects and effectiveness are difficult to quantify. However, the lived experience of its operation is tangible, with thousands of workers recruited into an institutionalized system of monitoring, risk-assessing and informing on opinions and behaviours.

## Notes

1 Counter-Terrorism and Security Act 2015, s.5.
2 University and College Union, 'The Prevent Duty: A Guide for Branches and Members' (2015) www.ucu.org.uk/media/7370/The-prevent-duty-guidance-for-branches-Dec-15/pdf/ucu_preventdutyguidance_dec15.pdf (accessed 27 July 2018).
3 National Union of Students, 'Preventing Prevent – We are Students Not Suspects @ NUS connect' (2018) www.nusconnect.org.uk/campaigns/preventing-prevent-we-are-students-not-suspects (accessed 27 July 2018).
4 Communities and Local Government, *Preventing Violent Extremism: Next Steps For Communities* (Department for Communities and Local Government 2008) 12.
5 Ibid.
6 P Bracchi, 'Britons who HATE Britain: The Muslim extremists hell-bent on segregation rather than integration' (2009) www.dailymail.co.uk/news/article-1161855/Britons-HATE-Britain-The-Muslim-extremists-hell-bent-segregation-integration.html accessed 27 July 2018, D Gardham, 'Mainstream Islamic organisations "share al-Qaeda ideology"', *Telegraph* (5 August 2010) www.telegraph.co.uk/news/uknews/7928377/Mainstream-Islamic-organisations-share-al-Qaeda-ideology.html (accessed 27 July 2018).
7 *Independent*, 'Profiles of the 4 bombers who killed 52 people in London on 7/7' (2015) www.independent.co.uk/news/uk/home-news/77-bombings-london-anniversary-live-profiles-of-the-four-bombers-who-killed-52-people-in-london-10369984.html (accessed 27 July 2018).
8 Intelligence and Security Committee, *Could 7/7 Have Been Prevented?: Review of the Intelligence on the London Terrorist Attacks on 7 July 2005* (2009) 50.

9 Communities and Local Government Committee, 'Preventing Violent Extremism: Sixth report of 2009–2010' (2010) https://publications.parliament.uk/pa/cm200910/cmselect/cmcomloc/65/6502.htm (accessed 27 July 2018).
10 D Cameron, 'PM's speech at Munich Security Conference – GOV.UK' www.gov.uk/government/speeches/pms-speech-at-munich-security-conference (accessed 21 February 2018).
11 Ibid.
12 Ibid.
13 Ibid.
14 M Sedgwick, 'The Concept of Radicalization as a Source of Confusion' *Terrorism and Political Violence* 22, no. 4 (2010): 479–94.
15 Ibid.
16 Ibid.
17 R Borum, 'Rethinking radicalization', *Journal of Strategic Security* 4, no. 4 (2011): 1–6.
18 Ibid.
19 PR Neumann, 'The trouble with radicalization', *International Affairs* 89, no. 4 (2013): 873–93.
20 A Richards, 'The problem with 'radicalization': the remit of 'Prevent' and the need to refocus on terrorism in the UK', *International Affairs* 87, no. 1 (2011): 143–52.
21 National Union of Students, 'NUS' No Platform Policy @ NUS connect' (2017) www.nusconnect.org.uk/resources/nus-no-platform-policy-f22f (accessed 22 February 2018).
22 Joint Committee on Human Rights, 'Oral evidence – Freedom of Speech in Universities – 10 January 2018' http://data.parliament.uk/writtenevidence/committeeevidence.svc/evidencedocument/human-rights-committee/freedom-of-speech-in-universities/oral/76710.html (accessed 22 February 2018).
23 A Packham, 'Boris, Tatchell, Greer: were they actually no-platformed?' *Guardian* (5 May 2016) www.theguardian.com/education/2016/may/05/boris-tatchell-greer-were-they-actually-no-platformed. www.theguardian.com/education/2016/may/05/boris-tatchell-greer-were-they-actually-no-platformed (accessed 22 February 2018).
24 Joint Committee on Human Rights, 'Oral evidence – Freedom of Speech in Universities – 10 Jan 2018', C Turner, 'Sussex University free speech society told to submit guest's speech for approval in case it violates 'safe space' policy' *Telegraph* (30 October 2017) www.telegraph.co.uk/education/2017/10/30/sussex-university-free-speech-society-told-submit-guests-speech (accessed 22 February 2018).
25 Equality and Human Rights Commission, *Freedom of Expression* (2015).
26 Education (No. 2) Act 1986, s.43.
27 Joint Committee on Human Rights, 'Oral evidence – Freedom of Speech in Universities – 15 November 2017' (2017) 13 http://data.parliament.uk/writtenevidence/committeeevidence.svc/evidencedocument/human-rights-committee/freedom-of-speech-in-universities/oral/74027.pdf (accessed 22 February 2018).
28 Joint Committee on Human Rights, 'Oral evidence – Freedom of Speech in Universities – 6 December 2017' (2017) 3 http://data.parliament.uk/writtenevidence/committeeevidence.svc/evidencedocument/human-rights-committee/freedom-of-speech-in-universities/oral/75335.pdf (accessed 22 February 2018).
29 Ibid.
30 This was affirmed in a ECtHR decision on the 'Gündüz' case, ibid.
31 European Court of Human Rights, *Factsheet – Hate Speech* (2018).
32 Joint Committee on Human Rights, 'Oral evidence – Freedom of Speech in Universities – 6 December 2017'.
33 For a detailed account of the law on free speech in universities, see I Cram and H Fenwick, 'Protecting Free Speech and Academic Freedom in Universities' *The Modern Law Review* 81, no. 5 (2018): 825–73.

34 Joint Committee on Human Rights, 'Oral evidence – Freedom of Speech in Universities – 6 December 2017'.
35 Ibid.
36 Ibid.
37 Ibid.
38 Education (No. 2) Act 1986.
39 HM Government, *Prevent Duty Guidance for Higher Education in England and Wales* (2015) 4.
40 Ibid.
41 Ibid.
42 Joint Committee on Human Rights, 'Oral evidence – Freedom of Speech in Universities – 29 November 2017' (2017) 7 http://data.parliament.uk/writtenevidence/committeeevidence.svc/evidencedocument/human-rights-committee/freedom-of-speech-in-universities/oral/74974.pdf (accessed 22 February 2018).
43 Joint Committee on Human Rights, 'Oral evidence – Freedom of Speech in Universities – 10 January 2018'.
44 Ibid.
45 Ibid.
46 Ibid.
47 University and College Union, 'Business of the recruitment, organising and campaigning committee 2015' www.ucu.org.uk/article/7523/Business-of-the-recruitment-organising-and-campaigning-committee-2015. www.ucu.org.uk/article/7523/Business-of-the-recruitment-organising-and-campaigning-committee-2015#62 (accessed 22 February 2018).
48 NUS Black Students, *Preventing Prevent: A student handbook on countering the PREVENT agenda on campus* (2015).
49 Joint Committee on Human Rights, 'Oral evidence – Freedom of Speech in Universities – 29 November 2017'.
50 Heriot-Watt University Student Union Executive Committee, 'Written evidence from the Heriot-Watt University Student Union Executive Committee (FSU0024)' (2018). http://data.parliament.uk/writtenevidence/committeeevidence.svc/evidencedocument/human-rights-committee/freedom-of-speech-in-universities/written/75657.html (accessed 27 July 2018).
51 Joint Committee on Human Rights, 'Oral evidence – Freedom of Speech in Universities – 15 November 2017'.
52 Ibid., Joint Committee on Human Rights, 'Oral evidence – Freedom of Speech in Universities – 10 January 2018'.
53 Joint Committee on Human Rights, 'Oral evidence – Freedom of Speech in Universities – 10 January 2018'.
54 Joint Committee on Human Rights, 'Oral evidence – Freedom of Speech in Universities – 29 November 2017'.
55 Ibid.
56 Ibid.
57 Joint Committee on Human Rights, 'Oral evidence – Freedom of Speech in Universities – 15 November 2017'.
58 Joint Committee on Human Rights, 'Oral evidence – Freedom of Speech in Universities – 29 November 2017'.
59 Joint Committee on Human Rights, 'Oral evidence – Freedom of Speech in Universities – 6 December 2017'.
60 HM Government, *Prevent Duty Guidance for Higher Education in England and Wales.*
61 Ibid.
62 HM Government, *Prevent strategy* (The Stationery Office London 2011) 107.
63 J Dawson and S Godec, 'Counter-extremism policy: an overview (Commons Briefing papers CBP-7238)' (2017) http://researchbriefings.parliament.uk/ResearchBriefing/Summary/CBP-7238 (accessed 27 February 2018).

64 M Townsend, 'Theresa May's counter-terrorism bill close to "sinking without trace"' *Guardian* (29 January 2017) www.theguardian.com/politics/2017/jan/29/theresa-may-counter-terrorism-bill-sinking-without-trace-extremism-british-values www.theguardian.com/politics/2017/jan/29/theresa-may-counter-terrorism-bill-sinking-without-trace-extremism-british-values (accessed 27 February 2018).
65 Joint Committee On Human Rights, 'Oral evidence – Legislative Scrutiny: Counter-extremism Bill – 9 March 2016' http://data.parliament.uk/writtenevidence/committeeevidence.svc/evidencedocument/human-rights-committee/legislative-scrutiny-counter extremism-bill/oral/30366.html accessed 27 February 2018, Joint Committee on Human Rights, *Counter-Extremism: Second Report of Session 2016–17* (2016).
66 Joint Committee on Human Rights, 'Oral evidence – Freedom of Speech in Universities – 6 December 2017'.
67 Ibid.
68 IRoT D Anderson Q.C., *The Terrorism Acts In 2014: Report of the Independent Reviewer on the operation of the Terrorism Act 2000 and Part 1 of The Terrorism Act 2006* (2015) 65.
69 Joint Committee on Human Rights, 'Oral evidence – Freedom of Speech in Universities – 6 December 2017'.
70 Joint Committee on Human Rights, 'Oral evidence – Freedom of Speech in Universities – 10 January 2018'.
71 Joint Committee on Human Rights, 'Oral evidence – Freedom of Speech in Universities – 6 December 2017'.
72 *Salman Butt* v. *Secretary of State for the Home Department* (High Court of Justice).
73 Joint Committee on Human Rights, 'Oral evidence – Freedom of Speech in Universities – 6 December 2017'.
74 Ibid.
75 Joint Committee on Human Rights, *Freedom of Speech in Universities inquiry* (UK Parliament, 2018) 4.
76 Ibid.
77 Ibid.
78 AW Neal, 'Legislative practices', in Mark B Salter and Can E Mutlu (eds.), *Research Methods in Critical Security Studies: An Introduction* (New York, Routledge, 2012).
79 House of Commons, 'Counter-Terrorism and Security Bill Second Reading, HC Deb 2 December 2014, vol. 589, cols 207–257' (2014) https://publications.parliament.uk/pa/cm201415/cmhansrd/cm141202/debtext/141202-0004.htm (accessed 28 February 2018).
80 House of Lords, 'Counter-Terrorism and Security Bill Second Reading, HL Deb 13 January 2015 vol 758, cols 661–772' (2015) https://publications.parliament.uk/pa/ld201415/ldhansrd/text/150113-0003.htm (accessed 28 February 2018).
81 House of Lords, 'Lords Amendments: Counter-Terrorism and Security Bill (3rd February 2015)' (2015) https://publications.parliament.uk/pa/bills/lbill/2014-2015/0092/amend/ml092-II.htm (accessed 27 July 2018).
82 Counter-Terrorism and Security Bill 2014 (HC Bill 127).
83 Counter-Terrorism and Security Act 2015.
84 House of Lords, Counter-Terrorism and Security Bill Second Reading, HL Deb 13 January 2015 vol 758, cols 661–772.
85 C Heath-Kelly, 'The geography of pre-criminal space: epidemiological imaginations of radicalisation risk in the UK Prevent Strategy, 2007–2017' *Critical Studies on Terrorism* 10, no. 2 (2017): 297–319, 301.
86 Ibid.
87 Ibid.
88 K Spiller, I Awan and A Whiting, 'What does terrorism look like?': university lecturers' interpretations of their Prevent duties and tackling extremism in UK universities, *Critical Studies on Terrorism* 11, no. 1 (2018): 130–50, 131.

89 Ibid., F Ragazzi, 'Preventing radicalisation in the EU: pre-emption, rights and effectiveness' presentation of the report 'Preventing and Countering Youth Radicalisation in the EU' (Access Europe annual conference), F Ragazzi, 'Countering terrorism and radicalisation: Securitising social policy?' *Critical Social Policy* 37, no. 2 (2017): 163–79.
90 HM Government, *Prevent Duty Guidance for Higher Education in England and Wales.*
91 K Spiller, I Awan and A Whiting, 'What does terrorism look like?': university lecturers' interpretations of their Prevent duties and tackling extremism in UK universities.
92 Ibid.
93 C Heath-Kelly and E Strausz, 'The banality of counterterrorism "after, after 9/11"? Perspectives on the Prevent duty from the UK health care sector' *Critical Studies on Terrorism* 11, no. 1 (2018): 1–21, 2.
94 Ibid.

# 6 Prevent in schools after the *Trojan Horse Affair*

*Helen Fenwick and Daniel Fenwick*

## Introduction

This chapter will consider the impact of the Prevent strategy, placed on a statutory footing by Part 5 of the Counter-Terrorism and Security Act 2015 (CTSA), on freedom of expression in schools.[1] The duty under Part 5, s26 requires 'specified authorities', which includes schools,[2] to have 'due regard' to 'the need to prevent people from being drawn into terrorism' when carrying out their functions. Guidance, fleshing out the statutory duty, directs schools as to what steps they should take to fulfil this duty (s29(2) CTSA).[3] This guidance indicates that schools should have regard in particular to disrupting promoters of terrorism, to identify and support those at risk of being drawn to terrorism, and to prevent the promulgation to school pupils of extremist ideology that could be linked to drawing them into terrorism.[4]

The terms 'terrorism, 'radicalization', and 'extremism' are pivotal in the s26 duty and Prevent guidance as they relate to the impact of the Prevent policy in schools. Therefore, they require elaboration and explanation. It could be argued that such terms are misused in UK law and policy, either because they are too broad or because their meaning is unclear. The term 'radicalization' could be said to have a positive meaning in the sense of becoming an individual who seeks to criticize conventional assumptions and orthodox beliefs; thus 'radicalization' could be said to be linked to critical thinking taught in schools and universities.[5] In contrast, the Prevent definition of 'radicalization' is much narrower and, where the term is used below, it relies on that definition. It covers the process by which individuals are brought to, or come to support terrorist groups and 'extremist ideology' linked to terrorism.[6] The definition reflects the typical use of the term in contemporary counter-terror theory and practice. Given that radicalization covers the rejection of the liberal-democratic values of contemporary western society, it therefore encompasses rejection of critical thinking associated with such values applied to assumptions underpinning the involvement of extreme religious or far-right groups or individuals in terrorist activity. Therefore, as expanded on below, the term is used in contradistinction to the encouragement of pluralistic, critical thinking in schools.[7] But given the necessity of a link to terrorism, the mere expression of support for anti-western values, without more, would not mean that radicalization would be viewed as having occurred.

'Terrorism' is defined in s1 Terrorism Act 2000 (TA) to mean the 'use or threat of action' which 'involves serious violence against a person' or 'involves serious damage to property' or 'endangers a person's life, other than that of the person committing the action' or 'creates a serious risk to the health and safety of the public or a section of the public', or 'is designed seriously to interfere with or seriously to disrupt an electronic system'. Further, the act/threat must be designed to 'influence the government … or to intimidate the public or a section of the public', and be 'made for the purpose of advancing a political, religious, racial, or ideological cause'.[8] The breadth of the definition of terrorism may be criticized for encompassing actions, or the threat of actions, designed to further liberal, democratic, political, or ideological causes that seek to influence totalitarian governments.[9] However, if a pupil in school merely expressed support for, for example, establishing a Kurdish state in support of the PKK, without expressing a threat of action as covered by s1, it is possible that this would not indicate that the pupil could be 'drawn into terrorism' for the purposes of Prevent, since such expression is not itself within the definition, despite the fact that, in theory, a terrorist offence could apply.[10]

The term 'extremism' used in the guidance is, at face value, more problematic. Extremism is defined in the guidance to include 'vocal or active opposition to fundamental British values, including democracy, the rule of law, individual liberty and mutual respect, and tolerance of different faiths and beliefs.'[11] The duty to counter such 'extremism' in order to prevent pupils being radicalized, with the possibility of being drawn into terrorism,[12] clearly covers expression in schools that is directly an incitement to terrorism or to violence. It would cover praising the actions of terrorist groups or supporting terrorism, as amounting to the expression of violent extremism capable of creating the risk in question. Therefore, it would be covered by both the guidance and s26. But the wording of the guidance also extends to opposing expression amounting to non-violent extremism; it could therefore lead to the curbing or suppression of forms of political expression in schools critical of 'British values', such as a commitment to the rule of law and fundamental liberties.[13] This chapter will consider, therefore, whether or how far the width of the term can be viewed as affecting the application of the Prevent policy in schools. The question is also raised whether the impact of the duty, as reflected in the guidance, is compatible with or supports another fundamental British value – freedom of speech, as a common law value and as guaranteed by Article 10 ECHR.

This chapter will proceed as follows. First, it will consider the background to the introduction of the statutory Prevent duty, focussing on its links with the Trojan Horse affair.[14] Second, it will examine and evaluate the content of the Prevent duty and guidance to schools. Third, it will consider the impact of enhanced safeguarding measures under Prevent as applied to pupils considered vulnerable to being radicalized. Fourth, it will consider the emphasis upon the promotion of British values in schools as a counter to extremism. Fifth, it will consider the enforcement mechanisms accompanying Prevent. Sixth, it will consider other duties to promote free, pluralistic debate in schools, and, finally, it will come to conclusions as to the need to apply Prevent on a statutory basis in schools as – in part – a response to the Trojan Horse affair.

## 1 Background to the statutory Prevent duty as applied in schools; the Trojan Horse affair

The Prevent strategy is one of the four pillars of Contest, the government's overall strategy for countering the terrorist threat to the UK post-9/11.[15] The Contest strategy prior to 2009, under the then Labour government, referred to the need to disrupt *violent* extremism which was designed to draw people into terrorism.[16] It was adopted after the 7/7 terrorist attacks in London, leading to the shift in the Contest strategy to address domestic terrorism.[17] The underlying aim of this strategy, as it related to schools, was partially articulated previously by the Department for Children, Schools and Families in 2008.[18] The expressed aim was to safeguard children from extremism on the basis that if, via classroom materials and teaching, they were exposed to an ideology linked to violent extremism while at school, and therefore at an impressionable age, it would be possible that such exposure might, to varying degrees depending on individual circumstances, have a radicalizing impact on them.[19] However, after 2008, the revised Contest strategy increasingly emphasized the role of non-violent extremism, or 'material and arguments which create a climate of intolerance and distrust in which violence as a tool of political discourse becomes acceptable'[20] as an important initial stage in the process of individuals being drawn into terrorism.[21]

In 2011, the Liberal-Conservative coalition government published a comprehensive Prevent strategy document which also emphasised the role of non-violent extremism in the initial phases of radicalization.[22] In 2012, the Home Affairs Select Committee identified problems of radicalization in prisons, religious institutions, and via the internet, which had featured in the backgrounds of current and former Islamic terrorists.[23] In 2013, the Prime Minister's anti-extremism taskforce, created after the murder of Drummer Lee Rigby by two Islamic extremists,[24] recommended that the Prevent strategy should be made a legal requirement in 'certain areas of the country where extremism is of particular concern' to enable local authorities to carry out their role in delivering 'Prevent'.[25] It was against this background of an increasing emphasis in the Prevent strategy on the need to address *both* non-violent extremism, and the initial phases of radicalization, that the Trojan Horse affair occurred.

Prior to that affair, and shortly after the Liberal-Conservative coalition government took office, the issue of radicalization in educational settings, and the appearance of a lack of an effective response to those concerns, was vividly illustrated when an undercover reporter for Channel 4 released footage from the Darul Uloom school in Birmingham.[26] This showed a student speaker addressing younger students – under the supervision of staff – in a speech which reproduced extremist ideology, describing British society in general as evil and singling out certain groups, such as Hindus, for ridicule.[27] This, and similar revelations concerning Islamist groups operating in universities,[28] in addition to the involvement of an assistant teacher, Mohammed Sidique Khan, in the 7/7 attacks, created pressure on the Department for Education (DfE) and Ofsted to do more to address extremism in schools.[29]

The Channel 4 revelations about radicalization in educational settings provided the context to the even more dramatic allegations arising from the Trojan Horse affair in 2014. This affair began when an anonymous letter was sent to the Leader of Birmingham City Council describing a process of five steps by which a number of schools in Birmingham could be 'taken over' in order to ensure that they were run on strict Islamic principles. The steps included the use of pressure from activist groups of parents, and especially from governors, to pressurize staff to align the organization of the school, including teaching, with such principles. It also set out methods of coercing staff and head teachers into resigning from the schools in question if they were unsympathetic to the imposition of such principles. The letter set out a blue-print for similar takeovers in other schools.[30] It purported to be from one Islamist to another outlining a conspiracy to take over schools in the ways described, but this was never established, and it may have been merely a whistle-blowing ruse[31] adopted to draw the issues to the attention of the Council.[32] The Council strongly affirmed that the problems it drew attention to genuinely arose.[33]

Birmingham City Council informed the police, who decided to take the matter no further; however, the Department for Education ultimately received a copy of the letter from the police (via the Home Office). The letter drew attention to concerns that had already been raised with the Department for Education by senior teachers in Birmingham schools, such as head teacher Mr Tim Boyes,[34] and – when the DfE received the letter – a national campaigning organization put the DfE in contact with further whistle-blowers at Park View school.[35] The contents of the letter, and the concerns raised by the whistle-blowers, resulted in various inquiries with various remits. There were two investigations concerning the substance of the allegations made in the Trojan Horse letter by the Education Commissioner, Peter Clarke, (the Clarke Report) appointed by the Department for Education,[36] and the report of Ian Kershaw, appointed by Birmingham City Council.[37]

The Kershaw review leading to the report had a remit which included investigation into the substance of the allegations made in the letter. It found that there was evidence of pressure to change the ethos of schools to be run on strict Islamic principles,[38] but did not find enough evidence to sustain the claim that there was a 'systematic plot' to take over schools as envisaged by the letter.[39] The Clarke Report's remit was more generally to: establish what had occurred in the schools of concern, focusing on governance; to gather evidence going beyond the specific Trojan Horse issues, to include the issue of safeguarding generally; and to 'understand the implications for the school system', both in Birmingham and nationally.[40] The Clarke Report echoed the Kershaw Report's conclusion as regards pressure being applied to change the character, ethos, and staff in some Birmingham schools.[41] It found that 'there are a number of people, associated with each other and in positions of influence in schools and governing bodies, who espouse, endorse, or fail to challenge extremist views.'[42] In particular, it found evidence of hard line or extremist views among certain staff associated with the Park View Educational Trust, and indications that this had influenced the delivery of personal, social, and health education, so that discussion about extremist practices, such as female genital mutilation, and the Prevent duty, were omitted or were taught from a narrow Islamic perspective, as were elements of sex and relationship education.[43]

The Clarke Report further found that certain governors and teachers were promoting, via lessons, materials, and external speakers, an Islamic ideology which if 'left unchecked ... would confine schoolchildren within an intolerant, inward-looking monoculture that would severely inhibit their participation in the life of modern Britain'.[44] It was also found that the curriculum was limited in some schools, that gender segregation was imposed in some lessons,[45] and that extremist speakers had been brought in to speak in school assemblies.[46] The report also accepted that there had been abuses of power in the schools and that some governing bodies had been able to change the ethos of the school.[47] Finally, it also found that measures had been taken to disguise the extent of the changes from sources of accountability, such as the DfE, Birmingham Local Education Authority, Ofsted, or staff or parent whistle-blowers. They included the discrediting of critical head teachers, staff, or governors, and the obscuring of practices such as narrowing the curriculum, so that parents and inspectors were not aware of their occurrence or extent.[48]

The Clarke report also considered the extension of an invitation to Shaykh Shady Al-Suleiman to speak at an assembly about exam revision.[49] The invitation was challenged in the Clarke report on the basis that senior staff either were, or should have been, aware of his politicized ultra-orthodox Sunni views, which had reportedly included supporting the Mujahideen (who oppose the west generally, and specifically in Afghanistan), as well as defending Sharia punishments for homosexuality and adultery.[50] The lack of a policy vetting individuals such as Shaykh Shady, and other institutional failings that resulted in his invitation, were cited in the Ofsted Report for Park View subsequent to the inquiry.[51] It was found, *inter alia*, that its vetting policy was inadequate, which resulted in an intervention that included the replacement of senior staff in management positions.[52] The individuals involved were also subject to sanctions, and Tahir Alam in particular was barred from acting as a governor (although proceedings against senior teaching staff largely collapsed due to mismanagement of the evidence).[53]

Some of the evidence in the Clarke Report was disputed at length by the Park View Educational Trust,[54] as well as by certain academics,[55] and the necessarily anonymous nature of many of the whistle-blowing allegations, has resulted in some speculation as to the veracity of the evidence cited in the report.[56] The series of disciplinary hearings brought before the National College for Teaching and Leadership,[57] concerning certain teachers involved in the Trojan Horse affair (and the evidential basis of some of the claims in the Clarke Report), was subject to additional scrutiny.[58] One example concerned a reference in the report to a 'lesson worksheet', which stated that wives must consent to sex with their husbands.[59] On cross-examination of the witness as part of the hearing, it was revealed that the document was not part of the course materials, or distributed by the teacher, but, rather, was from an internet source and distributed to the class in front of the teacher by students.[60]

The Clarke Report resulted in a number of recommendations to the Department for Education (DfE). These included that it

> should ensure that the governing body of every school extends the responsibilities of the teacher designated Child Protection Officer to include Prevent within his/her role … [and that the] mandatory … training undertaken by these responsible teachers should include the Prevent Strategy.[61]

Another recommendation was that 'Ofsted should consider whether the existing inspection framework and associated guidance is capable of detecting indicators of extremism and ensuring that the character of a school is not changed substantively without following the proper process.'[62] The DfE, under Michael Gove, pre-empted these recommendations to an extent by announcing a consultation into the 'active promotion of British values' in schools, which culminated in a report issued in November 2014, discussed further below.[63] The DfE also published a progress report which suggested that 'all the recommendations have been implemented or are on track.'[64] The result of the Trojan Horse inquiry into 21 Birmingham schools found two to be outstanding, but six schools, including Park View, were found to be failing and were put into special measures.[65]

The findings of the Kershaw and Clarke Reports were published in July 2014 and were referred to in the debates on the Counter-Terrorism and Security Bill in 2014.[66] The reference to schools as a designated authority to be subject to the legal duty to have due regard to Prevent was not, however, a direct response to their findings, but rather a response to the recommendations of the Prime Minister's taskforce on radicalization and extremism.[67] This taskforce recommended that the 'government must do more to address extremism in locations where it can exert control, such as prisons, and increase oversight where it is needed, such as in some independent and religious schools'.[68] However, rather than a general legal duty to enforce Prevent, the taskforce recommended a legal duty to enforce that was specific to 'areas of the country where extremism is of particular concern'.[69] These recommendations were interpreted in the 2014 Contest strategy to be 'in line with' the proposals for the new statutory duty placed on schools in the Counter-Terrorism and Security Bill.[70] It is probable that this evolution in policy was the result of pressure on the Home Department, created by the high profile of the Trojan Horse affair, to demonstrate, in particular, that it was taking a strong stance on Prevent and was seeking to limit the discretion given to individual schools or local authorities to implement it. This pressure was created partly by the DfE under Michael Gove, which had emphasized the importance of 'promoting British values' at the time of the Trojan Horse affair, leading to a public fallout between Mr Gove and Theresa May.[71] Another example of this pressure is evident in the debates on the Bill itself in the statement of Khalid Mahmood, a Birmingham MP who had been instrumental in supporting whistle-blowers in the Trojan Horse schools, who was critical of what he perceived as a lack of support from Birmingham City Council for his efforts.[72]

## 2 The Prevent duty and regulatory framework in schools: introduction

The focus of the Prevent strategy under the previous Labour government was on violent extremism.[73] The current strategy, largely captured in s26 CTSA and the Prevent duty guidance, also covers the harms of non-violent extremism, such as social division and the encouragement of isolation.[74] The current strategy is based, as discussed above, on the identification of evidence of extremism in institutions, including the school system, as a particular concern, referring to the Trojan Horse affair and the Clarke Report.[75] The key requirements of the Prevent duty are now set out in the revised Prevent duty guidance,[76] and dedicated guidance for schools.[77]

The guidance emphasizes at the outset that

> the Prevent duty is not intended to stop pupils debating controversial issues … [and] schools should provide a safe space in which children, young people and staff can understand the risks associated with terrorism and develop the knowledge and skills to be able to challenge extremist arguments.[78]

Nevertheless, concerns have been raised by Islamist activists regarding the impact of the Part 5 Prevent duty on expression in schools[79] in relation to two key related areas: first, the reporting/referring of pupils who express extremist views, and, second, methods of preventing such views being expressed by speakers in schools, and the promotion of 'British values'. The legal/regulatory framework of Prevent relevant to both areas is discussed in turn in the two sections below.

In the second reading of the Counter-Terrorism and Security Bill, Khalid Mahmood MP (Labour), who had originally pressured Birmingham Council over the Trojan Horse letter and the concerns raised, welcomed the new duty in Part 5.[80] He considered its most significant contribution to be that it could address the lack of official support that he had experienced in raising concerns about the pressure brought to bear on head teachers and staff to accept Salafi-aligned schooling.[81] The need to do more to support schools and other public institutions to counter extremism was also emphasized by the government in its response to a number of critical parliamentary committee reports concerning the Trojan Horse affair, in particular that of the Education Committee. It was also emphasised in the government's response – after CTSA Part 5 had come into force – to a 2015 consultation on the Prevent duty guidance.[82]

## 3 Countering extremism by enhanced safeguarding of pupils

The Prevent duty guidance states that schools are required to demonstrate that they are able 'to assess the risk of children being drawn into terrorism, including support for extremist ideas that are part of terrorist ideology,'[83] while the DfE guidance states that schools must have a 'specific understanding of how to identify individual children who may be at risk [of radicalization] ... and what to do to support them'.[84] The relevant support is to refer a pupil who demonstrates signs of radicalization to the 'Channel' programme, which is a non-compulsory de-radicalization programme[85] designed to counteract influences that draw individuals into terrorism. In addition to the fulfilment of s26, such support is required to fulfil statutory duties placed on school governors and Local Education Authorities (LEAs) to put in place arrangements for the safeguarding of pupils and the promotion of their welfare, under s175 Education Act 2002 for maintained schools, and under the Education (Independent School Standards) Regulations 2014[86] in relation to independent schools.

Claims that Prevent 'criminalizes' the expression of certain viewpoints[87] are, therefore, obviously false, since Channel cannot lead to a criminal conviction and non-participation carries no criminal penalty.[88] Similarly, claims that Prevent is simply a duty to report pupils to the police are not correct in legal terms. The relevant statutory duty imposed under s26 makes no reference to referrals. The departmental guidance concerning safeguarding suggests that the fulfilment of the s26 duty requires schools to have 'clear procedures in place for protecting children at risk of radicalization' as well as to co-operate with relevant safeguarding and Prevent bodies.[89] A failure to refer could indicate that an institution or individual had failed to have regard to the Prevent duty since it might – but need not – indicate that the clear procedures were not in place.[90] So, a duty to refer could arise indirectly.

Furthermore, claims that there are large number of referrals, including many frivolous or mistaken ones,[91] should be viewed in the light of the filtering mechanism provided by designated safeguarding leads (staff specifically concerned with safeguarding pupils under Prevent)[92] and the Chief of Police, who must refer a pupil to a local authority panel only if there are reasonable grounds to believe that the individual is vulnerable to being drawn into terrorism.[93] However, the involvement of the police could be seen as an intimidatory measure, especially given the ages of the pupils who might be referred. Moreover, some risk-averse schools may have taken an over-cautious approach to the guidance, possibly motivated by concern about negative publicity, which could chill the expression of some school pupils.[94] Uncertainty as to the demands of the guidance in relation to the promotion of 'British values' (the term is discussed below) could also foster a risk-averse approach, although as Prevent 'beds in' that risk appears to be diminishing.[95]

It is argued that a further difficulty with the Prevent scheme concerns the extremely broad criteria for reference to Channel due to an individual's engagement 'with a group, cause, or ideology' associated with terrorism, which is one of the three key 'dimensions' in the vulnerability assessment framework set out in the Channel guidance (the other two being 'intent to cause harm' and 'capability to cause harm').[96] The guidance refers to such engagement factors as: 'needs, susceptibilities, motivations and contextual influences and together map the individual pathway into terrorism ... [including].... Feelings of grievance and injustice.... A need for identity, meaning and belonging.... A desire for political or moral change.'[97]

If these factors for a referral were taken in isolation then they would be extremely concerning in terms of the potential to interfere with debate in schools on issues of fundamental political and moral significance, and for the expression of individual identity. However, it is important to emphasize, contrary to the perception of prominent critics of Prevent,[98] that the guidance does not direct that referrals should be made on such a basis, but – in common with safeguarding good practice[99] – is instead directed towards a pupil's behaviour as a whole, and to the specific question of whether there are reasonable grounds to believe that he or she is vulnerable to being drawn into terrorism. Nevertheless, the Channel criteria, which are based on a model developed by forensic psychologists working in a probation context,[100] have been subject to criticism both by academics and civil society NGOs in terms of the quality of the model adopted and the research at its foundation.[101] Greer and Bell, writing in support of Prevent in general in the university context, concede that it is 'not an exact science'.[102] The breadth of the criteria lends some weight to the criticism that referrals could be made on the basis of ignorance of and antipathy to certain political viewpoints and religious convictions.[103]

The primary means by which schools can demonstrate that they have fulfilled the safeguarding aspect of the Prevent duty as set out in the guidance is 'at a minimum' to demonstrate that the safeguarding lead has undergone Prevent training so that Prevent procedures are implemented effectively.[104] The cornerstone of such training is the 'Workshop to Raise Awareness of Prevent' (WRAP) developed by the Home Office, based on research into specific examples of radicalized individuals who have gone on to commit terrorist acts.[105] WRAP workshops have a standard structure and emphasize, by reference to 14 specific case-studies, the range of behaviours associated with different radicalized individuals. They also emphasise that a referral should be based upon considered concerns about behaviour that are checked and shared with a Local Safeguarding Children Board before action is taken.[106] The workshop and similar guidance go some way to addressing concerns about the breadth of the Channel criteria, since they emphasize the holistic nature of the decision to refer, and that the expression of political viewpoints or religious beliefs are not in themselves a sufficient basis for referral.[107]

The implementation of the Prevent duty in schools that receive government or local government funding is overseen, primarily, by Ofsted, although there are additional official inspectorates for independent schools which operate on a similar framework and are required to be inspected in accordance with the same standards.[108] In 2015, Ofsted revised the relevant Inspectors' Handbook – the key framework for Ofsted assessments of school performance – to assess the ability of schools to identify and address radicalization risks. The assessment of such arrangements is relevant in particular to key assessment criteria relating to the 'quality of leadership and management' in a school and also to 'the personal development, behaviour and welfare of children and learners'.[109] Inspectors are required to assess staff awareness of the methods of responding when they suspect that a pupil is vulnerable to extremism or radicalization,[110] and also the arrangements schools have in place to 'promote pupils' welfare' and prevent radicalization and extremism.[111] Such an assessment includes checking policy and procedures for vetting and monitoring the actions of visitors to the school, and the guidance gives the example of the need to check that there are policies on external speakers at school assemblies.[112] Staff training arrangements are evaluated, which includes examining whether staff have undergone Home Office online training or attended the standardized Prevent workshop (WRAP), or similar training.[113] Inspectors must also assess policy and performance relating to pupil awareness of radicalization as a safeguarding risk, including, in particular, on-line risks such as pupils becoming aware of friends online whose behaviour indicates that they may be becoming radicalized. Schools are also required to monitor IT use: '… governing bodies and proprietors should ensure appropriate filters and appropriate monitoring systems are in place'.[114]

An illustration of the operation of Ofsted in relation to the safeguarding duty in a failing school is provided by the inspection of a Muslim faith primary school in Luton, which found that the implementation of Prevent (and other safeguarding duties) was inadequate due to a lack of consistency in the training of new staff.[115] In contrast, the inspection report for another Muslim faith primary school in Luton found that the safeguarding policy was suitable, as it was accessible and key staff demonstrated a good understanding of the Prevent duty on inspection.[116]

The broad indication from reports into the effectiveness of Prevent in 2017, is that the number of frivolous or mistaken referrals has diminished as understanding of the nature of the Prevent safeguarding duty has improved, which may be credited to a greater awareness of radicalization as a safeguarding issue due to the emphasis now placed on staff training in this area by the DfE and Ofsted.[117] However, the effectiveness of the scheme, in terms of making proportionate referrals that avoid political or religious bias and which have little impact on the free expression of school pupils, is difficult to assess due to a lack of clarity in terms of reporting on the outcomes of Prevent.[118] A particular difficulty with the 'engage' aspect of Channel referrals is the potential for the link with terrorism to be unclear, with the result that they can readily be represented as a tool of ideological repression, as various Islamist groups have, indeed, sought to do.[119] The result may be that the prospect of Channel referrals has a chilling effect that is out of proportion to the actual benefit of the measures, but the data does not conclusively support such a conclusion, and it may be doubted due to the results of one academic study as to the impact of Prevent in schools.[120]

## 4 Countering extremism by promoting 'British values' in schools

### *Introduction*

Turning from the safeguarding aspect of Prevent to the more general countering of extremist narratives in schools, the departmental guidance explaining the Prevent duty states that schools can satisfy s26 by building pupils' 'resilience' to radicalization 'by promoting fundamental "British values" and enabling them to challenge extremist views'.[121] As mentioned above, the relevant values include: 'democracy, the rule of law, individual liberty and mutual respect, and tolerance of different faiths and beliefs.'[122] The emphasis on the active promotion of such values represented a decisive shift from the approach of the previous Labour government, from challenging terrorist-linked violent extremism that most obviously draws individuals into terrorism to countering non-violent extremism where that link is less apparent. As the guidance makes clear, the promotion of such values does not mean that students are required to adopt a state-sponsored understanding of such values, as occurs in nationalistic or ideological schooling, which is associated with indoctrination.[123] It is clear that by 'British values' it is not meant that these are the values of the current government or of the British state in general. Nor is the promotion of 'British values' designed to inculcate a framework of ideas in a manner that marginalizes any viewpoint about their nature, since the guidance states that schools should provide 'a safe environment for debating controversial issues and helping [pupils] to understand how they can influence and participate in decision-making'.[124] One commentator, giving evidence to the Joint Committee on Human Rights, criticized a lack of clarity and predictability as to the values that are being promoted,[125] but the focus on open debate militates against an attempt to set out an authoritative definition of such values.

In contrast to the safeguarding concern, the relationship between challenging opposition to the promotion of British values in schools, and fulfilment of the s26 duty, is less apparent.[126] As discussed, the safeguarding aspect of Prevent concerns the identification of a specific risk that an *individual* will be drawn into terrorism, and provides a clear basis for intervention on an individual basis, while the aim of supporting 'British values' relates to a more diffuse outcome.[127] This lack of clarity has contributed to the perception that the expression of certain viewpoints that contradict 'British values' will result in referral to Channel (and the various misconceptions concerning the criminalization of Muslims that have been associated with that process).[128] Furthermore, in the absence of a specific risk of an individual being drawn into terrorism, taking account of the 'engagement', 'intent', and 'capacity' dimensions of risk in the Channel framework, the satisfaction of this aspect of the duty requires a close focus on the definition of extremism. The breadth of the definition, which is 'vocal or active opposition to fundamental British values', has been claimed to be a failing of Prevent,[129] notably by the Joint Committee on Human Rights.[130]

However, there are two matters that should be taken into account in order to argue that such concerns can now be viewed as less significant.

### *Disapplication of aspects of the schools' Prevent guidance*

First, following the *Butt* case,[131] the Prevent guidance can be disapplied if it conflicts with the provisions of s26. That case arose in a university context, but it is argued that its findings as to the status of the guidance to higher education providers[132] should also be applied to schools' guidance. Butt's challenge to the lawfulness of the guidance failed,[133] partly on the basis that it is merely expressed to be 'guidance', and s26 only requires that 'due regard' should be given to preventing persons being drawn into terrorism. It does not state that the guidance is binding.[134] It was found that the guidance is not law, in contrast to the duty under s26, and that it is not *ultra vires* to that duty since it was not found to 'equate non-violent extremism with terrorism'. It was found: 'If there is some non-violent extremism, however intrinsically undesirable, which does not create a risk that others will be drawn into terrorism, the guidance does not apply to it', but it was not found that the inclusion of non-violent extremism went beyond what the Prevent duty lawfully permits, so long as in the circumstances it *could* be linked to the risk of drawing persons into terrorism.[135]

The claimant in *Butt* further argued that the guidance could not be shown to be necessary in terms of Article 10(2) ECHR, on the basis that there was insufficient evidence that non-violent extremism contributed to drawing people into terrorism. Justice Ousley accepted that the forms of expression of non-violent extremism that can draw people into terrorism were not susceptible to precise definition or to being clearly evidenced,[136] and noted that the Secretary of State had not produced evidence of individual case-studies or statistics that demonstrated that individuals had been drawn into terrorism partly due to encountering non-violent extremist expression.[137] However, it was found that, due to the complexity of the issue, the emphasis placed on protecting fundamental freedoms in combatting non-violent extremism in the guidance, the approval of parliament for the guidance, and the expertise of the Home Office in assessing the risks posed by non-violent extremism, the courts would require clear evidence that non-violent extremism could not draw people into terrorism.[138] Justice Ousley found that no such evidence had been presented.[139] After *Butt*, evidence linking non-violent extremism with terrorism would be more likely to be available since the Home Office then began to release statistics on Prevent and to make specific case-studies available, such as those used in WRAP training.[140]

That last point could be taken to mean that while some faith schools, such as Charedi schools, may well teach aspects of the curriculum in ways that do not comport with British values, and so aspects of expression in such schools could be deemed to fall within the category of non-violent extremism, the schools' Prevent guidance on such extremism could be disapplied. That is because the link drawing pupils towards terrorism appears to be missing, given that ultra-orthodox Jewish groups have no tradition of engaging in terrorist-related activity in the UK. (But other statutory duties, including the equality duty discussed below, might be found to be breached in such schools due to certain practices, including gender segregation.)[141]

*Butt* provided an important clarification of the relationship between the Prevent guidance and the s26 duty. Clearly, it may take some time for the impact of *Butt*, in the schools' guidance, to filter through to schools. Further, where some aspects of the schools' guidance reflect *other* statutory duties imposed on schools, apart from s26, it would need to be applied. The schools' Prevent guidance now needs to be updated to reflect *Butt*, and also to make it clearer as to which aspects reflect which duties. But it can be concluded that the breadth of the guidance is of less concern than previously appeared to be the case.

### *Overlap of Prevent with existing duties*

Second, as the DfE's advice on the Prevent guidance makes clear, the active defence of and promotion of British values in schools is relevant not only to the Prevent duty, but to a number of education-related statutory duties and to government policy,[142] particularly that of the Department for Education which has direct responsibility for the running of state schools and which has an oversight role in relation to almost all educational services. Indeed, governmental references to the promotion of British values suggest that it is seen primarily as a goal of education policy and secondarily as an aspect of home security,[143] *unlike* the safeguarding aspect of Prevent. An assessment of education law and policy in general is beyond the scope of this chapter, so what follows is merely a brief overview intended to provide context to the discussion of the impact of Prevent on expression in schools.

Maintained schools (i.e. those controlled by Local Education Authorities) are required under s78 Education Act (EA) 2002 to follow the national curriculum and to promote the 'spiritual, moral, social and cultural development' of pupils. Department for Education (DfE) guidance on the fulfilment of the s78 duty now includes more explicit references to British values, aligning it with Prevent.[144] Furthermore, s38 Education and Inspections Act 2006 imposes a duty on such schools to promote community cohesion. Independent Schools (i.e. privately controlled or academies with a funding agreement with the DfE) have a similar duty, set out in s157 EA 2002, which is further specified in the Independent School Standards Regulations 2010 (amended 2014) to include promotion of 'British values' aligned with Prevent[145] and to 'further tolerance and harmony between different cultural traditions'.[146] Maintained or independent schools that are faith schools, whether maintained or (more typically) independent, are also subject to the s78 or s157 EA 2002 requirements, but the content of communal worship and religious instruction is understood to conform to the values of the school's adopted religion and is overseen by a nominated religious authority (s5(7) and s48 Education Act 2005). The statutory duties applicable to maintained and independent schools relate both to the content of the curriculum as well as to its delivery and the organization of the school environment.

In certain respects, the move to a more explicitly Prevent-aligned understanding of the s78 and s157 EA 2002 requirements is uncontroversial, it is argued, in free speech terms. Defending values of democracy, the rule of law, and liberty involves, as the Prevent guidance makes clear, support for a mutually respectful debate about politics, religion, and culture reflecting a plurality of views, which is at the core of the value of free speech, as discussed further in Section 6, below (and, indeed, rights to free expression and to non-discrimination are mutually supportive of civil rights). However, the movement towards a Prevent-aligned understanding of 'mutual respect and tolerance' conflicts with the expression of certain socially conservative, and usually religiously-based, viewpoints of pupils and parents within certain religious sects.[147] It also conflicts with socially conservative viewpoints associated with secular far-right groups such as 'For Britain' or 'National Action'; where a parent is a member of, or associated with, such a group, the child might well bring the views of its parents into school.[148] The DfE has made it clear that mutual respect is incompatible with notions that individuals who are members of certain groups (defined, in particular, by religion, race, sexuality, or gender) are either morally inferior or superior to members of another group. It is also made clear that maintaining such respect is not compatible with the view that members of a particular group are more or less entitled to enjoy freedoms and benefits than others due to their status as members of such a group. Promotion of 'British values', therefore, requires teachers, to an extent, to educate against and challenge such views when expressed by pupils, and to make it clear that such views are not acceptable or welcome in a school environment – partly because they may have a directly adverse impact on the welfare of other pupils and members of the 'inferior' group, as such views are often a justification for physical and emotional abuse ('bullying'). While pupils, depending on their age, might be expected to tolerate being disturbed by the expression of others' views, that would not be expected to extend to systematically enduring discriminatory expression, especially when condoned or disregarded by the school. It should be emphasized that while this understanding of 'mutual respect' is clearly a key aspect of the Prevent guidance, it is far from unique to Prevent, since the requirement that schools operate in a manner that does not undermine mutual respect and tolerance under s149 Equality Act 2010 (the Public Sector Equality duty) has increasingly been interpreted by the DfE, Ofsted, and the courts in a similar manner.[149] Toleration of the promotion of discriminatory ideologies in schools may be more likely to be found to represent a failure to implement the Equality duty than the Prevent duty.[150]

### *Fostering 'British values' as a viewpoint-based attack on faith/ political groups?*

Opponents of Prevent and of DfE policy on 'British values' have characterized the Prevent-DfE's approach as an 'attack' on political or faith groups that hold convictions and beliefs contrary to those values, including Islamist groups, such as Engage Dewsbury, who oppose violent extremism but have claimed that

Prevent has no credibility and is perceived to be anti-Muslim.[151] But the characterization of the Prevent-DfE's approach as an attack on political/faith groups exaggerates and obscures, it is argued, the type of pressure being brought against members of such groups who express discriminatory views, contrary to promoting 'mutual respect' between groups, in two ways. It is important to address them briefly in order to establish whether that pressure is illegitimate in free speech terms.[152]

First, challenging expression that is incompatible with mutual respect in schools is not an attack on the group, nor on the private holding of such views, but rather opposes their expression in the school environment on grounds of safeguarding the welfare of pupils who might be intimidated or humiliated by others due to such expression. Furthermore, the requirement is not necessarily to challenge the expression of a certain *viewpoint*, but rather to open the viewpoint up to reasoned debate; for example, racist or homophobic views typically rely on morally loaded assumptions about the target group, such as that homosexuals are promiscuous, which may only be addressed if those assumptions are explored. Second, the challenge is not to 'group doctrine' as a whole but, rather, certain aspects of it that may be expressed in schools by pupils. Even if the contentious aspect of certain doctrines might be deemed fundamental to 'group doctrine' by some members, beyond the most basic assertions, the identification of any aspect as 'fundamental' is likely to be contestable – and this is even more likely to be the case in relation to sophisticated and long-standing religious, political, and cultural traditions, such as are encapsulated in Islam.[153] Therefore, an apparently fundamental challenge to an aspect of 'group doctrine' from the perspective of certain group members, such as the assertion that women who enjoy sexual freedoms are not evil, would not represent a challenge to a fundamental aspect of it for others.[154]

Furthermore, as seen in the case of ultra-conservative Salafi Islam, those who challenge the 'fundamental' status of certain contentious values can be subject to extreme pressure from other members in the group, which could lead to an understandable reluctance to express such views publicly, thus giving the impression of a false unanimity.[155] Bearing these important distinctions in mind, it is nevertheless clear that a degree of pressure is brought to bear on pupils who hold views contrary to the DfE-Prevent approach to 'mutual respect'. As discussed above, the fact that Prevent is a project of the Home Office, which closely involves the police, could create a degree of intimidation and could contribute to a perception that coercive measures will be brought against individuals who express such views.[156] But such a perception could be dispelled if the workings of Prevent in schools were communicated much more transparently to parents and others.

In 2016 and 2017 a number of Charedi and Islamic faith schools came under pressure to comply with the DfE-Prevent approach to 'mutual respect'.[157] In one instance, an Islamic faith school was reported by the Chief Inspector of Ofsted to have literature defending medieval Islamic views on the treatment of women, in particular a tract entitled *Women Who Deserve to go to Hell*, a polemical that reinforces Qur'anic justifications for the control of wives by husbands on pain of violence, and also emphasizes that women who do not wear Islamic clothing are evil ('wear garments yet be nude').[158] But the consequences that followed would have arisen regardless of Prevent; the school hosting such material was unregistered and since lack of registration is illegal, the school was therefore closed (see further below in relation to enforcement of the Prevent duty).[159] However, Ofsted used the example to emphasize the point that schools require greater government regulation, including via Prevent (and the Equality duty). Another example of the promotion of equality as a 'British value,' which took Prevent into account, is provided by the 2015 Ofsted inspection of the Darul Uloom Islamic high school,[160] which became notorious as one of the Islamic faith schools in which extremism and child abuse was exposed (by Channel 4), as referred to above.[161] The report found that:

> [d]espite pupils' understanding of fundamental British values, leaders do not consistently practise the values that they teach. For example, inspectors were concerned that when they met with members of the governing body, a female governor sat in an adjacent room to the main meeting and contributed through a doorway. This practice, which governors informed inspectors was their usual arrangement, does not demonstrate equality and respect, and undermines the school's work to promote British values.[162]

In general, however, while over a third of independent Jewish faith schools were found inadequate between 2016 and 2017, and over a quarter of Muslim faith schools were found inadequate in the same period, most have, more recently, achieved compliance with the DfE-Prevent approach.[163] An indicative example of compliance is provided by the Ofsted report for the Olive Tree Primary school in London, a registered independent Islamic faith school.[164] In relation to the quality of education provided, the school had come under pressure to do more to challenge negative views about homosexual relationships, and an example was given of a positive development whereby the governors had adopted a strategy for doing so by engaging with pro-gay charities.[165]

For the reasons given above, it is argued that the Prevent duty guidance and the DfE approach to that duty appear to create minimal interference with free debate about religion, politics, and culture in schools. Further, it should be emphasized that this approach *supports* such debate. The importance of giving students the confidence to interrogate cultural, religious, and political assumptions is consistently emphasized within the DfE guidance for schools and, to an extent, in the Prevent guidance itself,[166] as emphasized above, as the most important factor in preventing radicalization.[167] For example, where teachers or pupils are concerned as to those measures that favour only one political or religious narrative in schools, through a narrowing of the curriculum to focus mainly on such a narrative – a key issue in the Trojan Horse affair – Ofsted is now required to take such concerns into account.[168] Therefore, a Catholic school would not be prevented from teaching the majority Catholic view that abortion is a mortal sin, but it would be prevented from denying pupils access to minority Catholic positions critical of that view, or to other religious and secular commentary critical of the assumptions underpinning it. To take some further examples: school pupils would not be prevented from criticizing US/UK bombing in Syria under Prevent, but it would not be expected that the school would promote only one narrative concerning that action. A pupil would not be prevented from expressing a positive view about Sharia law, but again the school would not be expected to promote only one, favourable, view of that law. It would not be in accordance with Prevent for the teacher simply to challenge that view as unacceptable, or, alternatively, to shut down a minority Muslim opinion opposed to Sharia. If, on the other hand, a pupil whose parents were members of a far-right group brought leaflets into school supporting the ideas of that group, such as that Muslims should leave the UK, the school, in furtherance of the 'British value' of tolerance of minorities under the Prevent guidance, but also under the Equality duty, should prevent their distribution. The direct link with a far-right group would also appear to satisfy s26.

### *Conclusions*

Thus, Prevent can foster a 'more speech' solution to the narrowing of pupils' perspectives in some faith schools, given that it opposes religiously or politically-based closing down of a plurality of views.[169] Additionally, the Prevent duty reinforces measures to promote equality and encourages teachers to foster a critical attitude among pupils towards, for example, restrictions linked to gender and sexuality. The importance of supporting such attitudes has been repeatedly re-emphasized by high profile liberal Muslims such as Irshad Manji, who has complained that where conservative Islamic discourse is allowed to predominate in schools, LGBT Muslims and sympathizers are rendered 'invisible' because they fear violent rejection if they express their views.[170] Sara Khan has made a similar point in relation to feminist Islamic perspectives, which she argues are also suppressed if conservative Sunni Islamic doctrine is not challenged in UK schools.[171]

## 5 Enforcement of the Prevent duty in schools

### *Regulation of schools*

If maintained schools funded by the local authority fail to remedy breaches of the Prevent duty, that failure is primarily overseen by Ofsted and could result in intervention measures, such as school closure or the imposition of special measures.[172] In respect of academies funded by central government, failure to remedy such breaches could result in the withdrawal of the funding agreement.[173] After 2015, Ofsted used powers to conduct no-notice inspections in order to reduce the likelihood that schools could present a false image of their practices.[174] These powers were a direct response to criticisms that Ofsted had failed to identify problems of extremism in the Trojan Horse schools, particularly Park View (one of the schools at the centre of the affair) which had been rated as 'outstanding'.[175] Privately funded schools can choose to be inspected by Ofsted or by an independent inspectorate, and such inspections can trigger formal enforcement measures. All 'independent educational institutions' must be registered under s96 Education and Skills Act 2008, and Ofsted has powers to inspect and close such institutions if unregistered.[176]

There is at present no requirement for supplementary schooling to be registered, despite the fact that evidence of extremism has been found repeatedly in madrassas.[177] Proposals for such a registration requirement, which were a significant aspect of the Command paper in which the Conservative government's revised counter-terrorism strategy was set out in 2015,[178] would have formed part of the Counter-Extremism and Safeguarding Bill 2016, but were ultimately dropped from the government's legislative agenda, and the proposals have not so far been revived. This failure has been strongly criticized, notably by Dame Louise Casey,[179] who regarded it as indicative of general government inaction in light of the recommendations in her report, as well as by Ofsted.[180] Similarly, parents who are educating their children at home are not required to register,[181] making it easier for some parents to send their children to illegal, unregistered schools.[182] This phenomenon has come under scrutiny recently, in part due to counter-extremism efforts linked to Prevent; raids had found the presence of extremist literature on the premises of unregistered schools.[183] The Chief Inspector has consistently recommended enhanced regulation of children who are home-schooled to the government, but this recommendation has also not yet been acted upon.[184]

### *Role of the Charity Commission*

In addition to enforcement through Ofsted, or another inspectorate, educational trusts are regulated by the Charity Commission, which is also required to enforce the Prevent duty. An example of the interaction between the two bodies arose recently in relation to the Lantern of Knowledge Educational Trust. After a critical Ofsted report cited failures of management and safeguarding concerns, the Commission embarked on a statutory inquiry into the charity, which included an assessment of '… the management and supervision of staff at the school with access to children or young people'.[185] It is also possible, although very unlikely, that a judicial review of a school (if it was a qualifying public body) could provide a basis for enforcing the Prevent duty.

### *Bars on employment/service against teachers/governors*

It is not only schools and educational trusts that are subject to pressure to comply with the Prevent duty; individual teachers and governors, either involved in or who fail to challenge extremism in schools, may also be subject to sanctions, although private litigation for breach of the Prevent duty is prevented by s34

CTSA 2015. Failure to observe the Prevent duty could amount to a failure to satisfy the statutory teaching standards, which is a ground for dismissal or for a refusal to award Qualified Teacher Status.[186] Furthermore, in particularly serious cases, the Teaching Regulation Agency professional conduct hearing panel could impose a prohibition order, barring the individual from teaching.[187] The promotion of extremism in schools is singled out in particular as a factor weighing in favour of the imposition of such an order, and specific reference is made to the 'exposure of pupils to [extremist] actions or behaviours' by inviting speakers known to espouse extreme views to speak at school events.[188] Individual governors can also be barred from serving by direction of the Secretary of State under s142 of the Education Act 2002 or s128 of the Education and Skills Act 2008. This sanction was applied to Tahir Alam, former governor of Park View high school, one of the schools at the centre of the Trojan Horse affair. In the prohibition direction published by the Department for Education, the Secretary of State found that Tahir Alam's activities as governor were most responsible for the issues raised in the Clarke Report, which were aimed at undermining 'British values'. The notice cited, in particular, activities such as inviting extremist speakers to address pupils as well as 'the narrowing of curricula in non-faith schools to make them conform with conservative religious teachings....'[189] This notice was later upheld on appeal.[190]

## 6 Duties to foster pluralistic, free debate in schools

The impact of the Prevent/DfE approach in avoiding the imposition of a narrow, monocultural curriculum in schools, and in fostering the promotion of a range of viewpoints, has been considered above. But a range of other duties are also imposed on schools, which are designed to further similar ends – although no specific duty to promote free expression in schools, similar to that imposed on universities under s31 CTSA, is imposed. Freedom of speech finds positive legal protection under Article 10 ECHR,[191] given further effect by the Human Rights Act 1998 (HRA). S6 HRA provides that it is 'unlawful' for public bodies, which includes the government, LEA-funded schools, and Ofsted, to act in a way that is incompatible with a convention right.

The rights of children, and especially mature school children, to express and receive ideas in education is recognized by Article 13 of the United Nations Convention on the Rights of the Child 1989, which has been ratified by the United Kingdom. Prevent may be said to be aligned with Article 13 since it is partly intended to prevent the narrowing of children's minds due to the imposition upon them of a rigid, religiously or politically driven ideological curriculum, affording them greater opportunities to receive a range of ideas.[192]

Protocol 1, Article 2 ECHR provides a right to education. Its core content is understood to be the protection of the individual from political indoctrination by the state, and that discussion of matters that are the subject of beliefs or convictions should be addressed 'in an objective, critical and pluralistic manner' that reflects the core democratic values of the ECHR.[193] The right to education in

Article 2 emphasizes that anti-liberal indoctrination is a particular concern within school settings.[194] This concern is emphasized in *Campbell and Cosans* v. *UK*,[195] in which it was found that the scope of the convictions and beliefs that merit protection under Article 2 are those that 'are worthy of respect in a "democratic society" and are not incompatible with human dignity....'[196]

The combination of the requirements of Article 10, Article 2, Protocol 1, Article 13, and the DfE/Prevent approach could pose problems for literalist approaches to religious texts in faith schools, since the assumptions underpinning the texts could not be explored without challenging that approach. One method to avoid falling foul of requirements to promote free speech and debate would be to separate religious instruction based on a literalist approach from teaching other aspects of the curriculum, such as relationships and sex education, biology, and history.

It is clear that the 'promotion of British values' aspect of Prevent is not merely compatible with the rationale of Article 2, and with the values underlying the ECHR as a whole, including Article 10,[197] but is actually supportive of them, because those ECHR values are reflected in the Prevent guidance.[198] Exposure of pupils to extremist speakers, combined with attempts to isolate pupils from exposure to forms of art, music, dance, knowledge of key world religions, and ideas as to non-discrimination against homosexuals,[199] could aid in isolating some Muslim pupils from British society. Creation of isolationism was linked in *Butt* to the risk of drawing persons towards terrorist-related activity. Justice Ousley considered whether, given the disputed nature of the evidence, a possible connection between non-violent extremism and drawing people into terrorism could be shown as being relevant to the link between the schools' Prevent guidance and s26 CTSA. He found that non-violent extremism could create a 'framework of a sense of separateness, alienation, victimhood ... at one with a rigid and pure version of religion or ideology' that was capable of justifying violence.[200] He found that when a view is part of a 'rigid and pure' ideology that seeks to change UK law to reflect that ideology through non-violent democratic means, then this was non-violent extremism and, *furthermore*, created a risk of drawing others into terrorism, because '[t]he argument might lead others, persuaded by it of the merit of the aim, to reject the [democratic, non-violent] means.'[201] These findings would apply equally – or more strongly – to schools, given the greater vulnerability of schoolchildren to persuasion from authority figures, as compared to students.

## Conclusions

In conclusion, it is argued, based on the findings above, that Prevent is neither a policy of mass surveillance of children, nor mass propaganda designed to pressure schoolchildren to adopt any particular viewpoint, as opponents of Prevent have suggested since its inception.[202] Rather, Prevent was designed to be a policy that was complementary to pre-existing approaches to handling 'sensitive and controversial issues' in schools,[203] which recognized the importance of a

'... climate in which children can express a point of view that may differ from those held either by their teachers/practitioners or their peers'.[204] But the hyperbole about Prevent deployed by the anti-Prevent lobby[205] is, it is argued, obscuring impartial, objective analysis of Prevent as it operates in schools, making it hard to disentangle its real impact in terms of the stigmatization of Muslims from the impact of the Prevent myths.[206] The image of Prevent that has been created by the anti-Prevent lobby is intended to indicate that it is having counterproductive effects in schools and so should be abandoned. The use of exaggeration, and the distortion of its effects, are intended to feed feelings of persecution within certain communities in order to provide a basis for that argument; it has, therefore, to an extent become a tool of extremist propaganda itself. The most high-profile narratives about Prevent appear to have arisen from the school context.[207]

Thus, certain activist groups have sought to arouse anxiety in some Muslim communities as to the effect of Prevent in schools, and have sought to present the strategy as a further argument for furthering Muslim isolationism and suspicion of the 'West'.[208] This effect could be particularly heightened in a community, such as the socially conservative Deobandi Muslim community, meaning that pupils from that community could be seen as the 'target' of apparent ideological repression. Obviously, it is extremely difficult to assess the extent or impact of such concerns, but some faith groups and some academics have highlighted this as an issue.[209] It is questionable, however, whether the solution to such concerns is to abandon Prevent, as opposed to challenging the narrative of persecution, especially as there is evidence that the anti-Prevent campaign is losing ground as Prevent 'beds in'.[210] Echoing the recommendations of the Joint Committee on Human Rights (JCHR) in relation to the impact of Prevent in universities,[211] the solution appears to be to retain Prevent but to ensure that parents, pupils, teachers, and school governors are educated much more effectively about the operation of Prevent in schools. In general, the creation of greater transparency in respect of its real impact in schools is needed in order to counter Prevent myths.[212] The announcement of a Commission for Countering Extremism could play a part in achieving these goals, but until it is known what recommendations the Commission will make to the government it is unclear how the legal environment may be affected.[213]

However, on the basis that a number of activist groups are deliberately seeking to distort the effects of Prevent in schools,[214] they are unlikely to be receptive to attempts at creating greater transparency. If their intention is to use distortion and exaggeration in order to fuel feelings of grievance in some communities, with a view to then using the argument that due to its counterproductivity Prevent should be abandoned, which could then give such groups a freer hand in relation to radicalization in schools, that project would obviously be disturbed if the true impact of Prevent could be made to reach ordinary parents and pupils. It might, therefore, be concluded that there is a case for abandoning Prevent on grounds of proportionality since it overlaps with existing duties; on the one hand, there is limited evidence that it has had an impact in countering extremism among pupils,[215] while, on the other, activist groups have to an extent succeeded in using Prevent as an aid to radicalization in some communities. But that would be likely to aid in the creation of a limited and stunted educational experience for some pupils,[216] leaving them less able to obtain employment and post-school qualifications and, possibly, more open to seeking isolation within society, rendering some of them more vulnerable to radicalization. While it is not argued that Prevent has created decisive change, its abandonment would also tend to disempower once again those such as Khalid Mahmood who sought unsuccessfully to draw the attention of the authorities to such limited educational experiences in Birmingham as one aspect of the Trojan Horse affair.[217] Also Muslim and/or non-Muslim parents and teachers, resistant to the imposition of a narrowed curriculum on the pupils, would similarly face a diminution in their avenues of challenge. So, efforts to educate communities about Prevent should be increased, especially on the basis that it is now working more effectively, given that teachers and others in schools have had time to undergo training and gain greater experience as to its true impact.

The modern Prevent policy as it applies to schools has in some respects changed substantially from that adopted by the Labour governments between 2003 and 2010, but it retains a commitment to the creation of complementarity to existing law/policy on the safeguarding of pupils, and on inculcating knowledge about political and moral values as well as setting standards of behaviour in conformity with those values. It is contended that, as applied in schools, Prevent has the potential to support rather than inhibit expression since, in company with other statutory duties of schools, including the Equality duty, it supports the broadening of pupils' minds rather than the narrowing of them due to the imposition of a narrow curriculum based on socially conservative values. Thus, insofar as Prevent in schools is linked to the Trojan Horse affair, it is argued that the affair has led to an impact in schools more in tune with the promotion of free speech values than inhibitory of them. Insofar as it supports the expression of a plurality of views in schools, as opposed to promoting their isolation from such plurality, it is also likely to diminish the risk of pupils being drawn towards terrorism.

## Notes

1 'Schools' refers to institutions of primary and secondary education, as specified in the Education Act 1996 s2(2),(2A), including sixth forms that are part of state schools (i.e. maintained or academy schools). Institutions involved in 'further education' and 'higher education,' which are subject to different statutory frameworks to those applying to primary and secondary educational institutions, are therefore beyond the scope of this chapter.

2 Sched 6 CTSA.

3 HM Government, *The Revised Prevent Duty Guidance*, (issued 12 March 2015, revised 16 July 2015); see www.gov.uk/government/publications/prevent-duty-guidance (accessed 10.8.18).

4 Ibid. [6].

5 Numerous commentators have highlighted the fact that many historic figures who are today viewed as important figures in the development of humanism and liberalism, such as Michael Servetus, were considered to be a danger to society due to their

radical, heretical, views; see, for example, AC Grayling, *Towards the Light: The Story of the Struggles for Liberty and Rights that Made the Modern West* (Bloomsbury Publishing, 2007) pt 1.

6 See n. 3 above at [6].

7 See A Moffat, *Reclaiming Radical Ideas in Schools: Preparing Young Children for Life in Modern Britain* (Routledge, 2017).

8 It should be noted that in *R (Miranda)* v. *Secretary of State for the Home Department* [2016] EWCA Civ 6 at 51–5, the definition of terrorism was significantly refined: it was found that the acts listed in s1(2)(a) and (b) should be understood to contain a mental element of awareness of involvement in the damage/ violence.

9 See, for example, A Greene, 'Defining terrorism: one size fits all?' (2017) 66(2) ICLQ 411, 415–19.

10 The offence of supporting a proscribed organisation – s12 of TA 2000 (since the PKK is proscribed), or the offence of glorifying terrorism (s1 TA 2006).

11 See n. 3 at [7]. It should be noted that the relationship between non-violent extremism and radicalization is strongly disputed; see, for example, J Holmwood and T O'Toole, *Countering Extremism in British Schools?* (Bristol, Policy Press, 2017), 54–7. The authors are of the view that the term should be understood in light of the contemporary context of terrorist violence against the UK state and its citizens. The authors agree with Justice Ouseley's finding in *Butt* v. *Secretary of State for the Home Department* [2017] EWHC 1930 (Admin) that the 'radicalization' process by which an initially non-violent extremist could ultimately engage in terrorism involves a 'framework of a sense of separateness, alienation, victimhood … at one with a rigid and pure version of religion or ideology' (at [137]). However, it must be emphasized that the association between such a framework and the commission of terrorist acts is not a close one; the adoption of an extremist ideology is only *one* indicator among many that an individual may commit: such acts and such an indicator must be treated with caution in order to avoid unjustifiably implicating a broader religious community; see, for example, J Taylor, '"Suspect Categories," Alienation and Counterterrorism: Critically Assessing PREVENT in the UK' *Terrorism and Political Violence* 1 (2018): 1156. See on counter-terrorism law and social division generally: M-S Abbas, 'Producing "Internal Suspect Bodies": Divisive Effects of UK Counter-Terrorism Measures on Muslim Communities in Leeds and Bradford' *British Journal of Sociology* 1 (2018); F Ragazzi, 'Suspect Community or Suspect Category? The Impact of Counter-Terrorism as "Policed Multiculturalism"' (2016) *Journal of Ethnic and Migration Studies* 42 no. 5 (2016): 724. See further below text to n. 135.

12 See further, I Cram and H Fenwick 'Protecting Free Speech and Academic Freedom in Universities' MLR 81, no. 5 (2018): 825 at 835 for discussion and criticism of the linkage between radicalization and participation in terrorism-related activity.

13 Note that the government has stated that the overall counter-extremism strategy was designed to help to address the harms of extremism – in particular the support or justification of violence: Home Office, *Counter-Extremism Strategy* (Cm 9148, 2015) para 7.

14 See: P Clarke, 'Report into allegations concerning Birmingham schools arising from the "Trojan Horse" letter' (HMSO 2014); J Holmwood and T O'Toole, *Countering Extremism in British Schools? The truth about the Birmingham Trojan Horse affair* (Bristol, Policy Press, 2018).

15 Home Office, *Countering International Terrorism: The United Kingdom's Strategy* (Cm 6888, 2006).

16 Ibid.

17 Ibid. [3].

18 See Department for Schools, Children and Families, 'Learning Together to be Safe' (London, 2008); see at http://dera.ioe.ac.uk/8396/1/DCSF-Learning%20Together_bkmk.pdf (accessed 10.8.18).
19 Ibid. 3.
20 Cabinet Office, *The National Security Strategy of the United Kingdom: Update 2009 security for the Next Generation* (Cm 7590, 2009), para 6.36.
21 Ibid.
22 Home Office, *Prevent Strategy* (Cm 8092, 2011) paras 5.35–5.37; see at www.gov.uk/government/publications/prevent-strategy-2011 (accessed 10.8.18).
23 Home Affairs Select Committee, *Roots of violent radicalisation* (HC 2010–12, 1466-I), chap 3.
24 Prime Minister's Taskforce on Tackling Radicalisation and extremism, 'Tackling extremism in the UK' (Dec 2013); see at https://assets.publishing.service.gov.uk/government/uploads/system/uploads/attachment_data/file/263181/ETF_FINAL.pdf (accessed 10.8.18).
25 Ibid. para 4.1.
26 R Butt, 'Lessons in Hate and Violence: the same old story' *Guardian* (17 February 2011); see at www.theguardian.com/commentisfree/belief/2011/feb/17/lessons-in-hate-and-violence-muslim-extremism (accessed 10.8.18).
27 Birmingham Post, 'Hate preacher expelled from Birmingham Islamic school featured on TV documentary' (14 February 2011); see at www.birminghampost.co.uk/news/local-news/hate-preacher-expelled-birmingham-islamic-3923609 (accessed 10.8.18).
28 See E Husain, *The Islamist* (Penguin, 2007), and Maajid Nawaz, *Radical* (Lyons Press, 2012).
29 Home Office, *Prevent Strategy* (Cm 8092, 2011), para 10.30.
30 I Kershaw, 'Investigation report Trojan Horse letter' (Eversheds Northern Education 2014); www.birmingham.gov.uk/download/downloads/id/1579/investigation_report_trojan_horse_letter_the_kershaw_report.pdf (accessed 10.8.18).
31 In contrast, Islamist activist group MEND, formerly iENGAGE, claimed that the letter was a hoax and held events seeking to link the letter to a general stigmatisation of Muslims in education: MEND, 'Trojan Horse – The Facts' (The Bordersley Centre, Birmingham, 3 November 2017).
32 See: Kershaw, 'Investigation report,' n. 30 above; R Adams, 'Is the Trojan horse row just a witch hunt triggered by a hoax?' *Guardian* (8 June 2014); see at www.theguardian.com/education/2014/jun/08/trojan-horse-extremism-political-storm-michael-gove-ofsted (accessed 10.8.18).
33 See Birmingham Mail, 'Birmingham Council insists Trojan Horse did happen and promises to challenge those who deny it' (3 November 2017); see at www.birminghammail.co.uk/news/midlands-news/birmingham-council-insists-trojan-horse-13852775 (accessed 10.8.18).
34 Education Committee, 'Extremism in Schools: the Trojan Horse Affair' (HC 2014–2015, 473), 13. See also R Garner, 'Trojan Horse: Headteacher received death threats for speaking out against homophobia' *Independent* (3 May 2015); see at www.independent.co.uk/news/education/schools/trojan-horse-headteacher-received-death-threats-for-speaking-out-against-homophobia-10222271.html (accessed 10.8.18).
35 P Clarke, 'Report into allegations concerning Birmingham schools arising from the "Trojan Horse" letter' (HMSO 2014), para 2.5.
36 Ibid. para 1.1.
37 Kershaw, 'Investigation report,' n. 30.
38 Ibid. para 22.
39 Ibid. para 22.
40 P Clarke, 'Report into allegations concerning Birmingham schools arising from the "Trojan Horse" letter' (HMSO 2014), para 1.1.

41 Ibid. paras 1.1, 11.1.
42 Ibid. paras 1.1, 11.1.
43 Ibid. para 4.16.
44 Ibid. para 5.1.
45 Ibid. para 4.43.
46 Ibid. para 7.25:

> Speakers were found to include the following individuals: Shaykh Yusuf Estes – a speaker who has caused controversy in the past for reportedly advocating wife beating and the killing of homosexuals. Shaykh Shady al-Suleiman – a preacher who has reportedly called on God to 'destroy the enemies of Islam'. Al-Suleiman has also asked God to 'give victory to the Muslims in Afghanistan and Chechnya', to 'give victory to all the Mujahideen all over the world' and to 'prepare us for the jihad'. Ustadh Hamza Tzortis – a speaker who has reportedly said that Muslims reject the idea of freedom of speech and even the idea of freedom.

47 Ibid. para 4.3.
48 Ibid. para 4.20. See also Mr Khalid Mahmood, HC Deb 2 December 2014, vol. 603, col. 248.
49 P Clarke, 'Report into allegations concerning Birmingham schools arising from the "Trojan Horse" letter' (HMSO 2014) , para 4.30.
50 Ibid. para 7.25.
51 Ofsted, 'Inspection Report for Park View Academy of Mathematics and Science on 5–6 March and 17–18 March 2014'; see at https://files.api.beta.ofsted.gov.uk/138059__3.PDF (accessed 10.8.18).
52 Ibid. 1.
53 See below re T Alam, n. 190, and re the collapse of the proceedings, n. 60.
54 Park View Educational Trust, 'Statement from Park View Educational Trust on Ofsted reports on Park View, Golden Hillock and Nansen schools' (9 June 2014); see at www.mohammedamin.com/Community_issues/PVET/PVET-statement-9-6-2014-on-Ofsted-reports.pdf (accessed 10.8.18).
55 See in particular J Holmwood and T O'Toole, *Countering Extremism in British Schools?* (Bristol, Policy Press, 2018), chapter 8.
56 Ibid. chapter 8.
57 Now the Teaching Regulation Agency.
58 *NCTL* v. *Monzoor Hussain* decision of 1 March 2017; see at www.matrixlaw.co.uk/wp-content/uploads/2017/03/02.03.17.pdf (accessed 10.8.18); see further J Holmwood and T O'Toole, *Countering Extremism in British Schools?* (Bristol, Policy Press, 2018): 89.
59 P Clarke, 'Report into allegations concerning Birmingham schools arising from the 'Trojan Horse' letter' (HMSO, 2014), para 4.20.
60 *NCTL* v. *Monzoor Hussain*, Transcript of Proceedings, Day 4, 22 October 2015 p. 89, cited in *Countering Extremism in British Schools?* (Bristol, Policy Press, 2018), 223. As a result of these evidential irregularities the hearings collapsed, although dismissal of certain teachers involved in the 'scandal', such as Razwan Faraz, was subsequently upheld: N Johnston, 'Trojan horse teacher called gays "animals"' *The Times* (13 August 2018) www.thetimes.co.uk/article/trojan-horse-teacher-called-gays-animals-kfbbzmv3k (accessed 13.8.18).
61 Op cit. 98.
62 Ibid. 98.
63 Department for Education, 'Promoting fundamental British values as part of SMSC in schools' (November 2014); see at https://assets.publishing.service.gov.uk/government/uploads/system/uploads/attachment_data/file/380595/SMSC_Guidance_Maintained_Schools.pdf (accessed 10.8.18).
64 HC Deb, 29 January 2015, vol. 591, col. 1015.

65 M Wilshaw, 'Advice notes on academies and maintained schools in Birmingham' 8th July 2016; see at https://assets.publishing.service.gov.uk/government/uploads/system/uploads/attachment_data/file/535976/HMCI_advice_note_to_the_Secretary_of_State_on_Birmingham_8_July_16.pdf (accessed 10.8.18).
66 HC Deb 2 December 2014, vol. 603, cols 248, 265.
67 Prime Minister's Taskforce on Tackling Radicalisation and extremism, 'Tackling extremism in the UK' (Dec 2013); see at https://assets.publishing.service.gov.uk/government/uploads/system/uploads/attachment_data/file/263181/ETF_FINAL.pdf (accessed 10.8.18).
68 Ibid. 5.
69 Ibid. 4.
70 Home Office, *Contest Annual report* (Cm 9048, 2014) para 2.34.
71 R Adams, 'Is the Trojan horse row just a witch hunt triggered by a hoax?' *the Guardian* (8 June 2014); see at www.theguardian.com/education/2014/jun/08/trojan-horse-extremism-political-storm-michael-gove-ofsted (accessed 10.8.18); see also in relation to the link between Prevent and 'British values': S Miah, *Muslims, Schooling and Security: Trojan Horse, Prevent and Racial Politics* (Palgrave, 2018) chap 5.
72 HC Deb 2 December 2014, vol. 603, cols 248, 265.
73 Home Office, *Countering International Terrorism: The United Kingdom's Strategy* (Cm 6888, 2006) para 6.
74 Home Office, *Counter-Extremism Strategy* (Cm 9148, 2015) para 7.
75 P Clarke, 'Report into allegations concerning Birmingham schools arising from the 'Trojan Horse' letter' (HMSO, 2014).
76 HM Government, *The Revised Prevent Duty Guidance* (Issued 12 March 2015, revised 16 July 2015); see at www.gov.uk/government/publications/prevent-duty-guidance (accessed 10.8.18).
77 Department for Education, 'The Prevent duty: Departmental advice for schools and childcare providers' (June 2015); see at https://assets.publishing.service.gov.uk/government/uploads/system/uploads/attachment_data/file/439598/prevent-duty-departmental-advice-
v6.pdf. (accessed 10.8.18).
78 Ibid. 4.
79 See J Mohammed and A Siddiqui, 'The PREVENT strategy: A cradle to grave police-state' (CAGE, 2013); see at www.cage.ngo/prevent-strategy-cradle-grave-police-state (accessed 10.8.18).
80 HC Deb 2 December 2014, vol. 603, col. 246.
81 Ibid., col 246.
82 Department for Education, 'Review into possible warnings to DfE relating to extremism in Birmingham schools' (January 2015); see at https://assets.publishing.service.gov.uk/government/uploads/system/uploads/attachment_data/file/396211/Review_into_possible_warnings_to_DfE_relating_to_extremism_in_Birmingham_schools.pdf (accessed 10.8.18); Secretary of State for Education, *Government response to the Education Select Committee report: Extremism in schools: the Trojan Horse affair* (Cm 9094, 2015) 1:

> We are collaborating with the Home Office and Police to develop advice and material to support schools in meeting their new duty to prevent young people from being drawn into terrorism, as part of the Counter-Terrorism and Security Act 2015.

83 HM Government, *The Revised Prevent Duty Guidance* (issued 12 March 2015, revised 16 July 2015); see at www.gov.uk/government/publications/prevent-duty-guidance (accessed 10.8.18) para 67.
84 Department for Education, 'The Prevent duty: Departmental advice for schools and childcare providers' (June 2015); see at https://assets.publishing.service.gov.uk/

government/uploads/system/uploads/attachment_data/file/439598/prevent-duty-departmental-advice-v6.pdf (accessed 10.8.18) 5. This duty is supplementary to the statutory duty under s11 Children Act 2004 which imposes a duty on schools to have regard to the need to safeguard and promote the welfare of children.

85 Ibid.

86 SI 3283/2014.

87 See, for example, J Mohammed, 'Britain's Counter Extremism Policies are Criminalising Muslim thought and expression' (Public Spirit, October 2015); see at www.publicspirit.org.uk/assets/Jahangir-Mohammed-Final.pdf (accessed 10.8.18).

88 Section 34 CTSA 2015.

89 Local Safeguarding Children Boards (LSCB) and Prevent co-ordinators (in areas which have been identified as Prevent Priority areas).

90 For the legal status of the Guidance see discussion of the *Butt* case, n. 133 below, and associated text.

91 L Casey, 'The Casey Review: A review into opportunity and integration' (Department of Communities and Local Government, 2016); see at https://assets.publishing.service.gov.uk/government/uploads/system/uploads/attachment_data/file/575973/The_Casey_Review_Report.pdf (accessed 10.8.18) 152 *et seq*; J Mohammed and A Siddiqui, 'The PREVENT strategy: A cradle to grave police-state' (CAGE, 2013); see at www.cage.ngo/prevent-strategy-cradle-grave-police-state (accessed 10.8.18), paras 3.8–3.9.

92 'The Prevent duty: Departmental advice for schools and childcare providers,' n. 84 above, 5.

93 CTSA 2015 s36(1), (3). National Union of Teachers, 'Education and Extremism: Advice for Members' (11 May 2015); see at www.teachers.org.uk/equality/equality-matters/education-and-extremism (accessed 10.8.18) para 39. Between April 2016 and March 2017 there were 1,078 Prevent referrals related to Islamist concerns from Education: Home Office, 'Individuals referred to and supported through the Prevent Programme, April 2016 to March 2017' (Home Office Statistical Bulletin, March 2018) Annex A; see at www.gov.uk/government/statistics/individuals-referred-to-and-supported-through-the-prevent-programme-april-2016-to-march-2017 (accessed 10.8.18) para 1.1.

94 See in support: J Busher, T Choudhury, P Thomas and G Harris, 'What the Prevent duty means for schools and colleges in England: An analysis of educationalists' experiences' (Centre for Peace, Trust and Social Relations Coventry University and Aziz Foundation, 2017); see at http://azizfoundation.org.uk/wp-content/uploads/2017/07/What-the-Prevent-Duty-means-for-schools-and-colleges-in-England.pdf (accessed 10.8.18) para 4.4; Joint Committee on Human Rights, *Counter Extremism* (2016–17, HL Paper 39, HC 105) 15.

95 See text to n. 124. See also the recent study by Busher *et al.*, ibid. para 4.4. It found no widespread direct resistance or opposition to the duty, with staff confidence bolstered by the feeling that it is an extension of their existing safeguarding responsibilities.

96 HM Government, 'Channel: Vulnerability assessment framework' (October 2012); see at https://assets.publishing.service.gov.uk/government/uploads/system/uploads/attachment_data/file/118187/vul-assessment.pdf (accessed 10.8.18).

97 Ibid.

98 J Mohammed and A Siddiqui, 'The PREVENT strategy: A cradle to grave police-state' (CAGE, 2013); see at www.cage.ngo/prevent-strategy-cradle-grave-police-state (accessed 10.8.18) para 3.8.

99 'The Prevent duty: Departmental advice for schools and childcare providers,' n. 84 above, 5.

100 S Webster, J Kerr and C Tompkins, 'A Process Evaluation of the Structured Risk Guidance for Extremist Offenders' (HM Prison and Probation Service, 2017); see

at https://assets.publishing.service.gov.uk/government/uploads/system/uploads/attachment_data/file/661787/process-evaluation-srg-extremist-offender-report.pdf (accessed 10.8.18).

101 A Qureshi, 'The science of pre-crime: the secret "radicalisation" study underpinning Prevent' (CAGE, 2016); see at https://cage.ngo/wp-content/uploads/2016/09/CAGE-Science-Pre-Crime-Report.pdf (accessed 10.8.18).

102 S Greer and L Bell 'Counter-terrorist law in British universities: a review of the "prevent" debate' [2018] PL 84, 94. It should be noted that Greer's rejection of the notion that counter-terror laws and policies such as Prevent demonstrate that British Muslims are a 'suspect community' – S Greer, 'Anti-terrorist laws and the UK's suspect Muslim community: A Reply to Pantazis and Pemberton' *The British Journal of Criminology* 50 (2010): 1171 – is controversial and has been criticised: C Pantazis and S Pemberton, 'Restating the case for the suspect community: A Reply to Greer' *The British Journal of Criminology* 51 (2011): 1054.

103 See for example J Halliday and V Dodd, 'UK Anti-Radicalisation Prevent Strategy a "Toxic Brand,"' *Guardian* (9 March 2015); see at www.theguardian.com/uk-news/2015/mar/09/anti-radicalisation-prevent-strategy-a-toxic-brand (accessed 10.8.18).

104 'The Prevent duty: Departmental advice for schools and childcare providers,' n. 84 above, 5.

105 HM Government, *Channel Duty Guidance: Protecting vulnerable people from being drawn into terrorism* (2015); see at https://assets.publishing.service.gov.uk/government/uploads/system/uploads/attachment_data/file/425189/Channel_Duty_Guidance_April_2015.pdf (accessed 10.8.18).

106 See for example HM Government, 'Workshop to Raise Awareness of Prevent: Full Workshop Script' (December 2014); see at https://assets.documentcloud.org/documents/2520075/wrap-full-workshop-script-december-2014-14-09.pdf (accessed 10.8.18): 'What will those signs that someone needs our help look like? In truth, they will look a lot like other troubling behaviour.' See also A Ali, 'Workshop to Raise Awareness of PREVENT' (Birmingham Education Support Services, 2017); see at www.birmingham.gov.uk/.../workshop_to_raise_awareness_of_prevent.pptx (accessed 10.8.18).

107 See for discussion, J Lewis, 'Prevent as an Intractable Policy Controversy: Implications and Solutions' (2018) *Journal for Deradicalization* 15 (2018): 113.

108 The Education (Independent School Standards) Regulations 2014, SI 3283/2014.

109 Ofsted, 'Ofsted School inspection handbook: Handbook for inspecting schools in England under section 5 of the Education Act 2005' (Ref: 150066, 2018) 42.

110 Ibid. para 148.

111 Ibid. para 148.

112 Ofsted, 'Inspecting safeguarding in early years, education and skills settings' (Ref: 160047, 2016); see at www.gov.uk/government/publications/inspecting-safeguarding-in-early-years-education-and-skills-from-september-2015/inspecting-safeguarding-in-early-years-education-and-skills-settings (accessed 10.8.18); Ofsted, 'Inspecting Safeguarding in Maintained Schools and Academies' (Ref: 140143, 2015); see at http://dera.ioe.ac.uk/21736/1/Inspecting_safeguarding_in_maintained_schools_and_academies_-_a_briefing_for_section_5_inspections.pdf (accessed 10.8.18) 14.

113 Ibid.

114 Department for Education, 'Keeping children safe in education Statutory guidance for schools and colleges' (September 2016) para 63; see at www.gov.uk/government/publications/keeping-children-safe-in-education-2 (accessed 10.8.18). This requirement has been criticized for having the potential to limit access to viewpoints touching on extremist themes and to intrude into online privacy, e.g. Big Brother Watch, 'Classroom Management Software – Another Brick in the Wall?' (2016); see at www.bigbrotherwatch.org.uk/wp-content/uploads/2016/11/Classroom-Management-Software-Another-Brick-in-the-Wall.pdf (accessed 10.8.18).

115 Ofsted, 'Inspection Report for Olive Tree Primary School, 23–25 May 2017' (July 2017); see at https://reports.ofsted.gov.uk/inspection-reports/find-inspection-report/provider/ELS/131825 (accessed 10.8.18).

116 Ofsted, 'Inspection Report for Rabia Girls' and Boys' School, 12–14 April 2016' (May 2016); see at https://reports.ofsted.gov.uk/provider/files/2567089/urn/130331.pdf (accessed 10.8.18).

117 In 2015–16, the education sector referred almost 2,539 individuals, 'Individuals referred to and supported through the Prevent Programme, April 2015 to March 2016' (Home Office Statistical Bulletin, March 2017); see at www.gov.uk/government/statistics/individuals-referred-to-and-supported-through-the-prevent-programme-april-2015-to-march-2016 (accessed 10.8.18) para 1.1; while in 2016–17 this number dropped to 1976 referrals (Home Office, 'Individuals referred to and supported through the Prevent Programme, April 2016 to March 2017' (Home Office Statistical Bulletin, March 2018); see at www.gov.uk/government/statistics/individuals-referred-to-and-supported-through-the-prevent-programme-april-2016-to-march-2017 (accessed 10.8.18) para 1.1; see also Joint Committee on Human Rights, *Counter Extremism* (2016–17, HL 39 HC 105) Appendix A.

118 JCHR, ibid, at 15.

119 Ibid.

120 B Durodie, 'Securitising education to prevent terrorism or losing direction?' *British Journal of Educational Studies* 64 (2016): 21, 24 *et seq*. Home Office, 'Individuals referred to and supported through the Prevent Programme, April 2015 to March 2016,' n. 117 above, para 2.7. See also J Busher, T Choudhury, P Thomas and G Harris, 'What the Prevent duty means for schools and colleges in England: An analysis of educationalists' experiences' (Centre for Peace, Trust and Social Relations Coventry University and Aziz Foundation, 2017); see at http://azizfoundation.org.uk/wp-content/uploads/2017/07/What-the-Prevent-Duty-means-for-schools-and-colleges-in-England.pdf (accessed 10.8.18) which concluded that 'Most of the respondents did not perceive the Prevent duty to have had a "chilling effect" on discussion and debate.…' (at 65).

121 'The Prevent duty: Departmental advice for schools and childcare providers,' n. 84 above, 8; HM Government, *The Revised Prevent Duty Guidance* (Issued 12 March 2015, revised 16 July 2015); see at www.gov.uk/government/publications/prevent-duty-guidance (accessed 10.8.18) para 58.

122 *The Revised Prevent Duty Guidance*, ibid, para 7

123 See for example YW Leung, 'Nationalistic Education and Indoctrination' *Citizenship, Social and Economics Education* 6(2) (2004): 116.

124 'The Prevent duty: Departmental advice for schools and childcare providers,' n. 84 above, 8.

125 Joint Committee on Human Rights, *Counter Extremism* (2016–17, HL Paper 39, HC 105) para 90, per Professor Rivers.

126 See for example A Kundnani, 'A decade lost: Rethinking Radicalisation' (London, Claystone, 2015).

127 See text to n. 84.

128 Joint Committee on Human Rights, *Counter Extremism* (2016–17, HL Paper 39, HC 105) paras 48–50; L Casey, 'The Casey Review: A review into opportunity and integration' (Department of Communities and Local Government, 2016); see at https://assets.publishing.service.gov.uk/government/uploads/system/uploads/attachment_data/file/575973/The_Casey_Review_Report.pdf (accessed 10.8.18) 152 *et seq*; S Warsi, *The Enemy Within* (Penguin, 2018) 87; Islam21c, 'Muslims in Luton display remarkable unity against Prevent' 19/11/2016; www.islam21c.com/special/web-posts/muslims-in-luton-display-remarkable-unity-against-prevent/ (accessed 10.8.18).

129 See M Versi, 'Concerns on Prevent: Meeting between David Anderson QC and the MCB' (Muslim Council of Britain 2015); see at www.mcb.org.uk/wp-content/uploads/2015/10/20150803-Case-studies-about-Prevent.pdf (accessed 10.8.18).

130 Joint Committee on Human Rights, *Counter Extremism* (2016–17, HL Paper 39, HC 105) para 50.
131 *Butt* v. *Secretary of State for the Home Department* [2017] EWHC 1930 (Admin).
132 HM Government, *The Revised Prevent Duty Guidance*, (Issued 12 March 2015, revised 16 July 2015); see at www.gov.uk/government/publications/prevent-duty-guidance (accessed 10.8.18).
133 The case was brought by Salman Butt, since he had been named in a Downing Street press release about the use of the Prevent duty to stop extremists radicalizing students on university campuses. He was listed as one of six speakers who had given talks on campuses, and in the release he was said to have views that violated British values 'such as democracy, free speech, equality and the rule of law', including supporting FGM. He challenged his listing in the release as having such views, as well as the non-violent extremism aspects of the guidance, although, as the court found, he had not been de-invited by a university under the guidance and so was not a victim of the alleged breach of Article 10: *Butt* v. *Secretary of State for the Home Department* [2017] EWHC 1930 (Admin) [87]-[95].
134 Ibid. at [61]; it was found that the Guidance was 'guidance not direction' and that '[i]nstitutions are responsible for their own decisions'.
135 Ibid. [30].
136 Ibid. [132].
137 Ibid. [132].
138 Ibid. [134].
139 Ibid. [134].
140 Home Office, 'Individuals referred to and supported through the Prevent Programme, April 2016 to March 2017,' n. 117; HM Government, *Channel Duty Guidance: Protecting vulnerable people from being drawn into terrorism* (2015); see at https://assets.publishing.service.gov.uk/government/uploads/system/uploads/attachment_data/file/425189/Channel_Duty_Guidance_April_2015.pdf (accessed 10.8.18); Educate Against Hate, 'Teachers' Q&As: Intervention Working' (2018); see at https://educateagainsthate.com/teachers/are-there-real-world-examples-of-cases-where-successful-interventions-have-stopped-a-young-person-being-radicalised-2/ (accessed 10.8.18).
141 See *HM Chief Inspector of Education, Children's Services and Skills* v. *The Interim Executive Board of Al-Hijrah School* [2017] EWCA Civ 1426.
142 'The Prevent duty: Departmental advice for schools and childcare providers,' n. 84 above, 8.
143 See for example Department for Education, 'Promoting fundamental British values as part of SMSC in schools' (2014); see at https://assets.publishing.service.gov.uk/government/uploads/system/uploads/attachment_data/file/380595/SMSC_Guidance_Maintained_Schools.pdf (accessed 10.8.18).
144 Ibid.
145 The Education (Independent School Standards) Regulations 2014, SI 3283/2014, Sched 1 Para 5.
146 Ibid. Sched 1 para 5(v).
147 Such socially conservative viewpoints are found in the ultra-orthodox Charedi schools; for example, the Charedi Talmud Torah Tashbar school was closed in January 2016. Ofsted inspectors found that the school taught 'cultural and ethnic insularity because it is so narrow and almost exclusively rooted in the study of the Torah' and no lessons were taught in English: British Humanist Association, 'BHA reveals illegal Jewish school allowed to stay open for years despite repeated Ofsted warnings' (January 2016); see at https://humanism.org.uk/2016/01/15/bha-reveals-illegal-jewish-school-allowed-to-stay-open-for-years-despite-repeated-ofsted-warnings/ (accessed 10.8.18). Such viewpoints are also found in certain Salafi-dominated schools; for example, in the Bordesley Independent School in

Birmingham, Ofsted inspectors closed the school after finding that the curriculum was 'narrow and inadequate' and that 'Religious education dealt only with Islam to the exclusion of any other religion' in addition to finding extremist literature: National Secular Society, 'Head of unregistered Islamic school banned from teaching' 15 January 2018; see at www.secularism.org.uk/news/2018/01/nss-banned-head-of-unregistered-islamic-school-should-be-prosecuted (accessed 10.8.18).

148 See, for example, Home Office, 'CONTEST The United Kingdom's Strategy for Countering Terrorism: Annual Report for 2015' (Cm 9310, 2016); Devon and Cornwall Police, 'Case study: how Channel helped' (2015); see at www.devon-cornwall.police.uk/advice/your-community/prevent-extreme-views/a-case-study-how-channel-helped/ (accessed 10.8.18).

149 *HM Chief Inspector of Education, Children's Services and Skills* v. *The Interim Executive Board of Al-Hijrah School* [2017] EWCA Civ 1426; 'Promoting fundamental British values as part of SMSC in schools,' n. 143; Ofsted, 'Talmud Torah Machzikei Hadass School: Independent school additional inspection report' (15 July 2015); see at https://reports.ofsted.gov.uk/inspection-reports/find-inspection-report/provider/ELS/100294 (accessed 10.8.18) 2.

150 Equality and Human Rights Commission, 'Gender Segregation at Events and Meetings: guidance for universities and Students' Unions' (17 July 2014); see at www.equalityhumanrights.com/en/publication-download/gender-segregation-events-and-meetings-guidance-universities-and-students (accessed 13.8.18).

151 See, for example, R Shabi, 'Deradicalising Britain: the activists turning young Muslims away from extremism' *Guardian* (13 March 2016); see at www.theguardian.com/uk-news/2016/mar/18/deradicalising-britain-the-activists-turning-young-muslims-away-from-extremism (accessed 10.8.18). One individual who worked for Engage Dewsbury claimed that Prevent was 'Islamophobic' and designed to 'de-Islamise Islam' (ibid.).

152 S Greer and L Bell 'Counter-terrorist law in British universities: a review of the "prevent" debate' [2018] PL 84, 97–9.

153 See I Bowen, *Medina in Birmingham, Najaf in Brent: Inside British Islam* (Hurst, 2014); I Manji, *Allah, Liberty and Love: The Courage to Reconcile Faith and Freedom* (The Free Press, 2011).

154 See Manji, *Allah, Liberty and Love*, ibid; U Hasan, 'The Veil – Between Tradition and Reason, Culture and Context', in R Hannan and T Gabriel (eds.) *Islam and the Veil: Theoretical and Regional Contexts* (Continuum Books, 2011).

155 Such as Dr Usama Hassan – a former prominent Salafi cleric – who challenges the emphasis placed on mainstream conservative Islamic ideas such as veiling. See Dr Hasan's profile at Quilliam (a counter-extremism think tank): www.quilliaminternational.com/about/staff/usama-hasan/. See also S Khan, *Battle for British Islam* (Saqi 2016) 160–4, 195–6. See generally, Z Sardar, *Desperately Seeking Paradise* (Granta Books, 2005).

156 See n. 94; also Open Society Justice Initiative, 'Eroding Trust: The UK's PREVENT Counter-Extremism Strategy in Health and Education' (Open Society Foundations, 2016), 17.

157 An example of the closure of a Charedi school is the Talmud Torah Tashbar school, which was closed in January 2016.

158 MA Hakim, *Women Who Deserve to go to Hell* (Darul Ishaat 1901).

159 See text to n. 176 *et seq.*

160 Ofsted, 'Inspection Report for Darul Uloom Islamic High School 13 October 2015' (Ofsted 2015); see at https://reports.ofsted.gov.uk/inspection-reports/find-inspection-report/provider/ELS/103586 (accessed 10.8.18).

161 The head teacher and key staff at the school were replaced by the DfE subsequently to the Channel 4 revelations, Channel 4, 'Dispatches Mosque teacher jailed' (Nov

2011); see at www.channel4.com/info/press/news/dispatches-mosque-teacher-jailed (accessed 10.8.18).

162 Ofsted, 'Inspection Report for Darul Uloom Islamic High School 13 October 2015' (Ofsted 2015) 5; see at https://reports.ofsted.gov.uk/inspection-reports/find-inspection-report/provider/ELS/103586 (accessed 10.8.18).

163 Ofsted, 'The Annual Report of Her Majesty's Chief Inspector of Education, Children's Services and Skills 2016/17 (2017, HC 618).

164 Ofsted, 'Inspection Report for Olive Tree School 12 and 19 September' (November 2017); see at https://reports.ofsted.gov.uk/inspection-reports/find-inspection-report/provider/ELS/134400 (accessed 10.8.18).

165 Ibid. 2.

166 See text to n. 124.

167 'The Prevent duty: Departmental advice for schools and childcare providers,' n. 84 above.

168 Ofsted, 'School inspection handbook: Handbook for inspecting schools in England under section 5 of the Education Act 2005' (Ref: 150066, 2018) 42–4.

169 See further below text to n. 197. See also a recent study by Busher *et al.* (n. 94) which found little evidence that educational professionals perceive the duty to have led to a 'chilling effect' on free speech in schools and colleges (p. 53). It also found 'considerable support (41 per cent of respondents) for the view that the Prevent duty had resulted in more open discussions around such topics as extremism, intolerance and inequality' (p. 51).

170 I Manji, *Allah, Liberty and Love: The Courage to Reconcile Faith and Freedom* (The Free Press, 2011).

171 S Khan, *The Battle for British Islam* (Saqi, 2016) 125.

172 Education and Inspections Act 2006, Part 4.

173 Academies Act 2010, ss2A and 2D.

174 Ofsted, 'School inspection handbook: Handbook for inspecting schools in England under section 5 of the Education Act 2005' (Ref: 150066, 2018) para 48. Section 8 Education Act 2005.

175 Education Committee, 'Extremism in Schools: the Trojan Horse Affair' (HC 2014–15, 473) paras 30–41. Ofsted responded to the committee's recommendations, saying that one the reason for change was a 'culture of fear and intimidation' in such schools after the Trojan Horse affair: Education Committee, 'Extremism in schools: Ofsted Response to the Committee's Seventh Report of Session 2014–15' (HC 2015–16, 324).

176 Ofsted, 'Handbook for conducting inspections of unregistered schools' (September 2015); see at www.gov.uk/government/publications/inspections-under-section-97-of-the-education-and-skills-act-2008-handbook-for-inspectors (accessed 10.8.18).

177 Channel 4, *Dispatches: Lessons in Hate and Violence*.

178 Home Office, *Counter-Extremism Strategy* (Cm 9148, 2015) para 24.

179 National secular society, 'Islamic faith schools endorsing misogyny, dossier reveals' (28 November 2017); see at www.secularism.org.uk/news/2017/11/islamic-faith-schools-endorsing-misogyny-dossier-reveals (accessed 10.8.18); see also Louise Casey, 'The Casey Review: A review into opportunity and integration' (Department of Communities and Local Government, 2016); see at https://assets.publishing.service.gov.uk/government/uploads/system/uploads/attachment_data/file/575973/The_Casey_Review_Report.pdf (accessed 10.8.18) paras 7.55–7.57.

180 See for example, The Annual Report of Her Majesty's Chief Inspector of Education, Children's Services and Skills 2016/17 (2017, HC 618) 15; Ofsted's chief operating officer Mathew Coffey, 'We have no ability to inspect out-of-school settings, such as madrassas, and we believe greater powers in this area could help keep children safe in the future.' See J Grierson, 'Isis follower tried to create jihadist child army in east London' (2 March 2018); see at www.theguardian.com/uk-news/2018/mar/02/

isis-follower-umar-haque-jihadist-child-army-east-london-radicalise (accessed 10.8.18). See also R Long, 'Counter-extremism policy in English schools' (CBP 07345, 20 January 2017) para 2.6.

181 See Home Education UK, 'De-registration: the basics;' see at www.home-education.org.uk/legal-dereg.htm (accessed 10.8.18).

182 'The Casey Review' n. 179 above, para 7.49. M Wilshaw, 'Advice notes on academies and maintained schools in Birmingham' (8 July 2016); see at https://assets.publishing.service.gov.uk/government/uploads/system/uploads/attachment_data/file/535976/HMCI_advice_note_to_the_Secretary_of_State_on_Birmingham_8_July_16.pdf (accessed 10.8.18).

183 National secular society, 'Islamic faith schools endorsing misogyny, dossier reveals' (28 November 2017); see at www.secularism.org.uk/news/2017/11/islamic-faith-schools-endorsing-misogyny-dossier-reveals (accessed 10.8.18).

184 M Wilshaw, 'Advice letter from Sir Michael Wilshaw, Her Majesty's Chief Inspector, in respect of suspected illegal schools' (16 May 2016); see at https://assets.publishing.service.gov.uk/government/uploads/system/uploads/attachment_data/file/523694/Unregistered_schools_advice_note_16_May_2016.pdf (accessed 10.8.18). See R Long, 'Counter-extremism policy in English schools' (CBP 07345, 11 April 2018) para 2.7.

185 Charity Commission, 'New charity investigation: Lantern of Knowledge Educational Trust' (2 March 2018); see at www.gov.uk/government/news/new-charity-investigation-lantern-of-knowledge-educational-trust (accessed 10.8.18).

186 Department for Education 'Teacher's Standards' (July 2011, updated June 2013); see at https://assets.publishing.service.gov.uk/government/uploads/system/uploads/attachment_data/file/665520/Teachers__Standards.pdf (accessed 10.8.18).

187 Teaching Regulation Agency, 'Teacher misconduct: The prohibition of teachers: Advice on factors relating to decisions leading to the prohibition of teachers from the teaching profession' (April 2018); see at https://assets.publishing.service.gov.uk/government/uploads/system/uploads/attachment_data/file/700607/Teacher_misconduct-the_prohibition_of_teachers.pdf (accessed 10.8.18). A breach could amount to a finding of 'unacceptable professional conduct' or 'conduct that may bring the profession into disrepute'.

188 Ibid. 13.

189 Department for Education, 'Regulation of school managers and governors: prohibition direction' 3 September 2015; see at www.gov.uk/government/publications/direction-tahir-alam-barred-from-managing-independent-schools (accessed 10.8.18).

190 See for the rejection of his appeal against the banning order: 'Ruling on ex-chair of governors at "Trojan Horse" school kept under wraps' *Times Educational Supplement* (2 January 2018); see at www.tes.com/news/ruling-ex-chair-governors-trojan-horse-school-kept-under-wraps (accessed 10.8.18). Unusually, this ruling was not published, despite the hearing being in public.

191 Article 10 provides in paragraph 1 that '[e]veryone has the right to freedom of expression … to receive and impart information and ideas without interference by public authority', subject to paragraph 2 which states that 'the exercise of these freedoms, since it carries with it duties and responsibilities, may be subject to such formalities, conditions, restrictions or penalties as are prescribed by law and are necessary in a democratic society'.

192 See n. 124.

193 *Kjeldsen, Busk Madsen and Pedersen* v. *Denmark* (1979–80) 1 EHRR 711 para 53; *Campbell and Cosans* v. *UK* (1982) 4 EHRR 293 para 58.

194 Protocol 1 Article 2 states 'In the exercise of any functions which it assumes in relation to education and teaching, the state shall respect the rights of parents to ensure such education and teaching in conformity with their own religious and philosophical convictions'; see also *Kjeldsen, Busk Madsen and Pedersen* v. *Denmark*

(1979–80) 1 EHRR 711 para 53. See further Harris, Boyle, Bates and Buckley 'Law of the European Convention on Rights' (Oxford, OUP, 2009), 703; *Campbell and Cosans* v. *UK* (1982) 4 EHRR 293.

195 *Campbell and Cosans* v. *UK* (1982) 4 EHRR 293.

196 Ibid. para 58.

197 See: *Handyside* v. *United Kingdom* (1979–80) 1 EHRR 737; *IA* v. *Turkey* (2007) 45 EHRR 30 para 43.

198 See text to n. 124 above.

199 This was a central claim in the 'Clarke Report' in relation to the Trojan Horse affair (see n. 35). Tahir Alam, the chair of the governors at Park View School from 1997 to 2014, wrote a report representing the 'Muslim Council of Great Britain' in 2007 as a guide for schools termed 'Towards Greater Understanding: Meeting the Needs of Muslim Pupils in State Schools' which included the following:

> Muslims consider that most dance activities, as practised in the curriculum, are not consistent with the Islamic requirements for modesty as they may involve sexual connotations and messages when performed within mixed-gender groups or if performed in front of mixed audiences.... Muslims believe that God should not and cannot be represented in any form, whether two-dimensional or three-dimensional … girlfriend/boyfriend as well as homosexual relationships are not acceptable practices according to Islamic teachings.... All forms of music that may include the use of obscene and blasphemous language … arouse lustful feelings, encourage the consumption of intoxicants and drugs or contain unethical and un-Islamic lyrics would be considered objectionable. For this reason some Muslim parents may express concerns in the way music is taught in school and the extent to which their children may participate in it. Muslim pupils should not be expected to participate in drama or musical presentations associated with celebrating aspects of other religions, such as nativity plays or Diwali.... In Islam the creation of three dimensional figurative imagery of humans is generally regarded as unacceptable because of the risk of idolatress (*sic*) practices.... The school should avoid encouraging Muslim pupils from producing three dimensional imagery of humans.... When organising overnight trips involving Muslim pupils, mixed-gender groups should be avoided. This will encourage greater participation, particularly from Muslim girls'.

In relation to Nansen Primary School, Ofsted found evidence that a process similar to that outlined in Tahir Alam's report had occurred: Ofsted's 'Inspection report for Nansen Primary School – A Park View Academy 2 April 2014' (9 June 2014), found that 'Pupils do not get a broad education. The governing body has removed some subjects, such as music, from the timetable,' and 'Pupils have limited knowledge of religious beliefs other than Islam.'

200 *Butt* v. *Secretary of State for the Home Department* [2017] EWHC 1930 (Admin) [137].

201 Ibid. [138].

202 J Mohammed and A Siddiqui, 'The PREVENT strategy: A cradle to grave police-state' (CAGE, 2013); see at www.cage.ngo/prevent-strategy-cradle-grave-police-state (accessed 10.8.18).

203 'The Prevent duty: Departmental advice for schools and childcare providers,' n. 84 above, 8.

204 Department for Education, 'Keeping children safe in education. Statutory guidance for schools and colleges' (September 2016); see www.gov.uk/government/publications/keeping-children-safe-in-education-2 (accessed 10.8.18).

205 L Casey, 'The Casey Review: A review into opportunity and integration' (Department of Communities and Local Government, 2016); see at https://assets.publishing.service.gov.uk/government/uploads/system/uploads/attachment_data/file/575973/

The_Casey_Review_Report.pdf (accessed 10.8.18). See also J Lewis, 'Prevent as an Intractable Policy Controversy: Implications and Solutions' *Journal for Deradicalization* 15 (2018): 113. The Joint Committee on Human Rights has stated 'that it is very easy for dangerous myths to be spread about Prevent. The only way for these to be dispelled is for there to be rigorous and transparent reporting about the operation of the Prevent Duty' in *Counter Extremism* (2016–17, HL Paper 39, HC 105) para 50.

206 See Busher *et al.* 'What the Prevent duty means for schools and colleges in England' (n. 94) which covered this issue but did not seek to disentangle the two factors, finding concerns about increased stigmatisation of Muslim students in the context of the Prevent duty – although such concerns tended not to focus on their own institution, where they perceived these issues to be being managed' (p. 65). The concern was found to have a general rather than a focused nature, possibly favouring the argument that where students and teachers focus on their own actual experience of stigmatisation it is found to be less pressing.

207 One widely reported example was a student who was reported to have been referred for a drawing that a teacher mistakenly thought was a 'cooker bomb' which was revealed to be a cucumber; another widely reported but apocryphal example was of a pupil who was visited by police after a teacher read in his homework that he lived 'in a terrorist house' apparently as a misspelling for 'terraced' (in his evidence to the JCHR David Anderson highlighted this referral as a 'myth' as the police investigation was in fact in relation to the suggestion that the uncle was abusing him): Joint Committee on Human Rights, *Counter Extremism* (2016–17, HL Paper 39, HC 105) para 49. In a significant report, The Open Society Justice Initiative has listed 11 case-studies of issues relating to schools, 'Eroding Trust: The UK's PREVENT Counter-Extremism Strategy in Health and Education' (Open Society Foundations, 2016), 65–89. Similarly, Professor Joe Cannatac, UN Special Rapporteur on the right to privacy, noted that representatives of Muslim communities had characterized Prevent as 'dividing, stigmatising and alienating communities' but stated that 'I was to date unable to gather sufficient evidence to substantiate such claims' and recommended that 'sufficient resources be allocated by the UK government to reinforce the evidence-base as to the precise impact of Prevent': L Dearden, 'UK government straying towards "thought crime" by criminalising viewing terrorist material, UN inspector says' (29 June 2018); see at www.independent.co.uk/news/uk/politics/thought-crime-uk-un-terrorism-government-viewing-material-offence-law-a8423546.html (accessed 10.8.18).

208 S Khan, *Battle for British Islam* (Saqi, 2016), 96 *et seq.*

209 See for example V Coppock, '"Can you Spot a Terrorist in Your Classroom?" Problematising the Recruitment of Schools to the "War on Terror" in the United Kingdom' *Global Studies in Childhood* 4, no. 2 (2014): 115, 116; Muslim Council of Britain, 'Parliamentary Briefing on introducing "Prevent" as a statutory duty for all public bodies' 18 January 2015; see at www.mcb.org.uk/wp-content/uploads/2015/01/MCB-Briefing-on-introducingPrevent-as-a-statutory-duty-for-all-public-bodies.pdf (accessed 10.8.18); Home Affairs Committee, 'Radicalisation: the counter-narrative and identifying the tipping point' (HC 2016–17, 135) Written evidence submitted by Faith Matters, A Kundnani, 'Spooked!: How not to prevent violent extremism' (London: Institute of Race Relations 2009), 25–8. See also J Taylor, '"Suspect Categories," Alienation and Counterterrorism: Critically Assessing PREVENT in the UK' *Terrorism and Political Violence* 1 (2018): 1156.

210 S Greer and L Bell 'Counter-terrorist law in British universities: a review of the "prevent" debate' [2018] PL 84, 94. See Busher *et al.* 'What the Prevent duty means for schools and colleges in England' (n. 94 above) which found that among school and college staff 'wholesale criticism of, much less opposition to, the duty was … very rare in the interview data' (p. 60).

211 See also Joint Committee on Human Rights, *Counter Extremism* (2016–17, HL 39 HC 105) at 15.

212 See n. 205.

213 See overview at 'Commission for Counter Extremism' at www.gov.uk/government/organisations/commission-for-countering-extremism (accessed 10.8.18). The Commissioner's brief is to examine the 'scale, influence and reach of extremism within Britain ... and look at the effectiveness of counter-extremism measures and policies....' The appointee, Sara Khan, has been publicly critical of the hyperbole surrounding Prevent and, as a Muslim, strongly advocates for compatibility between British values and the Prevent strategy. Her appointment was greeted with concern by some: see BBC, 'New counter-terrorism tsar faces calls to quit' (25 January 2018); see www.bbc.com/news/uk-politics-42807560 (accessed 10.8.18), including the former Conservative Party Chair Baroness Sayeedi Warsi, who has claimed that Khan is too close to the Home Office: see J Grierson, 'Choice of new UK anti-extremism chief criticised as "alarming"' *Guardian* (25 January 2018); see at www.theguardian.com/politics/2018/jan/24/leading-muslim-campaigner-sara-khan-head-anti-extremism-drive (accessed 10.8.18).

214 'The Casey Review,' n. 205 above, described 'an active lobby opposed to Prevent'. She found that 'elements of this lobby ... appear to have an agenda to turn British Muslims against Britain', whose activism to undermine Prevent she describes as making British Muslims 'feel even more alienated and isolated – and therefore more vulnerable to extremists and radicalisers'. She also found that the lobby had 'deliberately distorted and exaggerated cases' of Prevent delivery in an attempt to 'portray the programme at its worst' (p. 155). See also Greater Manchester Preventing Hateful Extremism and Promoting Social Cohesion Commission, 'A Shared Future' (Greater Manchester Combined Authority, July 2018); see www.greatermanchester-ca.gov.uk/downloads/file/780/a_shared_future (accessed 10.8.18) para 10.16.

215 Joint Committee on Human Rights, *Counter Extremism* (2016–17, HL 39 HC 105) paras 36–42.

216 See above n. 199.

217 HC Deb 2 December 2014, vol. 603, cols 248, 265.

# 7 Finding the right balance in counter-extremism

## Debates and policies in the UK and Europe

*Emma Webb*

European nations are being forced to self-reflect as extremism in Europe becomes ever more visible. At its heart is the fundamental question: *who are we?* Should the state be a neutral broker in the realm of ideas? What is it allowed to say about itself, and how should it be allowed to assert itself?

Individual liberty – freedom of expression, thought, of and from religion – is a cornerstone of the democratic system and necessary for its proper function. Yet, at the same time, Europe is confronted with the rise of extremism that corrodes social cohesion, subverts democracy, and, at worst, is fatal. Some might elevate tolerance above all others as being the ultimate value, tolerating even the most anti-democratic or intolerant speech, in the name of protecting the liberal ideal *in extremis.* Others feel that protecting the core values on which society is historically founded should be partly the role of the state, in order to protect the liberal democratic order and individual liberty for all, advocating minimal interference to accomplish this.

Finding the right balance is key to a just approach, respecting individual liberty while allowing the state to effectively defend the stability, welfare, and cohesion of body politic that allows democracy to properly function. This is necessary for preserving tolerance and the values that make liberal democracy possible. As philosopher Karl Popper famously articulated,

> unlimited tolerance must lead to the disappearance of tolerance. If we extend unlimited tolerance even to those who are intolerant, if we are not prepared to defend a tolerant society against the onslaught of the intolerant, then the tolerant will be destroyed and tolerance with them.[1]

The defence of democracy and the protection of freedom are not opposed, they are one and the same. The question has always been how to strike the right balance. In 1859, the father of liberalism, John Stuart Mill, pondered how liberty was to be maintained for all in the face of a diversity of ideas across time and place.[2] But for him, this question was more theoretical than it is now when rapidly changing demographics, multiculturalism, and prevailing relativism allow for competing views to exist side-by-side. A broad consensus or shared customs in any given time and place, that once may have provided a possible basis for peaceful co-existence, can no longer be taken for granted.[3]

How do you defend the political order against ideas that are subversive and destructive? The threat of communism provided a similar opportunity for reflection. As French philosopher and journalist Jean Francois Revel reflected 'Democracy can defend itself only very feebly; its internal enemy has an easy time of it because he exploits the right to disagree that is inherent in democracy.'[4] The questions we now face in relation to extremism – which have no place in totalitarian countries, or modern states like Saudi Arabia or Russia, where ideas do not compete on an even playing field or enjoy equal expression – are inherent to democracy. Democracy's foundations in consent, dissent, negotiation, respect, and compromise are both its strength and its weakness.

As Revel highlighted, democratic freedom can be easily exploited by anti-democrats, leading to the ironic situation in which those who seek to defend democracy can be 'pictured as repressive reactionaries', while 'those seeking to destroy democracy appear to be fighting for legitimate aims'.[5] Outlawing the expression of certain ideas is understandably distasteful to democrats. For that reason, European states have, by and large, taken an approach of not of forbidding, but challenging extremist ideas. This has taken place within the context of European nations trying to find their voice, asking 'who are we?'

Criticisms of counter-extremism policy can be unsubtle, but any reasonable and just approach will be couched in the same tradition through which democracy was born – one that solves one problem at a time, refining policies, seeking consent, feeling for the right balance to maintain and protect liberty from both extremism and the overreach of the state.

How is this to be done, and how are European states going about doing it? This chapter is written from a United Kingdom perspective, and while there is increasing recognition of the rising threat posed by far-right terrorism,[6] it will make primary reference to Islamist terrorism, because it remains the foremost threat in the UK.[7] Criticisms of counter-extremism policy are often framed in the abstract – encroachment on freedom of expression or religion, racism, or islamophobia – but the day-to-day reality of implementing counter-extremism policy across Europe is far removed, throwing up practical issues that require urgent responses. In reality, those designing and implementing policy work, within the boundaries permissible under international law, are seeking to solve pressing practical problems at a time while the larger difficult questions hover in the background.

The primary theses of this chapter are as follows: (1) challenging non-violent extremism is a legitimate activity of the state; (2) European countries are grappling to find the right balance when shaping these policies to remain effective whilst protecting individual liberty; (3) the United Kingdom's approach, though still in its infancy, is careful, reasonable, and defensible. The ultimate argument of this chapter is that states can and should challenge extremism, not *negatively* – through forbidding or banning the expression of extremist views – but *positively*, by robustly challenging these views and confidently asserting the historical values on which their democratic system is founded and interfering with expression only in limited ways in certain settings.

## Is challenging non-violent extremism a legitimate activity of the state?

Though connected, policies preventing individuals from being drawn into terrorism are distinct from those challenging non-violent extremist ideology. The legitimacy of preventing individuals from being drawn into terrorism is more straightforward. The state has a duty to protect itself and its citizens from violence and therefore must step in to prevent the proliferation of terrorism.[8]

Questioning the legitimacy of preventing individuals from being drawn into terrorism has become increasingly difficult in the face of the current scale of the threat, demonstrated in part by the unprecedented spate of large attacks in the UK between March and June 2017, with many more plots thwarted.[9] With disruption alone being an untenable long-term solution, it is widely accepted in Europe that preventative measures are necessary to stop individuals from being drawn into terrorism in the first place.

Some terrorist- or extremist-related actions can be prosecuted. For example, speech may be limited in certain instances, such as incitement to commit a terrorism offence (Terrorism Act 2006, 16 (5)(i)); inviting support of a proscribed organisation (Terrorism Act 2000, 12 (1)(a)); or hate speech (e.g. Public Order Act 1986; Racial and Religious Hatred Act 2006). The same is true of other European countries,[10] and there have been increasing Europe-wide efforts to tackle hate speech.[11] The public are right to be vigilant that any banning of speech does not go too far; for example, by limiting the free speech of comedians using offensive material. Rightly, any criminalization of speech should be constantly scrutinized.[12]

However, with the exception of some limited and legally justifiable exceptions, European governments have been hesitant to prohibit speech. Approaches to preventing individuals from being drawn into terrorism, as described below, tend to focus on safeguarding and seek to interfere with expression in only the most limited ways. At the same time, the issue of countering non-violent extremism is more contentious. Rather than banning non-violent extremist expression, states are developing positive ways to challenge it.

### *Where is the harm in non-violent extremism – and why challenge it?*

Is the harm inflicted on society by non-violent extremism enough to justify challenge from the government? Although non-violent extremists advocate peaceful – though often subversive – methods, and disagree with the use of violence to achieve their goals, they share the violent extremists' vision of an ideal society that is anti-democratic, restricts personal liberty, is discriminatory, and runs counter to human rights standards. If it is possible to recognize that this goal is objectionable and a risk to democratic society, then it is possible to see how challenging these ideas (though not banning them) could be a legitimate action of the state. At the very least, the state should not act in ways that help them further their goals, such as partnering with them, or allowing them to exploit state-affiliated intuitions or the public sector.

European governments are honing their approach to challenging these groups, with varying degrees of success. Some of the key players across Europe include: the Muslim Brotherhood; their South Asian counterpart Jamaat-e-Islami; Hizb ut-Tahrir; political Salafists; and lesser known groups such as the Turkish Islamist group Millî Görüş.[13] Some groups have a larger footprint in certain countries than in others, and though not ideologically identical they share a common agenda. Their non-violent activity is not illegal and the expression of their views cannot be justifiably banned outright. Some, for example, advocate the use of democratic means to affect change in line with their objectives.[14]

### *European governments' grappling with non-violent Islamist ideology*

Fears over the negative consequences of the spread of Islamist ideology are not new. In 2004, the Dutch General Intelligence and Security Service (AIVD) expressed concerns over the harmful effects of Salafist ideology, including anti-democratic and undemocratic radicalism and that which indirectly or unintentionally had the potential to 'hamper or undermine the functioning of the democratic legal order'.[15] Previously, Germany banned a Salafist group that 'act[ed] in opposition to the idea of constitutional order and multicultural understanding', but this was only possible because the group promoted violence to achieve its aims.[16] Under Article 21 of the Basic Law, Germany gives the Constitutional Court power to proscribe parties that 'seek to impair or do away with the liberal democratic order, or to endanger the existence of the Federal Republic of Germany' – but this would only be useful if Islamist groups formed political parties, which for the most part they do not.[17]

Countries such as Sweden[18] and the UK have been debating what to do about the influence of the Muslim Brotherhood.[19] The UK launched a review seeking to establish whether the Brotherhood risked damaging national interests. The decision was taken not to ban the organization, but the then Prime Minister, David Cameron, stated that 'both as an ideology and as a network it has been a rite of passage for some individuals and groups who have gone on to engage in violence and terrorism' and that individuals associated with the group had supported violence, including the affiliated proscribed terrorist group Hamas.[20] In addition, though it was recognized that the Brotherhood opposes the west and British values and democracy, the review concluded that there was not sufficient evidence to ban the group, even though membership or association may be considered an indicator of extremism.[21]

As discussed elsewhere in this collection, in the UK the government is increasingly seeking ways to deal with the societal harms associated with non-violent extremism. This has materialized primarily in the Counter-Extremism Strategy (2015) and the Integration Strategy (2017). Like many countries, the UK does not specify a single ideology, defining extremism as 'vocal or active opposition to our fundamental values, including democracy, the rule of law, individual liberty and the mutual respect and tolerance of different faiths and beliefs', as well as calling for the death of members of the armed forces.[22]

The Strategy notes that 'Extremists have attempted to coerce people not to participate in our democratic system or to subvert our democratic processes'[23] and outlines how extremists may target vulnerable institutions to further their agenda, including schools, universities, local authorities, charities, and prisons.[24] This was articulated well by the former Prime Minister, David Cameron, in a 2015 speech:

> You don't have to support violence to subscribe to certain intolerant ideas which create a climate in which extremists can flourish. Ideas which are hostile to basic liberal values such as democracy, freedom and sexual equality. Ideas which actively promote discrimination, sectarianism and segregation.[25]

On 4 June 2017, Prime Minister Theresa May reiterated this point in her speech following the Islamist attacks on London, when she spoke of an ideology that 'preaches hatred, sows division, and promotes sectarianism'.[26]

The effort to prevent individuals being drawn into terrorism (described below) and counter-extremism work are distinct and carefully separated. The UK appears to be working out a positive approach towards the latter. Rather than limiting expression of extremist views on the whole, it seeks to challenge them through the development of positive alternative narratives. We see this in the establishment in 2018 of the Commission for Countering Extremism to support the government by identifying extremism, advising on policy, supporting communities and the public sector, and promoting shared values and community cohesion.[27]

### *Non-violent extremism promotes segregation, inequality, and discrimination*

Why should the government challenge non-violent extremism? One of the key ways in which extremism damages society is by corroding social cohesion, encouraging segregation, and trampling on minority rights, particularly those of women and children. This is recognized the UK's Integration Strategy (2017) which responded to the review into opportunity and integration conducted by Dame Louise Casey in 2016.[28] The serious concerns raised by the review included high levels of segregation in schools, inequality of women (including those at risk of female genital mutilation (FGM), forced marriage and honour-based violence (HBV), and discrimination against LGBT people.[29]

Ideology contributing to the maintenance of these practices, unchallenged, makes it difficult, if not impossible, to create adequate policies bringing them to an end and improving social cohesion. The review highlighted, for example, the increasing prominence of the Deobandi revivalist movement, stating that 'although not necessarily supporting terrorism, they [Deobandi speakers] have promoted anti-Western and isolationist messages that are not conducive to integration'.[30]

The institutionalization of discriminatory religious laws and the solidifying of its influence can further serve to separate communities, having a negative impact on individuals within minority communities. 'Women's rights groups,' Casey noted, 'have accused Sharia Councils and other parallel legal systems of denying vulnerable women and children access to equality and human rights'.[31] The 'us versus them' world view, characteristic of extremist ideology, can negatively impact social cohesion.[32] The push for legal pluralism – different laws for different communities – has been identified as part and parcel of the Islamist approach to isolate Muslims from mainstream society. The purpose of Sharia councils is to accommodate the Muslim community, but sharia councils have no legal status or jurisdiction in England and Wales and cannot legally make rulings contrary to domestic or international law.[33] Participation should be voluntary, but the number of them operating is unknown and they are unregulated.[34] Concerns over 'jurisdiction creep' – to prevent the councils ruling beyond their jurisdiction and discriminating against women – led to the Arbitration and Mediation Services (Equality) Bill, which remains [as yet] unpassed.[35]

However, as highlighted by the Swiss-Yemeni academic, Elham Manea, Islamist extremists not only have a significant presence in the UK's sharia councils, but were a driving force in founding them. This has had an effect on how the councils have been used to affect communities.[36]

> Those working in the shari'a courts often display the ideological and political features of Islamism … these features include the emphasis on creating an Islamic state through incremental steps, on implementing shari'a, on jihad against enemies of Islam, and on the division of the world into two camps, believers and non-believers.[37]

Manea has presented the many ways in which this can negatively impact respect for human rights within minority communities. She argues that, as a consequence, discriminatory rulings against women and children occur on the pretext of respecting culture, or 'group rights', in areas of marriage, custody, divorce, maintenance, inheritance, and testimony.[38] The danger of allowing a parallel legal systems to develop is clear. Where this occurs, vulnerable members of communities, particularly women, become vulnerable to discrimination: 'once the state starts to situate rights within the frame of a group rather than within the individual, the likely outcome will be *segregation, inequality and discrimination.*'[39]

Dutch political scientist Machteld Zee likewise argued that multiculturalism has been complicit in allowing these plural systems to establish themselves.[40] Indeed, the European Court of Human Rights (ECtHR), as far back as 2001 in *Refah* v. *Turkey* (reiterated in *Gunduz* v. *Turkey*, 2003),[41] stated that:

> it is difficult to declare one's respect for democracy and human rights while at the same time supporting a regime based on sharia which clearly diverges from Convention values, particularly with regard to its criminal law and criminal procedure, its rules on the legal status of women and the way it intervenes in all spheres of private and public life in accordance with religious precepts.[42]

Does respect for religious freedom and personal autonomy mean that the state should tolerate the development and increasing influence of religious legal institutions? On the contrary, limiting Islamist extremist influence is required to protect the right to choose freely, because their growing influence has the potential to curtail free speech, personal autonomy, and freedom of religion.

### *Extremists seek to limit freedom of expression and religion*

Respect for religious freedom must be balanced with the need to protect individuals from having their autonomy dominated by religious or ideological imposition or discrimination. Extremists seek to prevent individuals from expressing their ideas freely – particularly those that are critical of their beliefs – and seek to hamper the right to freedom of/from religion. Community pressure, aggravated by segregation, threats of violence, and intimidation on the basis of apostasy or blasphemy charges (*takfir*) have the potential to limit the ability of individuals to act freely.

In what Professor Paul Cliteur describes as 'extrajudicial restraints on free speech', the influence of Islamist extremist groups has the potential to silence Muslims and non-Muslims alike.[43] The examples provided by Cliteur are abundant: the *Satanic Verses* affair, beginning with the publication of the book in 1988 and leading to protests, book burnings, and a fatwa against the author; the murder of Dutch filmmaker Theo Van Gogh in 2004; the *Jyllands-Posten* Danish cartoon affair; the attack on the staff of French satirical magazine Charlie Hebdo in January 2015, to name but a few.[44] Cliteur identifies the 'tension between the terrorist threat and civil liberties' as borne out in a plethora of examples of this kind, with the ongoing threat of intimidation or violence from those offended contributing to European self-censorship. Consistently giving into these threats by self-censoring and backing down is said, by Cliteur, to encourage the exertion of extremist power by appeasing those making the threats, ultimately eroding free speech in European society.[45]

Policies that do not adequately protect against this run the risk of adversely affecting the autonomy of individuals in minority communities. Alternatively, policies should be developed that balance respect for religious freedom with the need to protect individuals and society from extremism. One way it can do this is by positively defending the values historically important to the nation.

The UK has tried to do this through defining extremism – without any reference to a specific ideology – in opposition to British values.[46] The definition is an example of the state asserting that it is not value neutral. However, the issue of the definition remains contentious in a multicultural polity, with the idea of 'British' values being too controversial for some. Others feel that is too general; one argument could be that it would beneficial to refer to specific ideologies or to define extremism in terms of political subversion. Cases such as *Shakeel Begg* v. *BBC Broadcasting Corporation (2016)* show that specific definitions of Islamist extremism are being worked out on a case-by-case basis according to need.[47]

Would this mean that expressing support for Sharia law or criticizing foreign policy would be silenced under the pretext of counter-extremism? Certainly not, but in certain circumstances it is arguably legitimate to deny extremism a platform, such as within the public, educational, or charitable sectors. This would involve ensuring that extreme views are not given unbalanced platforms in universities; extremists are not given access to schools in ways that run counter to their purpose to educate the young minds; or allowed to form charities when providing a platform for extremists cannot be compatible with the requirement to be for the public benefit. Extremists have a right to free expression overall, but they have no specific right to propagate their subversive views on specific platforms without contestation. The state is entitled to proportionately limit these views and ensure that they are challenged.

## How should governments strike the balance? Debates and policies in Europe

### *International standards for balancing freedom and security*

Whether you agree with them or not, European countries must form their policies in line with international and domestic laws that are intended to balance individual rights with security, which requires states to protect freedom of expression and religion. The European Convention on Human Rights (ECHR) protects freedom of expression (Article 10) and freedom of thought, conscience, and religion (Article 9).[48] This was incorporated into UK domestic law by the Human Rights Act 1998. Article 10 of the Act protects an individual's right to freedom of expression including the 'freedom to hold opinions and to receive or impart information and ideas without interference by public authority and regardless of frontiers'. Article 9 protects freedom of thought, conscience, and religion, including the ability of an individual to change their religion or belief and to manifest that belief in worship, teaching, practice, and observance.[49]

The ECHR and Human Rights Act do allow for the restriction of these rights under certain conditions. According to the ECHR, these rights can be limited, for reasons 'necessary in a democratic society', including: national security; territorial integrity; public safety; prevention of crime; disorder; health or morals; and for the protection of the rights of others.[50] According to international human rights conventions, restrictions of certain rights, including freedom of expression, association, and assembly, must be: (a) clearly, precisely, and accessibly defined; (b) pursue a legitimate purpose, such as national security or public order; and (c) are necessary and proportionate, with a rational link to the objective.[51]

Article 19(3) of the International Covenant on Civil and Political Rights (ICCPR) is also relevant, which allows that everyone has the right to hold an opinion without interference and the right to freedom of expression. Again, this can be limited for the protection of national security, public order, health, or morals.[52] Article 26 of the ICCPR also protects the individual against discrimination on the basis of their opinion and other characteristics,[53] while Article 20 prohibits: (1) propaganda for war, or (2) advocacy of national, racial, or religious hatred constituting discrimination, hostility, or violence.[54]

The tension in the law results from the requirement to balance individual liberty with security and other national considerations to maintain freedom for all. As articulated by the United Nations (2008):

> Terrorism aims at the very destruction of human rights, democracy and the rule of law. It attacks the values that lie at the heart of the Charter of the United Nations and other international instruments: respect for human rights; the rule of law; rules governing armed conflict and the protection of civilians; tolerance among peoples and nations; and the peaceful resolution of conflict.[55]

States have a duty to combat terrorism because it has a direct impact on these rights – the rule of law, pluralistic civil society, democratic governance – and destabilizes governments;[56] however it is only balance that can achieve the optimum in freedom for individual citizens.

For example, in 2017 the UK Parliament's Joint Human Rights Committee on freedom of speech in universities noted the significance of competing legal obligations. Universities, like other public institutions, must have regard for the ECHR, the Human Rights Act, the Equalities Act 2010, and the public sector Equality duty. While having 'particular regard' for protecting free speech, these bodies must balance this carefully with the duties under the Counter Terrorism and Security Act (CTSA) 2015, which require specified public bodies to have due regard to preventing individuals in their care, or using their services, from being drawn into terrorism.[57]

The above relates primarily to the prevention of terrorism. However, there are other instances in which international law restricts behaviour associated with extremism, namely: gender discrimination, female genital mutilation (FGM), honour-based violence (HBV), forced marriage and child marriage, hate speech, and/or incitement to commit criminal acts. The state is entitled to restrict expressive acts in these contexts, to challenge them, and to counter such messages.

One example is the UN Convention on the Elimination of All Forms of Discrimination Against Women (CEDAW), which establishes the supremacy of gender equality when in conflict with cultural or religious practices, and is also relevant when dealing with religious extremism and its aims more broadly.[58] A general recommendation on Article 16 of CEDAW, issued by the United Nations 'Committee on the Elimination of Discrimination Against Women' (2013) recommended that states adopt legislation to 'eliminate the discriminatory aspects of their family law regimes, whether they are regulated by civil code, religious law, ethnic custom or any combination of laws and practices'.[59]

### *European policies in practice*

In reality, European countries rarely need to refer to this framework because they prefer to design policies that challenge, rather than limit speech. These policies are designed to have very limited and justifiable interference with free expression, and the focus on preventative approaches are primarily framed around safeguarding. Many take a multi-agency approach, like the UK, the Danish 'Aarhus' model,[60] and the Finnish approach,[61] focusing on social care, safeguarding and offering various forms of support.[62] As the Finnish Ministry of the Interior describes it, the aim 'relates to the core of maintaining public order and security: guaranteeing a safe living and operating environment and the safety of individuals and communities as well as protecting civil rights'.[63]

All European countries are seeking to find the right balance. There have been concerns that such approaches don't go far enough, with, for example, the Danish model being criticized for being too 'soft' and 'naïve' in its response to the problem of returning Isis fighters.[64] However, the French approach has been criticized for being too heavy handed, due to, for example, the creation of special voluntary centres to 're-engage' and 're-integrate',[65] where participants would study French history, religion, and philosophy, saluting the flag and singing the national anthem.[66]

Like other countries, the French have also struggled with finding the right approach, and are now exploring new ideas.[67] Under President Macron's government there have been signs that France is engaging with questions about the broader social context of non-violent extremism, with Prime Minister Edouard Philippe stating that they aim to combat segregation in French society and criticizing the previous 2014 strategy for focusing only on violent extremism.[68]

Finding the right approach also comes with practical and financial concerns. One of the criticisms of the French approach was its ineffectiveness and wastefulness. Senator Esther Benbassa, who authored the government's report on France's de-radicalization efforts said that they spent £88 million over three years on a host of associations: 'everybody opened an association, and they were not experts. All this work was done without evaluation, it was not controlled; everybody did what he wanted.'[69] These struggles are not unique to France.

### *The Dutch radicalization programme: radical ideas have radical consequences?*

The Netherlands provides an interesting case study of a country struggling to find the right balance. Following the murder of filmmaker Theo Van Gogh, who in the 2004 film *Submission* had criticized the treatment of women in Islam, the Netherlands began to seriously discuss Islamist extremism long before the rest of Europe[70] and produced national counter-radicalization policies to combat the threat, to be delivered on a municipal level.[71] Some municipalities, like Amsterdam, had been working to combat radicalization and polarization as early as 2004.[72] On a national level, this was further solidified by the *Comprehensive Action Programme to Combat Jihadism* (2014), which introduced measures of counter-radicalization to create resilience against Islamist extremist ideology.[73] The programme follows the same pattern as other European policies, focusing on safeguarding, alternative narratives, and challenging extremist views – not banning them. The aim was to disrupt the spread of extremism from multiple angles, including the dissemination of literature on and offline, and limiting the reach of hate preachers.[74]

The programme proposed a multi-agency approach developing cooperation on a national and local level, including civil society and the Muslim community to promote alternative narratives,[75] bolster trusted individuals within the community, and support, for example, education institutions to build resilience among the young.[76] In addition to training individuals across agencies and social neighbourhood teams to spot the signs of radicalization and encouraging information sharing, the programme is intended to propagate democratic values and the rule of law through debate initiatives to discuss 'conflicting values, the boundaries of the rule of law, and living together with differences'.[77]

However, as events in Amsterdam in 2017 to 2018 have shown, this went awry on a practical level. The primary challenges they faced were not big questions of individual liberty, but related to nepotism, integrity, and transparency that resulted in a failure to intervene when necessary.[78] The situation resulted in a Public Prosecution Service (OM) investigation following concerns relating to the nepotism and corruption of municipality advisors.[79] For example, as of July 2018, a former official of the programme was being investigated for knowingly approving false invoices filed by an individual with whom she is believed to have been in a close personal relationship.[80]

The troubling lack of transparency had also made accountability and accurate criticism difficult. This was seen in the controversy surrounding the hiring of extremists. One individual, known as Bilal L, working for an organization hired by the municipality was a former member of the Hofstad Group – the group connected to the murder of Theo Van Gogh – who had been sentenced to three years in prison in 2006 for preparing a terrorist attack.[81] The municipality decided to hire him through a subsidized organization, despite his being refused a 'declaration of behaviour' (which would have allowed him to be hired by the municipality) following a screening by government services. Believing his past experience would be beneficial, the Mayor of Amsterdam gave him an exemption allowing him to work for the programme.[82] Yet, in December 2017, *De Telegraaf* reported that as recently as 2013, when Bilal L had been a youth worker, he had recruited a 16-year-old who travelled to fight in Syria.[83] There has been a lack of public accountability in the Bilal L case; the answers to many legitimate questions were discussed under confidential terms within the council and have not been made publicly available.[84]

Thus, and notwithstanding the fact that in 2017, the municipality stated that they would no longer use former extremists in this way, these sorts of decisions were not publicly known until the time of the controversy, and could not, therefore, be fully scrutinized.[85] Professor Beatrice de Graaf, commissioned by the municipality to assess the programme, has recommended building trust through transparency and increasing checks and balances to avoid a repeat of these failures.[86]

The increased level of scrutiny triggered a public debate on the overall approach by Dutch authorities to the question of radicalization and specifically whether ideology was being properly taken into account.[87] Concerns were raised that the role of ideology was being downplayed. For example, in a 2015 policy letter, a key advisor influencing Amsterdam's programme claimed that ideology played little part in the recruitment of jihadists, serving only as an excuse, and therefore an approach giving weight to ideology would not be effective.[88] The leader of the Christian Democratic Appeal (CDA) party in Amsterdam criticized the programme for being led by someone who placed too much emphasis on social and economic causes, at the expense of addressing ideological influences.[89] The programme in Amsterdam had been described as a 'placebo'.[90] These concerns were put to the Mayor of Amsterdam in September 2017. Calling for extreme religious ideas to be taken into account, one council member stated 'Radicale ideeën hebben radicale consequenties' (Radical ideas have radical consequences).[91]

The debate around Salafism, the role of ideas, and what the Dutch state should do to tackle them, still continues apace. Despite the fact that in 2004 the AIVD reported the need to protect the democratic legal order from extremist ideologies, both violent or non-violent, whose 'main objective is the realisation of a form of government that is different from democracy', and that this, in turn, 'jeopardises fundamental rights such as freedom of expression and freedom of association with others, legal equality etc', the debate has reignited.[92]

These sentiments were again repeated in a 2015 joint report from the AIVD and National Coordinator for Security and Counterterrorism (NCTV).[93] Attempts were made to clarify where the line is drawn, emphasizing that, while the Dutch government respects the rights and freedoms of all irrespective of their religion or belief, 'this changes when religious or ideological beliefs serve as a basis for turning against the democratic order and established human rights.'[94] Significantly, the report states:

> It becomes even more problematic when religious or ideological beliefs lead to the pursuit of anti-democratic goals by using undemocratic means. By *undemocratic goals* we mean, for example, promoting a political system in which some sections of the population have fewer rights than others.[95]

In February 2018, a report commissioned to examine Amsterdam's programme found that within their approach considerable emphasis was placed on social and practical intervention, but that the role of ideology 'regularly remains unclear'. In particular, the report's authors remarked that the Amsterdam approach was not comfortable with the interface between terrorism and religion, and suffered 'religious cramp'. Unlike other cities, they found Amsterdam was not properly engaging with religious community leaders.[96]

How the programme should be improved off the back of this report remains under discussion, but an implicit struggle remains between those who think non-violent extremism is problematic, and those who do not. In June 2018, Amsterdam City Council responded with some actionable responses to De Graaf's recommendations. Referring to De Graaf's characterization of the programme as suffering from 'religious cramp', the Mayor recommended engaging more with orthodox, or Salafist, groups.[97] Three parties – the VVD, FvD and CDA – strongly objected to this interpretation, arguing that Salafists are inappropriate and ineffective partners in the fight against radicalization because of their regressive aims and rejection of Dutch society and its values.[98]

The same issues of transparency and struggles over how to deal with non-violent extremism arose again over the issue of foreign funding. Despite previous claims by the Dutch government that no such information was kept,[99] leaked government documents revealed significant funding from Saudi Arabia and Kuwait financing the spread of Salafist ideology through mosques and organizations in the Netherlands.[100] One MP complained, 'we have not progressed a millimetre in recent years.'[101] In a similar manner, there is likely to be ongoing discussion over what to do about the Turkish Islamist group Millî Görüş (MG) because of their increasing involvement in the Dutch education system.[102] The state of the debate in the Netherlands shows how difficult it is to design and implement effective policy and to discuss certain issues, such as ideology, ultimately slowing down the efficacy of the state's response to these problems.

### *The United Kingdom's Prevent strategy*

The UK's Prevent strategy, it should be noted, is a policy for countering violent extremism by preventing individuals from being drawn into terrorism, and is distinct from the counter-extremism strategy. However, by building the necessary resilience, individuals are safeguarded from being drawn into violent extremism, which inevitably touches on the ideology that motivates involvement in terrorism.

Since its creation in 2003 as part of the CONTEST counter-terrorism strategy, Prevent has been heavily criticized.[103] Many of these criticisms were constructive, particularly in the early days: the wasting of public money on unsuccessful initiatives or groups lacking correct expertise, and their lack of transparency, made it difficult to examine if schemes actually worked;[104] the clumsy handling of the relationship with, and poor communication between, the Home Office and British Muslims, which lead to accusations that it was unfairly targeting and alienating Muslims.[105]

The government has tried to respond to failures, with Prevent undergoing various iterations and reviews. The 2011 review of the strategy, for example, recognized the central need of dealing with the underlying ideology; areas were no longer to be prioritized according to demographics, but according to risk.[106] Responding to concerns relating to the lack of transparency and accountability, the government has worked to regularly release statistics of referrals to Channel, and has given greater recognition to the far-right threat in line with the increasing threat.[107] The most recent review of CONTEST, following the 2017 attacks, concluded that Prevent needed to emphasize disengaging those already radicalized, and improving communication and partnerships so that vulnerable individuals do not slip through the net.[108]

Under the Counter Terrorism and Security Act (CTSA) 2015, the UK's Prevent Strategy[109] became a statutory duty on specified public bodies, including universities, schools, local authorities, prisons, and the National Health Service (NHS). Accordingly, these public bodies must have 'due regard to the need to prevent people from being drawn into terrorism'.[110]

Individuals who are regarded as vulnerable to being drawn into terrorism should be referred to Prevent, where their case will be triaged by the police or local authority. Cases are then passed to be assessed by a multi-agency Channel panel, after which they will be given appropriate help – whether relating to extremism or a more relevant service, such as mental health. Participation in Channel, at present, is voluntary, confidential, and personal.[111]

Cases are assessed by the panel according to the Channel Vulnerability Assessment Framework (2012),[112] which lists the key indicators when an individual may be becoming radicalized. No single characteristic is to be taken in isolation and it is made clear that religion is not an indicating factor.[113] The conceptual framework underpinning this guidance is based on the Extremism Risk Guidelines (ERG 22+), developed by the National Offender Management Service (NOMS) using a broad evidence base.[114]

The Prevent strategy is a policy for countering violent extremism; however, by virtue of needing to engage with the ideological motivations behind terrorism, many of the criticisms of Prevent touch on the key themes and issues relating to individual liberty raised in this chapter. Prevent has been called a 'toxic-brand' by some, with its loudest critics wanting it scrapped altogether.[115] Many of these criticisms appear to have stuck largely as a result of what Dame Louise Casey has called an 'active lobby'[116] of groups and individuals pushing back with misleading criticisms. Some of these, notably, have connections with Islamist extremism.[117]

The campaigns that have popularized misconceptions and exaggerated criticisms of Prevent have involved the National Union of Students, the National Union of Teachers, and the University and College Union,[118] alongside the Muslim Council of Britain, CAGE,[119] Mend,[120] Prevent Watch, the Islamic Human Rights Commission, the Muslim Public Affairs Committee UK, and Stand Up To Racism (to name but a few).[121]

'In order to undermine Prevent,' Casey wrote, the programme's 'opponents have deliberately distorted and exaggerated cases'.[122] These groups may actually contribute through their narrative to the alienation of British Muslims,[123] making them more vulnerable to radicalization, and, importantly, they struggle to propose a viable alternative.[124] As one senior police officer put it, those who criticize it often 'don't understand properly how Prevent works [and] for a variety of different reasons, political or otherwise, just don't want Prevent to work in the first place'.[125] Misinformation and, in some cases, disinformation has a large role to play in some of the most common criticisms; in the public relations battle, the government has struggled to counter it.[126]

The most common criticisms include: Prevent is inherently islamophobic and racist, and deliberately targets the Muslim community; Prevent will result in a chilling effect on freedom of expression and political activism, particularly in the Muslim community; Prevent criminalizes Muslims and Islam itself; and Prevent violates basic human rights.[127] All of these belong to the same themes highlighted throughout this chapter: freedom of expression, religion, and human rights.

### *Prevent in the universities – the Butt case*

Dr Salman Butt, Chief Editor of the online Islamist publication Islam21c, was listed by the Extremism Analysis Unit (EAU) in a press release on 'hate speakers' frequenting UK campuses 'expressing views contrary to British values'. Butt subsequently brought a case against the Home Secretary in the High Court, making a number of challenges against Prevent (*Salman Butt* v. *Secretary of State for the Home Department*, 2017).[128]

Butt's lawyers challenged: (1) the lawfulness of the Prevent duty guidance; (2) argued that it doesn't comply with Section 31 of the CTSA Act (2015) insofar as having due regard for free speech in higher education institutions; and (3) argued that it breached the common law and EHRC rights to free speech, due to a lack of clarity, legitimate need, and proportionality.[129] Justice Ouseley's dismissal of these challenges restored some clarity against the background of exaggerations and misinformation of Prevent's more disingenuous critics.[130]

Any limitations of a right must be proportionate and serve a legitimate purpose, defined as: (1) rationally connected to its objective; (2) not more intrusive than required to achieve that objective; and (3) balancing the rights of the individual with the interests of the community (*Bank Mellat* v. *Her Majesty's Treasury*).[131] Does Prevent violate these rights, as critics claim? The UK government was particularly mindful of protecting freedom of speech and other human rights when passing the CTSA Act 2015.[132] Unless it [speech] falls within the categories outlined above (such as hate speech, incitement, glorification), the expression of extremist opinions is not criminalized and the level of interference with free speech is limited, particularly in a university context, though this can be applied more broadly to any public body. Individuals like Butt have no right to be invited to speak on university premises or to dictate how any event at which he speaks should be formatted; whether in a debate format or a balanced platform.[133] Rather than no platforming, interference with expression is likely to be restricted primarily to *challenge.* In other words, not allowing extremists to speak on uncontested platforms. In Justice Ouseley's words, 'the restriction may only bite to the extent that an external speaker may meet a controlled challenge to his views, or speakers expressing an alternative view as part of a reasoned public debate'.[134] In addition, there is no blanket limitation on speech; individuals like Butt can and do remain free to express their beliefs in other forums.

Where a speaker's views are challenged, this does not amount to a restriction of their rights under Article 10. Further, the statutory safeguarding duty (s26 CTSA 2015) does not override other duties, with which it must be balanced, such as ensuring freedom of expression (s31 CTSA 2015 and s43 Education (No. 2) Act 1986).[135] Justice Ouseley was clear that balancing these duties would mean having a speaker on a balanced platform, or a strong chair present able to challenge views that run against fundamental British values.[136]

In 2018, the Higher Education Funding Council of England (HEFCE) found that higher and further education institutions were 'adequately' balancing the Prevent duty and the duty to protect free speech.[137] The challenge will be to ensure extremism is still effectively challenged while free expression is respected: a 2017 report by *Student Right*s showed that in the 2016–17 academic year of the 112 events with extreme or intolerant speakers recorded only one was on such a balanced platform.[138]

Nonetheless, it stands testament to the UK's commitment to balancing countering extremism with free speech that a recent Joint Committee on Human Rights called for an independent review of the impact of Prevent on free speech, and for the government to update guidance documents in light of the clarity provided by the Butt case.[139] 'No platforming' has been a particular concern in the UK.[140] The Joint Committee on Human Rights on Freedom of Speech in Universities (2017) found concerns about 'no platforming', intimidating behaviour during events by protestors, and bureaucracy and confusion over Prevent.[141] Concerns have been raised of the chilling effect on free speech, particularly as a result of increased bureaucracy.[142] In the case of Salman Butt, the judge noted that the evidence of increased bureaucracy was actually due to the unwillingness of the participants to sign up to the university's policy of having a 'strong chair'.[143]

As with freedom of expression, there is little evidence to suggest the strategy unfairly targets a particular religion. The Prevent strategy, and the definition of extremism it employs,[144] makes no mention of a specific ideology and is explicit in that it deals with other extremist ideologies besides Islamist extremism.[145] Likewise, the government's Channel duty guidance is absolutely clear that the Channel panel must not discriminate on the basis of race, religion, or background,[146] stating that there is 'no single route to terrorism' and that an 'outward expression of faith, in the absence of any other indicator of vulnerability, is not a reason to make a referral to Channel'.[147]

A related and common criticism is that it is not justifiable to interfere with the expression of non-violent extremist ideas to prevent violent extremism. In this vein, Butt's lawyer argued that restrictions would only be legitimate and proportionate when dealing with those encouraging or condoning violent extremism or other unlawful acts, but not non-violent extremism.[148] However, Justice Ouseley clarified why challenging non-violent extremist views in some circumstances is justifiable to prevent individuals from being drawn into terrorism. Arguing that adulterers should be stoned to death, the Judge noted, is violent extremism:

> Arguing that the law should be changed through non-violent democratic Parliamentary means, so that adulterers can be stoned to death in fulfilment of a divinely given law, could be non-violent extremism, and could be seen to create a risk of drawing people into terrorism. This argument might lead others, persuaded by it of the merit of the aim, to reject the means, as an impious impediment to God's rule on earth.[149]

In some contexts, therefore, Justice Ouseley is clear that challenging non-violent extremist views may be justified to prevent individuals from being drawn into violent extremism.

The focus on Islamist extremism in this regard is a result of its prevalence rather than any focus on the religion of Islam itself. As Justice Ouseley stated, it is 'obvious that one target of the guidance is Islamist terrorism, and preventing Muslim and non-Muslim people being drawn into it through non-violent Islamist extremism'.[150] Justice Ouseley was clear in his judgement that the government has provided sufficient evidence to justify this approach, and that there was insufficient evidence that the guidance discriminates against Muslims.[151] 'The guidance,' he said, 'pursued the legitimate aims of protecting national security, public safety, prevention of disorder and crime, protecting health or the morals and rights of others'.[152] Importantly, if any individual felt that they had been unlawfully discriminated against, as highlighted by Professor Steven Greer and Lindsay Bell of the University of Bristol, it could be challenged before the courts.[153]

Finally, it is important to recall that Prevent operates within the remit of welfare and safeguarding.[154] 'Far from being a massive conspiracy,' one Prevent coordinator wrote, 'Prevent is coordinated and implemented from within communities and through grassroots organizations, not in a secret underground bunker or in cyber space. Prevent is about safeguarding vulnerable individuals from radicalization, preventing them from harm and from harming others.'[155]

## Conclusion

Traditional liberalism holds that one of the primary goals of government is to protect individual liberty. Interference may be justified only to protect the basis upon which that liberty is founded – democracy and the values and conditions necessary to allow its functioning. Compromise, consent, negotiation, and respect are all fundamental parts of the democratic process and the question of how the state can protect individual liberty whilst protecting itself from subversion is unavoidable. The only tenable answer is – balance. As illustrated, European states are seeking to negotiate this balance, preferring to challenge rather than ban extremist expression, simultaneously trying to solve day-to-day problems in implementing policy whilst seeking to answer the question 'who are we?'.

As with Prevent, 'Fine-tuning', not radical overhaul, is what is needed to find the right balance to protect society from extremism while protecting freedom of expression and other rights. No policy can come fully-formed, or ready-made, to address this problem. European states are not going to find the right balance, except by trial and error, working together over a period of time. The United Kingdom's current approach, as with other nations, is not perfect, but as Greer and Bell succinctly noted, Prevent is a 'democratically defensible and human-rights compliant response to palpable and urgent problems'.[156]

## Notes

1 Popper, K, *The Open Society and Its Enemies* (Routledge, 1947), p. 226.
2 Mill, JS, *On Liberty*, (Penguin Books, 1982), pp. 11–12.
3 Ibid.

4 Francois-Revel, J, *How Democracies Perish* (New York, 1983), p. 4.
5 Ibid. p. 5.
6 'Finsbury park attacker Darren Osborne jailed for minimum of 43 years', *BBC News*, 2 February 2018, available at: www.bbc.co.uk/news/uk-42920929 (last visited: 29 May 2018).
7 This chapter employs the definitions of Islamism and extremism used by the UK Government; 'Contest: The United Kingdom's Strategy for Countering Terrorism', HM Government, June 2018, available at: https://assets.publishing.service.gov.uk/government/uploads/system/uploads/attachment_data/file/713284/CCS207_CCS0218929798-1_CONTEST_3.0_WEB__003_.PDF (last visited: 26 September 2018, para. 4).
8 Slaughter, Anne-Marie, '3 responsibilities every government has towards its citizens', *World Economic Forum*, 13 February 2017, available at: www.weforum.org/agenda/2017/02/government-responsibility-to-citizens-anne-marie-slaughter/ (last visited: 26 September 2018).
9 For example, 'MI5: We prevented nine terror attacks in the past year', *Sky News*, 5 December 2017, available at: https://news.sky.com/story/nine-terror-attacks-prevented-in-past-year-11157431 (last visited: 29 May 2018); 'Seven terror plots foiled in six months, Sadiq Khan reveals', *Daily Telegraph*, 25 September 2017, available at: www.telegraph.co.uk/news/2017/09/25/seven-terror-plots-foiled-six-months-sadiq-khan-reveals/ (last visited: 29 May 2018); 'Far-right terror threat "growing" in UK as four plots foiled', *BBC News*, 26 February 2018, available at: www.bbc.co.uk/news/uk-43200966 (last visited: 29 May 2018). For example, the Netherlands threat level is substantial (level 4), and in Germany an attack is deemed 'highly likely', see: 'Dreiging verandert, niveau blijft nog wel op 4', Nationaal Coödinator Terrorismbestrijding en Veiligheid, 26 March 2018, available at: www.nctv.nl/organisatie/ct/dtn/dreiging-verandert-niveau-blijft-nog-wel-op-4.aspx (last visited: 29 May 2018); and 'Foreign travel advice: Germany', HM Government, available at: www.gov.uk/foreign-travel-advice/germany/terrorism (last visited: 29 May 2018).
10 'The Netherlands comprehensive action programme to combat jihadism', Ministry of Security and Justice, 29 August 2014, available at: https://english.nctv.nl/binaries/def-a5-nctvjihadismuk-03-lr_tcm32-83910.pdf (last visited: 26 September 2018, p. 13).
11 'Germany starts enforcing hate speech law', *BBC News*, 1 January 2018, available at: www.bbc.co.uk/news/technology-42510868 (last visited: 29 May 2018).
12 For example, the case of Jan Böhmermann in Germany, see: 'German Comedian Is Told Not to Repeat Lewd Lines About Erdogan', *New York Times*, 10 February 2017, available at: www.nytimes.com/2017/02/10/world/europe/jan-bohmermann-recep-tayyip-erdogan-poem.html (last visited: 26 September 2018); Dutch comedian Hans Teeuwen has also stood up for the right of comedians to be offensive, see: 'Hans Teeuwen: "It's time for a rebellion against political correctness', *Guardian*, 21 September 2016, available at: www.theguardian.com/stage/2016/sep/21/hans-teeuwen-dutch-comedian-islam-free-speech-interview (last visited: 29 May 2018).
13 For example, Werner Schiffauer, 'The Millî Görüş Community in Germany (Islamische Gemeinschaft Millî Görüş (IMG)' in Frank Peter and Rafael Ortega (eds.), *Islamic Movements of Europe: Public Religion and Islamophobia in the Modern World* (London and New York, I.B. Tauris, 2014): pp. 125–30.
14 For example, 'Advice on Voting By Sheikh Haitham al Haddad', *YouTube*, 6 May 2010, available at: www.youtube.com/watch?v=NdBDyXNX1yc&t=64s (last visited: 26 September 2018).
15 'From dawa to jihad: The various threats from radical Islam to the democratic legal order', Ministry of the Interior and Kingdom Relations', December 2004, available at: www.investigativeproject.org/documents/testimony/49.pdf (p. 15).

16 'Salafist Organization Banned in Germany', *Spiegel*, 14 June 2012, available at: www.spiegel.de/international/germany/germany-bans-salafist-organization-and-stages-police-raids-a-838832.html (last visited: 26 September 2018).
17 Paul Franz, 'Unconstitutional and Outlawed Political Parties: A German-American Comparison', *Boston College International and Comparative Law Review* 5 no. 1 (1982) available at: https://lawdigitalcommons.bc.edu/cgi/viewcontent.cgi?referer=&httpsredir=1&article=1554&context=iclr (p. 55).
18 'Debate rages in Sweden over Muslim Brotherhood report', *The Local SE*, 3 March 2017, available at: www.thelocal.se/20170303/debate-rages-in-sweden-over-muslim-brotherhood-report (last visited: 26 September 2018).
19 'Political Islam", and the Muslim Brotherhood Review", House of Commons Foreign Affairs Committee, 7 November 2016, available at: https://publications.parliament.uk/pa/cm201617/cmselect/cmfaff/118/118.pdf (last visited: 26 September 2018).
20 'UK will not ban Muslim Brotherhood, says David Cameron', *BBC News*, 17 December 2015, available at: www.bbc.co.uk/news/uk-35121792 (last visited: 28 September 2018).
21 Ibid.
22 'Counter-Extremism Strategy', HM Government, October 2015, available at: https://assets.publishing.service.gov.uk/government/uploads/system/uploads/attachment_data/file/470088/51859_Cm9148_Accessible.pdf (last visited: 26 September 2018).
23 Ibid., pp. 12–13.
24 Ibid., pp. 13–16; cf. Webb, E, 'Wolves in Sheep's Clothing: How Islamist Extremists Exploit the UK Charitable Sector', The Henry Jackson Society, 2018, available at: http://henryjacksonsociety.org/wp-content/uploads/2018/02/Wolves-in-Sheeps-Clothes.pdf (last visited: 26 September 2018).
25 'Extremism: PM speech', HM Government, 20 July 2015, available at: www.gov.uk/government/speeches/extremism-pm-speech (last visited: 26 September 2018).
26 'PM statement following London terror attack: 4 June 2017', HM Government, 4 June 2017, available at: www.gov.uk/government/speeches/pm-statement-following-london-terror-attack-4-june-2017 (last visited: 28 September 2018).
27 'Integrated Communities Strategy Green Paper', HM Government, March 2018, available at: https://assets.publishing.service.gov.uk/government/uploads/system/uploads/attachment_data/file/696993/Integrated_Communities_Strategy.pdf (p. 59).
28 Casey, L, 'The Casey Review: A review into opportunity and integration', Department for Communities and Local Government, December 2016, available at: https://assets.publishing.service.gov.uk/government/uploads/system/uploads/attachment_data/file/575973/The_Casey_Review_Report.pdf.
29 Ibid., p. 101.
30 Ibid., p. 129.
31 Ibid., p. 132.
32 *Begg* v. *British Broadcasting Corporation* [2016] EWHC 2688 (QB), 28 October 2016, available at: www.judiciary.gov.uk/wp-content/uploads/2016/10/shakeel-begg-v-bbc-judgment-final-20161028.pdf (para. 119).
33 'The Independent Review into the Application of Sharia Law in England and Wales', HM Government, February 2018, available at: https://assets.publishing.service.gov.uk/government/uploads/system/uploads/attachment_data/file/678478/6.4152_HO_CPFG_Report_into_Sharia_Law_in_the_UK_WEB.pdf (last visited: 26 September 2018).
34 Ibid.
35 Arbitration and Mediation Services (Equality) Bill, 2012, available at: https://publications.parliament.uk/pa/bills/lbill/2012-2013/0007/13007.pdf (last visited: 26 September 2018); Zee, M, *Choosing Sharia?* (The Hague, 2016), p. 153.
36 Manea, E, *Women and Sharia Law*, (London, 2016), pp. 136–82.

37 Ibid., p. 176.
38 Ibid., pp. 124–7.
39 Ibid., p. 54.
40 Zee, M, *Choosing Sharia?*, pp. 143–9.
41 Ibid., pp. 145–6; *Refah Partisi (the Welfare Party) and Others* v. *Turkey*, (App no s41340/98, 41343/98 and 41344/98), ECtHR 2001, available at: http://minorityrights.org/wp-content/uploads/old-site-downloads/download-384-Refah-Partisi-v.-Turkey.pdf (last visited: 26 September 2018, para. 19); *Gunduz* v. *Turkey*, (App no. 35071/97), ECtHR 4 December 2003, available at: www.legal-tools.org/doc/74a144/pdf/ (last visited: 26 September 2018, p. 51).
42 *Refah Partisi (the Welfare Party) and Others* v. *Turkey*, para. 123; Zee, M., *Choosing Sharia?* p. 147.
43 Cliteur, P *et al.*, 'The New Censorship: A Case Study of the Extrajudicial Restraints on Free Speech', in *Freedom of Speech Under Attack*, A Ellian and G Molier (eds.), (The Hague, 2015), available at: https://openaccess.leidenuniv.nl/bitstream/handle/1887/36279/Cliteur%2c%20Herrenberg%20and%20Rijpkema%20The%20New%20Censorship%202015_Redacted.pdf?sequence=1 (last visited: 26 September 2018).
44 'Charlie Hebdo attack: Three days of terror', *BBC News*, 14 January 2015, available at: www.bbc.co.uk/news/world-europe-30708237 (last visited: 26 September 2018).
45 Cliteur, P *et al.*, 'The New Censorship: A Case Study of the Extrajudicial Restraints on Free Speech', in *Freedom of Speech Under Attack* (The Hague, Eleven International Publishing, 23015), p. 131.
46 'Counter-Extremism Strategy', HM Government, October 2015.
47 *Begg* v. *British Broadcasting Corporation* [2016] EWHC 2688 (QB), 28 October 2016.
48 Council of Europe, *European Convention for the Protection of Human Rights and Fundamental Freedoms, as amended by Protocols Nos. 11 and 14 and supplemented by Protocols Nos. 1,4,6,16 and 13*, available at: www.echr.coe.int/Documents/Convention_ENG.pdf (last visited: 29 May 2018).
49 *Human Rights Act 1998*, available at: www.legislation.gov.uk/ukpga/1998/42/schedule/1/part/I/chapter/9 (last visited: 26 September 2018).
50 Ibid.
51 UN Office of the High Commissioner for Human Rights (OHCHR), *Fact Sheet No. 32, Human Rights, Terrorism and Counter-terrorism*, July 2008, No. 32, available at: www.ohchr.org/Documents/Publications/Factsheet32EN.pdf (last visited: 26 September 2018, pp. 23–4).
52 UN General Assembly, *International Covenant on Civil and Political Rights*, 16 December 1966, United Nations, Treaty Series, vol. 999, available at: https://treaties.un.org/doc/publication/unts/volume%20999/volume-999-i-14668-english.pdf (last visited: 26 September 2018); see, Shepherd, A., 'Extremism, Free Speech and the Rule of Law: Evaluating the Compliance of Legislation Restricting Extremist Expressions with Article 19 ICCPR', in *Utrecht Journal of International and European Law* 33, no. 85 (2017): pp. 62–83.
53 Shepherd, A., 'Extremism, Free Speech and the Rule of Law: Evaluating the Compliance of Legislation Restricting Extremist Expressions with Article 19 ICCPR', pp. 62–83.
54 UN General Assembly, *International Covenant on Civil and Political Rights*, 16 December 1966, United Nations, available at: www.ohchr.org/en/professionalinterest/pages/ccpr.aspx (last visited: 26 September 2018).
55 UN Office of the High Commissioner for Human Rights (OHCHR), *Fact Sheet No. 32, Human Rights, Terrorism and Counter-terrorism*, July 2008, No. 32, available at: www.ohchr.org/Documents/Publications/Factsheet32EN.pdf (last visited: 26 September 2018, p. 7).

56 Ibid., p. 7.

57 *Freedom of Speech in Universities*, Joint Committee on Human Rights Report, 27 March 2018, available at: https://publications.parliament.uk/pa/jt201719/jtselect/jtrights/589/589.pdf (last visited: 26 September 2018, pp. 13–14).

58 Zee, M., *Choosing Sharia?* (The Hague, 2016), p. 148.

59 UN General Assembly, *Convention on the Elimination of All Forms of Discrimination Against Women*, 18 December 1979, United Nations, Treaty Series, vol. 1249, available at: www2.ohchr.org/english/bodies/cedaw/docs/comments/CEDAW-C-52-WP-1_en.pdf (last visited: 26 September 2018, p. 149). Zee, M., *Choosing Sharia?* (The Hague, 2016).

60 Parker, D., and Davis J, 'Counter-Radicalisation at the Coalface: Lessons for Europe and Beyond', RUSI, February 2017, available at: https://rusi.org/sites/default/files/nb_vol.37_no1_davis_and_parker.pdf (last visited: 26 September 2018); 'A way home for jihadis: Denmark's radical approach to Islamic extremism', *Guardian*, 23 February 2015, available at: www.theguardian.com/world/2015/feb/23/home-jihadi-denmark-radical-islamic-extremism-aarhus-model-scandinavia (last visited: 26 September 2018).

61 'Annual Report 2017: National Action Plan for the Prevention of Violent Radicalisation and Extremism', Ministry of the Interior Finland, 2017, available at: http://julkaisut.valtioneuvosto.fi/bitstream/handle/10024/80731/SM_24_2017.pdf?sequence=1&isAllowed=y (last visited: 26 September 2018, p. 9).

62 Parker, D, and Davis, J, 'Counter-Radicalisation at the Coalface: Lessons for Europe and Beyond', RUSI, February 2017; 'A way home for jihadis: Denmark's radical approach to Islamic extremism', *Guardian*, 23 February 2015, available at: www.theguardian.com/world/2015/feb/23/home-jihadi-denmark-radical-islamic-extremism-aarhus-model-scandinavia (last visited: 26 September 2018).

63 'Annual Report 2017: National Action Plan for the Prevention of Violent Radicalisation and Extremism', Ministry of the Interior Finland, 2017, available at: http://julkaisut.valtioneuvosto.fi/bitstream/handle/10024/80731/SM_24_2017.pdf?sequence=1&isAllowed=y (last visited: 26 September 2018, p. 9).

64 'How do you deradicalise returning Isis fighters?' *Guardian*, 12 November 2014, available at: www.theguardian.com/world/2014/nov/12/deradicalise-isis-fighters-jihadists-denmark-syria (last visited: 26 September 2018).

65 'Inside France's "boot camp" for wavering radicals', *BBC News*, 25 September 2016, available at: www.bbc.co.uk/news/magazine-37454697 (last visited: 26 September 2018).

66 Ibid.

67 Ibid; 'How France hopes to help radicals escape jihadist net', *BBC News*, 28 February 2018, available at: www.bbc.co.uk/news/world-europe-43215027 (last visited: 26 September 2018).

68 'How France hopes to help radicals escape jihadist net', *BBC News*, 28 February 2018.

69 Ibid.

70 Van der Laan, E, 'Aanscherping Aanpak radicalisering (Tightening Approach to Radicalisation),' Letter from the Mayor of Amsterdam to Members of the City Council, 28 May 2015, available at: https://amsterdam.raadsinformatie.nl/document/2171936/1/document (last visited: 26 September 2018, p. 4).

71 'Evaluatie van het Actie programma Integrale Aanpak Jihadisme', Ministerie van Veilgheid en Justitie, September 2017, available at: www.inspectie-jenv.nl/binaries/inspectie-venj/documenten/rapporten/2017/09/06/evaluatie-van-het-actieprogramma-integrale-aanpak-jihadisme/Evaluatie+van+het+Actieprogramma+Integrale+Aanpak+Jihadisme.pdf (last visited: 26 September 2018, pp. 19–20).

72 'Written Questions', Amsterdam City Council (179), 4 August 2017, available at: https://amsterdam.raadsinformatie.nl/document/5573927/1/179boomsma (last visited: 26 September 2018).

73 'The Netherlands comprehensive action programme to combat jihadism', Ministry of Security and Justice, 29 August 2014.
74 Ibid., p. 14.
75 Ibid., p. 17.
76 Ibid., pp. 17–20.
77 Ibid., p. 20.
78 'Written Questions', Amsterdam City Council (179), 4 August 2017; 'Amsterdamse topambtenaar Saadia a. T. blunderde in zaak Syriëganger', *Elsevier*, 21 July 2017, available at: www.elsevierweekblad.nl/nederland/achtergrond/2017/07/amsterdamse-topambtenaar-saadia-a-t-schoot-tekort-in-begeleiding-524970/ (last visited: 26 September 2018); 'Topambtenaar gaf ronselpraktijk vrij baan', *De Telegraaf*, 4 August 2017, available at: www.telegraaf.nl/nieuws/288743/topambtenaar-gaf-ronselpraktijk-vrij-baan (last visited: 26 September 2018); Spoeddebat Amsterdams antiradicaliseringsbeleid belangrijke signalen zouden zijn gemist', *De Volkskrant*, 6 August 2017, available at: https://beta.volkskrant.nl/nieuws-achtergrond/spoeddebat-amsterdams-antiradicaliseringsbeleid-belangrijke-signalen-zouden-zijn-gemist~b4556b57/ (last visited: 26 September 2018); 'Frauderende' ambtenaar Amsterdam geschorst', *De Telegraaf*, 13 July 2017, available at: www.telegraaf.nl/nieuws/257145/frauderende-ambtenaar-amsterdam-geschorst (last visited: 26 September 2018).
79 'Frauderende ambtenaar Amsterdam geschorst', *De Telegraaf*, 13 July 2017.
80 'Saadia ait-Taleb voor rechter voor fraude met drie facturen van 18.000 euro', *AT5*, 18 July 2018, available at: www.at5.nl/artikelen/184472/saadia-ait-taleb-voor-rechter-voor-fraude-met-drie-facturen-van-18000-euro (last visited: 26 September 2018).
81 'Jongerenwerker Amsterdam maakte reclame voor jihad', *Elsevier*, 23 August 2017, available at: www.elsevierweekblad.nl/nederland/achtergrond/2017/08/jongerenwerker-amsterdam-maakte-reclame-voor-jihad-534515/ (last visited: 26 September 2018).
82 'Written Questions', Amsterdam City Council, 23 August 2017, available at: https://amsterdam.raadsinformatie.nl/document/5795556/1/09012f97821adaa1 (last visited: 26 September 2018, p. 4).
83 'De beerput van Bilal L. gaat open', *De Telegraaf*, 28 December 2017, available at: www.telegraaf.nl/nieuws/1478183/de-beerput-van-bilal-l-gaat-open (last visited: 26 September 2018).
84 See, for example, 'Beantwoording van vragen over radicalisering gesteld in de commissie AZ van 14 september 2017 en later aangevuld door verschillende raadsfracties', Amsterdam City Council, 3 October 2017, available at: https://amsterdam.raadsinformatie.nl/document/5795549/1/09012f97821adabf (last visited: 26 September 2018, pp. 25, 27).
85 Written Questions', Amsterdam City Council, 23 August 2017, p. 4.
86 'Quickscan Amsterdamse Aanpak Radicalisering en Terrorisme', University of Utrecht and University of Amsterdam, 14 February 2018, available at: https://amsterdam.raadsinformatie.nl/document/6209719/1/Quickscan_Amsterdamse_aanpak_radicalisering_en_terrorisme (last visited: 26 September 2018, pp. 2, 6).
87 'Diederik Boomsma: "Radicalisering los je niet op met stageplekken"', *Elsevier*, 28 August 2017, available at: www.elsevierweekblad.nl/nederland/achtergrond/2017/08/radicaliseringsbeleid-gemeente-amsterdam-is-placebo-535759/
88 Van der Laan, E., 'Aanscherping Aanpak radicalisering (Tightening Approach to Radicalisation),' Letter from the Mayor of Amsterdam to Members of the City Council, 28 May 2015, p. 7.
89 'Diederik Boomsma: "Radicalisering los je niet op met stageplekken"', *Elsevier*, 28 August 2017.
90 Ibid.
91 Minutes of the meeting of the General Affairs Council Committee, Council Commission Report, Amsterdam City Council, 14 September 2017, available at: https://

amsterdam.raadsinformatie.nl/document/5765204/1/20170914_definitief_verslag_Cie-AZ (last visited: 26 September 2018, p. 6).

92 'From Dawa to Jihad: The various threats from radical Islam to the democratic legal order', Ministry of the Interior and Kingdom Relations, December 2004, pp. 14–15.

93 'Salafism in the Netherlands: Diversity and dynamics', AIVD/NCVT, September 2015, available at: https://english.nctv.nl/binaries/publicatie-salafisme-eng-web_tcm32-84283.pdf (last visited: 26 September 2018).

94 Ibid.

95 Ibid.

96 'Quickscan Amsterdamse Aanpak Radicalisering en Terrorisme', University of Utrecht and University of Amsterdam, 14 February 2018.

97 'Follow up onderzoeken radicalisering', Mayor of Amsterdam – Amsterdam City Council, 21 June 2018, available at: www.parool.nl/rest/content/assets/d8405b7d-4c14-44f7-8703-f6d1d332d8b1 (last visited: 26 September 2018).

98 'Van Aartsen onderzoekt samenwerking met salafisten', *De Telegraaf*, 22 June 2018, available at: www.telegraaf.nl/nieuws/2203725/van-aartsen-onderzoekt-samenwerking-met-salafisten (last visited: 26 September 2018).

99 'Geheime lijsten financiering moskeeën onthuld', *NOS*, 23 April 2018, available at: https://nos.nl/nieuwsuur/artikel/2228686-geheime-lijsten-financiering-moskeeen-onthuld.html (last visited: 26 September 2018).

100 Ibid.

101 Ibid.

102 'Yusuf Altuntas vertelt waarom islamitisch onderwijs zo belangrijk is', *De Volkskrant*, 3 November 2017, available at: www.volkskrant.nl/nieuws-achtergrond/yusuf-altuntas-vertelt-waarom-islamitisch-onderwijs-zo-belangrijk-is~b336da49/ (last visited: 26 September 2018); 'Amsterdamse tak Millî Görüş start islamopleiding', *Het Parool*, 5 August 2017, available at: www.parool.nl/amsterdam/amsterdamse-tak-milli-gorus-start-imamopleiding~a4509733/ (last visited: 26 September 2018).

103 Malik, N, Wilson, T, Orton, K and Rushchenko, J, 'Understanding CONTEST: The Foundation and The Future', Henry Jackson Society, 2017, available at: http://henryjacksonsociety.org/wp-content/uploads/2017/07/FINAL-CONTEST.pdf (last visited: 31 May 2018).

104 For example, in 2016 the Liberal Democrat party expressed their wish to scrap the strategy, see 'Lib Dems aim to scrap "counter-productive" Prevent strategy', *Guardian*, 13 September 2016, available at: www.theguardian.com/politics/2016/sep/13/lib-dems-aim-to-scrap-counter-productive-prevent-strategy (last visited: 26 September 2018); Casciani, D, 'Analysis: The Prevent strategy and its problems', *BBC News*, 26 August 2014, available at: www.bbc.co.uk/news/uk-28939555 (last visited: 31 May 2018).

105 Casciani, D, 'Analysis: The Prevent strategy and its problems', *BBC News*, 26 August 2014.

106 Malik, N, Wilson, T, Orton, K and Rushchenko, J, 'Understanding CONTEST: The Foundation and The Future', Henry Jackson Society, 2017.

107 For example, the proscription of Far Right group National Action in December 2016, see: 'CONTEST', HM Government, June 2018; see also: 'Individuals referred to and supported through the Prevent Programme statistics', HM Government, available at: www.gov.uk/government/collections/individuals-referred-to-and-supported-through-the-prevent-programme-statistics (last visited: 26 September 2018).

108 'CONTEST: The United Kingdom's Strategy for Countering Terrorism,' HM Government, June 2018.

109 Ibid.

110 Counter-Terrorism and Security Act 2015, available at: www.legislation.gov.uk/ukpga/2015/6/pdfs/ukpga_20150006_en.pdf (last visited: 26 September 2018, para. 26).

111 'Individuals referred to and supported through the Prevent Programme, April 2016 to March 2017', Home Office, 27 March 2018, available at: https://assets.publishing.service.gov.uk/government/uploads/system/uploads/attachment_data/file/694002/individuals-referred-supported-prevent-programme-apr2016-mar2017.pdf (last visited: 26 September 2018).

112 Channel: Vulnerability assessment framework', HM Government, October 2012, available at: https://assets.publishing.service.gov.uk/government/uploads/system/uploads/attachment_data/file/118187/vul-assessment.pdf (last visited: 26 September 2018); see also 'Channel Duty Guidance: Protecting vulnerable people from being drawn into terrorism', HM Government, 2015, available at: https://assets.publishing.service.gov.uk/government/uploads/system/uploads/attachment_data/file/425189/Channel_Duty_Guidance_April_2015.pdf (last visited: 26 September 2018).

113 'Channel Duty Guidance: Protecting vulnerable people from being drawn into terrorism', HM Government, 2015, available at: https://assets.publishing.service.gov.uk/government/uploads/system/uploads/attachment_data/file/425189/Channel_Duty_Guidance_April_2015.pdf (last visited: 26 September 2018).

114 Lloyd, M and C Dean, 'The Development of Structured Guidelines for Assessing Risk in Extremist Offenders', *Journal of Threat Assessment and Management* 2, no. 1 (2015): p. 40.

115 This has included the mainstream Liberal Democrat Party, see: 'Lib Dems aim to scrap "counter-productive" Prevent strategy', *Guardian*, 13 September 2016, available at: www.theguardian.com/politics/2016/sep/13/lib-dems-aim-to-scrap-counter-productive-prevent-strategy (last visited: 16 September 2018); 'Prevent criticism "stems from ignorance" ', *BBC News*, 7 August 2017, available at: www.bbc.co.uk/news/uk-40845911 (last visited: 31 May 2018).

116 Casey, L., 'The Casey Review: A review into opportunity and integration', Department for Communities and Local Government, December 2016, p. 154.

117 Sutton, R., 'Preventing Prevent: Challenges to Counter-Radicalisation Policy on Campus', Henry Jackson Society, 2015, available at: http://henryjacksonsociety.org/wp-content/uploads/2015/10/Preventing-Prevent_webversion3.pdf (last visited: 26 September 2018); Sutton, R., 'Myths and Misunderstandings: Understanding Opposition to The Prevent Strategy', Henry Jackson Society, 2016, available at: http://henryjacksonsociety.org/wp-content/uploads/2016/10/Myths-and-Misunderstandings-PREVENT-Report-Final-29.09.2016.pdf (last visited: 26 September 2018).

118 Sutton, R., 'Myths and Misunderstandings: Understanding Opposition to The Prevent Strategy', Henry Jackson Society, 2016, p. 21.

119 For an example of CAGE's disinformation see: 'The "Science" of Pre-Crime: The Secret "Radicalisation" Study Underpinning Prevent', CAGE, 2016, available at: https://cage.ngo/wp-content/uploads/2016/09/CAGE-Science-Pre-Crime-Report.pdf (last visited: 26 September 2018); Sutton, R., 'Prevent isn't Perfect—but its critics should stick to the facts', *Left Foot Forward*, 4 October 2016, available at: https://leftfootforward.org/2016/10/prevent-isnt-perfect-but-its-critics-should-stick-to-the-facts/ (last visited: 26 September 2018).

120 Wilson, T, 'MEND: "Islamists Masquerading as Civil Libertarians", Henry Jackson Society, 2017, available at: http://henryjacksonsociety.org/wp-content/uploads/2017/10/HJS-Mend-Report.pdf (last visited: 26 September 2018).

121 These groups are listed in Malik, N, Wilson, T, Orton, K and Rushchenko, J, 'Understanding CONTEST: The Foundation and The Future', Henry Jackson Society, 2017, p. 3.

122 Casey, L, 'The Casey Review: A review into opportunity and integration', Department for Communities and Local Government, December 2016, p. 154.

123 For examples of the misinformation and distortion used by Prevent's opponents, see: Sutton, R, 'Myths and Misunderstandings: Understanding Opposition to The Prevent Strategy', Henry Jackson Society, 2016, p. 28.

124 Casey, L, 'The Casey Review: A review into opportunity and integration', Department for Communities and Local Government, December 2016, p. 154.
125 'Prevent criticism "stems from ignorance" ', *BBC News*, 7 August 2017, available at: www.bbc.co.uk/news/uk-40845911 (last visited: 31 May 2018).
126 Sutton, R, 'Preventing Prevent: Challenges to Counter-Radicalisation Policy on Campus', Henry Jackson Society, 2015.
127 These points are adapted from, and detailed further in Sutton, R, 'Myths and Misunderstandings: Understanding Opposition to The Prevent Strategy', Henry Jackson Society, 2016, p. 21; and 'Six myths about the Prevent duty in universities', *Times Educational Supplement*, 9 April 2018, available at: www.timeshighereducation.com/blog/six-myths-about-prevent-duty-universities#survey-answer (last visited: 26 September 2018).
128 *Butt* v. *the Secretary of State for the Home Department*, [2017] EWHC 1930 (Admin) (26 July 2017), available at: www.bailii.org/ew/cases/EWHC/Admin/2017/1930.html Para. 1.
129 Ibid., para. 2.
130 Ibid., para. 1.
131 Ibid., para. 111.
132 Ibid., para. 135.
133 Ibid., para. 71.
134 Ibid., para. 141.
135 Ibid., para 153.
136 Ibid., para 153. See also I Cram and H Fenwick, 'Protecting Free Speech and Academic Freedom in Universities' (2018) 81 *MLR* 825.
137 *Freedom of Speech in Universities*, Joint Committee on Human Rights Report, 27 March 2018, para. 70.
138 Black, R, 'Extreme Speakers and Events: In the 2016–17 Academic Year', *Student Rights* (September 2017), available at: http://henryjacksonsociety.org/wp-content/uploads/2017/09/Extreme-Speakers-and-Events-in-the-2016-17-Academic-Year-Final-1.pdf (last visited: 26 September 2018, p. 2).
139 *Freedom of Speech in Universities*, Joint Committee on Human Rights Report, 27 March 2018, paras. 69, 78.
140 Ibid., p. 21.
141 Ibid.
142 *Butt* v. *the Secretary of State for the Home Department*, [2017] EWHC 1930 (Admin) (26 July 2017), para. 75.
143 Ibid., para. 75.
144 'Counter-Extremism Strategy', HM Government, 2015.
145 'New figures show improved referrals to Prevent and a rise in far-right concerns', Home Office, 27 March 2018, available at: www.gov.uk/government/news/new-figures-show-improved-referrals-to-prevent-and-a-rise-in-far-right-concerns (last visited: 26 September 2018).
146 'Channel Duty Guidance', HM Government, 2015, available at: https://assets.publishing.service.gov.uk/government/uploads/system/uploads/attachment_data/file/425189/Channel_Duty_Guidance_April_2015.pdf (last visited: 28 September 2018, para. 71).
147 Ibid., para 54.
148 'Prevent Strategy', HM Government, 2011, available at: https://assets.publishing.service.gov.uk/government/uploads/system/uploads/attachment_data/file/97976/prevent-strategy-review.pdf (last visited: 26 September 2018, para. 128).
149 *Butt* v. *the Secretary of State for the Home Department*, [2017] EWHC 1930 (Admin) (26 July 2017), para 138.
150 Ibid., para. 151.
151 Ibid., para. 275.

152 Ibid., para. 143.
153 'Six myths about the Prevent duty in universities', *Times Educational Supplement*, 9 April 2018.
154 'Individuals referred to and supported through the Prevent Programme, April 2016 to March 2017', Home Office, 27 March 2018, pp. 5–6.
155 'Critics Have It Pegged As The Minority Report, But Prevent Really Isn't That Exciting', 13 March 2017, available at: www.huffingtonpost.co.uk/will-baldat/prevent_b_15281784.html (last visited: 31 May 2018).
156 'Six myths about the Prevent duty in universities', *Times Educational Supplement*, 9 April 2018.

# 8 Bad law

## How the United States Supreme Court mishandled the free speech issue in *Holder* v. *Humanitarian Law Project*

*James Weinstein and Ashutosh Bhagwat*

### Introduction

The Supreme Court's decision in *Holder* v. *Humanitarian Law Project* is a prime example of the old adage that hard cases make bad law.[1] Although the court arguably reached the correct result in this difficult case, it did so in a way that threatens to weaken the protective structure of American free speech doctrine. In addition, the court's disposition provided inadequate guidance to the lower courts on how to analyze First Amendment defences to prosecutions for providing material support to terrorist organizations. In this chapter, we will discuss in some detail why the court's free speech analysis in the *Humanitarian Law Project* case is ill conceived, and identify some potentially significant negative consequences of that analysis for free speech law in the United States. We close by suggesting how the court *should* have analyzed the free speech claims in that case.

### I The hard case

The case arose out of a constitutional challenge to 18 U.S.C. §2339B, the so-called material support statute, which prohibits 'knowingly provid[ing] material support or resources to a foreign terrorist organization.' The statute, in turn, defines 'material support or resources' broadly, to include, inter alia, any and all property, services, training, expert advice, and personnel.[2] A foreign terrorist organization (FTO) is defined as 'an organization designated as a terrorist organization'[3] by the Secretary of State, pursuant to his or her authority under 8 U.S.C. §1189.[4]

The plaintiffs in the litigation were US citizens and organizations who wished to provide expert training and advice to support the non-violent activities of two designated FTOs: the Kurdistan Workers' Party (PKK), an organization seeking the establishment of an independent Kurdish state in Turkey, and the Liberation Tigers of Tamil Eelam (LTTE or Tamil Tigers), an organization that sought the establishment of an independent Tamil state in Sri Lanka, but which had recently been defeated militarily by the Sri Lankan military.[5] The specific activities that the plaintiffs wanted to engage in were to provide expert training and advice to the PKK on the following topics:

> (1) 'train[ing] members of [the] PKK on how to use humanitarian and international law to peacefully resolve disputes'; (2) 'engag[ing] in political advocacy on behalf of Kurds who live in Turkey'; and (3) 'teach[ing] PKK members how to petition various representative bodies such as the United Nations for relief.'[6]

The military defeat of the LTTE mooted two of the specific the claims that had been litigated in the lower court.[7] The only specific claim concerning this FTO that remained alive was the plaintiffs' desire to 'engag[e] in political advocacy on behalf of Tamils who live in Sri Lanka'.[8]

The plaintiffs claimed that application of the material support statute to their activities violated their rights to freedom of speech and freedom of association protected by the First Amendment. The Supreme Court, in an opinion by Chief Justice Roberts, rejected both of these claims by a 6–3 vote.[9] The court devoted most of its First Amendment discussion to the free speech claim, giving short shrift to the freedom of association claim.

The court began its analysis of the free speech claim by considering the nature of the activity in which the plaintiffs wished to engage, and, consequently, the proper level of judicial scrutiny applicable to the statute's restriction of this activity. It rejected both the plaintiffs' and the government's positions on this issue as 'extreme'. With respect to the plaintiffs' claim that the statute banned their 'pure political speech', the court explained that the material support provision 'does not prohibit independent advocacy or expression of any kind'. It noted that under the statute, the plaintiffs could say anything they wished about the PKK, the LTTE, and the government of Turkey, and even advocate before the United Nations. For this reason, the court found that Congress has not 'sought to suppress ideas or opinions in the form of "pure political speech"' but, rather, has prohibited 'material support' which 'often does not take the form of speech at all'. And when the statute does apply to speech, the court emphasized, the law is 'carefully drawn to cover only a narrow category of speech', namely, 'speech to, under the direction of, or in coordination with' organizations that the speaker knows is an FTO.[10]

The court then rejected the government's argument that, because the only thing truly at issue in the case was 'conduct not speech', the restriction should be subject to 'intermediate scrutiny' applicable to a regulation of conduct that 'incidentally burdens speech'. In pressing this argument, the government relied on *United States* v. *O'Brien*,[11] which rejected a First Amendment challenge to a conviction under federal law which prohibited the destruction of draft cards – by a defendant who had burned his draft card to protest the draft. The court responded that '*O'Brien* does not provide the applicable standard for reviewing content-based restrictions on speech.'[12] The court found that the application of the material support provision in this case was a content-based restriction on speech because its application depends on what the plaintiffs say to the FTOs:

> If plaintiffs' speech to those groups imparts a 'specific skill' or communicates advice derived from 'specialized knowledge' – for example, training on

> the use of international law or advice on petitioning the United Nations – then it is barred. On the other hand, plaintiffs' speech is not barred if it imparts only general or unspecialized knowledge.[13]

Because the activity 'triggering coverage' under the material support provision 'consists of communicating a message' and because the regulation is 'related to expression', the court concluded that 'we are outside of *O'Brien's* test'. Consequently, rather than the 'intermediate scrutiny' urged by the government, the court held that it must 'apply a more demanding standard'.[14] Although the court sedulously avoids naming the type of scrutiny it found applicable, it is best understood as a variation of 'strict scrutiny'.[15]

The court easily concluded that the government's interest in combatting terrorism was 'an urgent objective of the highest order'.[16] The court then turned to the more difficult question of whether the application of the statute to the speech the plaintiffs wanted to engage in was 'necessary to further that interest',[17] and for three reasons found that it was.

First, the court accepted the government's assertion that even material support for an FTO's legal activities advances terrorism because it 'frees up other resources within the organization that may be put to violent ends'. In addition, the court agreed with the government's claim that support for legal activities of an FTO 'also importantly helps lend legitimacy to foreign terrorist groups – legitimacy that makes it easier for those groups to persist, to recruit members, and to raise funds – all of which facilitate more terrorist attacks'. Finally, and in a similar vein, the court accepted the government's argument that providing material support to FTOs 'also furthers terrorism by straining the United States' relationships with its allies and undermining cooperative efforts between nations to prevent terrorist attacks'.[18]

In coming to the conclusion that the ban on the activities that the plaintiffs wanted to engage in 'was necessary to further' the interest in combatting terrorism, the court relied on congressional findings that FTOs 'are so tainted by their criminal conduct that any contribution to such an organization facilitates that conduct'. In addition, it relied on an affidavit from the executive branch claiming that 'all contributions to foreign terrorist organizations further their terrorism'. Because the case implicated 'sensitive and weighty interests of national security and foreign affairs', the court held that these 'evaluation of facts' by the political branches were 'entitled to deference'.[19]

In rejecting the plaintiffs' free speech claim, the court added this cautionary statement:

> [W]e in no way suggest that a regulation of independent speech would pass constitutional muster, even if the Government were to show that such speech benefits foreign terrorist organizations. We also do not suggest that Congress could extend the same prohibition on material support at issue here to domestic organizations.[20]

Having rejected the free speech claim, the court then turned to the claim that application of the material support provision violated the plaintiffs' freedom of association. The court's discussion of this claim was brief, consisting of a mere three paragraphs. It held simply that the material support statute 'does not penalize mere association with a foreign terrorist organization', because the provision does not prohibit *membership* in an FTO, merely the provision of material support.[21]

Justice Breyer wrote a dissenting opinion, joined by Justices Ginsburg and Sotomayor.[22] Breyer emphasized that the plaintiffs' activities were political and so fell within the core of the First Amendment's protection.[23] He also repeatedly described the activities as implicating rights of both speech *and* association[24] rather than treating the associational claim as a poor stepchild, as the majority did. Indeed, Breyer emphatically rejected the majority's conclusion that the statute was constitutional because it prohibits only speech coordinated with an FTO. He pointed out that the First Amendment 'after all, also protects the freedom of association', citing cases that describe the right of freedom of assembly as an independent and 'cognate' right.[25] The dissent also pointed out that the previous cases had held 'that a person who associates with a group that uses unlawful means to achieve its ends does not thereby necessarily forfeit the First Amendment's protection for freedom of association'.[26] Finally, Breyer argued that the government's primary arguments in defence of the material support statute – that even peaceful support to FTOs is 'fungible', and that support for FTOs can 'legitimize' them – are either factually questionable or contrary to precedent.[27] Because the dissent concluded that the statute, as interpreted by the government, violates the First Amendment, the dissent would have imposed a limiting construction 'criminalizing First Amendment protected pure speech and association only when the defendant knows or intends that those activities will assist the organization's unlawful terrorist actions'.[28]

## II Making bad law

As we shall explain below, and as Chapter 4 also discusses, the result the court reached in *Humanitarian Law Project* is probably correct. The way the court reached this result, however, threatens to undermine the protection of freedom of speech in the United States in several ways. One way was the generalized and conclusory statements that the court accepted as discharging the government burden of showing that the restriction on the plaintiffs' speech was 'necessary to further' the interest in combatting terrorism. As Justice Breyer's dissent aptly notes:

> There is no *obvious* way in which undertaking advocacy for political change through peaceful means or teaching the PKK and LTTE, say, how to petition the United Nations for political change is fungible with other resources that might be put to more sinister ends in the way that donations of money, food, or computer training are fungible. It is far from obvious that these advocacy activities can themselves be redirected, or will free other resources that can be directed, towards terrorist ends. The Government has provided

> us with no empirical information that might convincingly support this claim. [Rather, it] points to [the Congressional findings and an Executive Branch affidavit discussed above]. The most one can say in the Government's favor about these statements is that they *might* be read as offering highly general support for its argument.[29]

The majority essentially acknowledges the accuracy of this critique: 'The Government, when seeking to prevent imminent harms in the context of international affairs and national security,' Chief Justice Roberts proclaimed, 'is not required to conclusively link all the pieces in the puzzle before we grant weight to its empirical conclusions'.[30]

An essential feature of searching judicial scrutiny – whether it is called 'strict scrutiny', 'the most exacting scrutiny' or, as in this case, remains coyly unnamed – is that the government must offer solid evidence that the regulation being challenged is actually needed to promote some extremely important interest. A major Supreme Court free speech decision that purports to apply rigorous scrutiny, but then upholds a law based on generalized assertions backed by no specific evidence, dilutes the strong protection of speech that rigorous judicial scrutiny was designed to provide. It provides a roadmap for the court to follow in the next case, in which a majority of the Justices, impelled by a blend of intuition and ideology, want to uphold a content-based restriction on speech based on a speculative evidentiary showing. Worse yet, it authorizes lower courts, in cases involving speech that strikes them as dangerous despite the lack of firm empirical proof of such danger, to engage in similar *faux* strict scrutiny.[31]

It could be argued that any dilution of speech protection in the wake of *Humanitarian Law Project* will be narrowly confined. In accepting the government's generalized claims as satisfying the requirement that the government had shown that the restriction was 'necessary to further' the interest in combating terrorism, the court explained that the government's 'factual evaluations' in a case concerning national security and foreign affairs was 'entitled to deference'.[32] However, the portion of the majority opinion in which the court expressly gives deference to key government 'factual evaluations' is a separate section at the end of the free speech discussion: prior to that section, the court accepted any number of other empirically weak assertions about how effectively combating terrorism requires prohibiting the plaintiffs' speech. The majority opinion thus supplies plenty of fodder for subsequent Supreme Court opinions and lower courts to weaken free speech protection beyond the realm of national security and foreign affairs.

But even if the diluting effects of speech protection were confined to areas of national security and foreign affairs, the speculative evidentiary showing that the court accepted in *Humanitarian Law Project* still poses a substantial threat to free speech. For instance, it would support limiting anti-war protests based on generalized congressional findings and conclusory statements in an executive branch affidavit that these protests were dispiriting our troops in the field and encouraging the enemy. The rigorous protection of dissent provided by contemporary free speech doctrine emerged largely in response to the appalling lack of protection that the court provided to protesters who objected to the United States' involvement in the First World War; cases in which the court accepted generalized and conclusory claims by government about harm to the war effort.[33] *Humanitarian Law Project* represents an unfortunate step back towards this inadequate protection for dissent in the areas of national security and foreign affairs.

Experience has shown, moreover, that judicial deference to factual assertions by the political branches in the areas of national security and foreign affairs can severely undermine civil liberties in the United States, including free speech. The court's deferential posture in *Humanitarian Law Project* brings to mind such questionable decisions as *Korematsu* v. *United States*[34] and *Dennis* v. *United States*[35] in which the court sacrificed basic civil liberties in the name of national security and deference to political and military authorities. The sweeping deference language of the *Humanitarian Law Project* majority opinion raises the possibility that in the 'Age of Terror' the court will retreat to a similar constitutional calculus.

The court's acceptance of the government's weak factual showing is, unfortunately, not the only way that the reasoning of *Humanitarian Law Project* makes bad law. Even more troubling is a dangerously broad rationale that the court accepted as justifying the prohibition of the plaintiffs' speech. The court found that any form of material support, including the speech in which the plaintiffs wished to engage, 'helps lend legitimacy to foreign terrorist groups – legitimacy that makes it easier for those groups to persist, to recruit members, and to raise funds – all of which facilitate more terrorist attacks'.[36] But, as Justice Breyer noted in his dissenting opinion, this argument 'applies as strongly to "independent" as to "coordinated" advocacy'. Indeed, speech in favour of a terrorist organization by a person having no connection with that group would ordinarily tend to be *more legitimating* than by a someone whose speech is made under that organization's 'direction or control'.[37]

As previously noted, towards the end of his opinion for the court, Chief Justice Roberts wrote: 'We in no way suggest that a regulation of independent speech would pass constitutional muster, even if the Government were to show that such speech benefits foreign terrorist organizations.'[38] But, this disclaimer notwithstanding, the holding that coordinated speech can be suppressed because it lends legitimacy to the organization, which in turn facilitates its terrorism, *strongly* suggests for the reasons just discussed that independent speech can be suppressed on this ground. It is telling that, despite the dissent's claim that this rationale would seem to apply to independent advocacy, the majority opinion made no attempt to explain why it would make a difference – insofar as legitimation is concerned – whether the speech was coordinated or independent.[39] This silence, alas, suggests that there is no credible distinction to be made.

The legitimation rationale would also seem to put in question the continued validity of *Brandenburg* v. *Ohio*, a cornerstone of contemporary free speech jurisprudence, at least as it applies to advocacy in favour of terrorist organizations. *Brandenburg* holds that the First Amendment protects the right of a speaker to advocate law violation, including violence, so long as that advocacy is not 'directed to inciting or producing imminent lawless action and … likely to incite or produce such action'.[40] But, if speakers have a First Amendment right to advocate *illegal* conduct subject to these narrow incitement limitations, then it follows *a fortiori* that they have a right to advocate in favour of *legal* activities. And they would have such a right, even if it is a criminal organization that is engaged in these activities, regardless of whether such advocacy tends to legitimize that organization. The dissent forcefully argues that *Brandenburg* should have 'led this Court to conclusions other than those it reached'.[41] But, as it did with the dissent's more general critique that the legitimation rationale would apply to independent as well as coordinated speech, the court simply ignores this argument. Indeed, despite its obvious relevance, the majority opinion does not even mention *Brandenburg*.

The legitimation rationale, therefore, would seem to create a terrorism exception to *Brandenburg*. Moreover, such an exception would seem to apply to domestic as well as foreign terrorist organizations. There is no reason to assume that advocacy in favour of the legal goals of foreign terror organizations will tend to legitimize those organizations any more than advocacy in favour of the legal goals of domestic terror groups will tend to legitimize those groups. Nor is there reason to believe that any such legitimation will lead to greater acts of terrorism by a foreign as compared to a domestic organization. Accordingly, like its *ipse dixit* regarding the scope of the legitimation rationale, the court's bald disclaimer that it does not 'suggest' that the legitimation rationale does not apply to domestic terrorist organizations is futile.

Finally, it should be emphasized that the legitimation rationale is so capacious that it encompasses not just advocacy tending to legitimize terrorist groups, but also speech that would tend to legitimize any organization that engaged in criminal activity, including political organizations such as the American Communist Party as it existed in the 1950s. American free speech doctrine has properly become more protective of radical dissent since 1951, when, in the *Dennis* case cited above, the court upheld the conviction of the leaders of the American Communist Party for conspiracy to advocate the overthrow of the Government of the United States.[42] It is most unfortunate that a key rationale of *Humanitarian Law Project* provides grounds for undercutting First Amendment protection of dissent in the United States. Of course, it is by no means certain that courts will use this rationale to uphold prosecutions of independent advocacy that 'tends to legitimize' criminal organizations, including political ones. Still, this dangerously broad rationale 'lies about like a loaded weapon'[43] that might well be used in fearful times to uphold suppression of dissent that, with hindsight of calmer times, will be seen as a mistake.[44]

## III Reconstructing Humanitarian Law Project

Was there a way in which this case could have been decided without destabilizing key aspects of American free speech doctrine? We believe that there was.

One obvious way was for the court to have actually applied the level of scrutiny it said was applicable to the case, and to have held that the government failed to show that banning the plaintiffs' speech was 'necessary to further' the interest in combatting terrorism. Admittedly, the court would have had to swallow hard to reach this conclusion. As Justice Breyer acknowledges in his dissent, it *might* be the case that the plaintiffs' speech would free up assets with which the FTOs can then devote to terroristic ends. It is well established, however, that under 'strict' or any other searching form of scrutiny, even reasonable speculation that speech 'might' cause serious harm is insufficient to warrant its suppression.[45]

The better approach, however, would have been for the court to have expressly held that the ban on the plaintiffs' speech was subject to the lenient scrutiny it actually applied. Contrary to Justice Breyer, the speech and association that the plaintiffs wanted to engage in was not 'the kind of activity to which the First Amendment ordinarily offers its strongest protection'.[46] Rather, as we now explain, it was 'the kind of activity to which the First Amendment ordinarily offers', at most, only modest protection.

Because the plaintiffs wished to act in coordination with – i.e. in association with – FTOs rather than simply advocating on their behalf independently, the court should have treated the case as being primarily about the right of association rather than, as it did, predominately about speech with the right of association treated merely as an afterthought. As Chapter 4 explained in more detail, there is no right to associate with a terrorist organization, even to promote its lawful ends. Once this case is seen for what it really was – an unmeritorious right of association claim – it becomes apparent, for reasons we will explain, that the free speech claim at most should have triggered the deferential scrutiny that the majority actually utilized.

We say 'at most' because it could be argued that the plaintiffs had no cognizable free speech claim because any such claim was subsumed in their free association claim. It is true that First Amendment cases involving the 'cognate' rights of free speech and right of association will, despite significant overlap, often involve distinct elements as well. In this case, however, the elements of the plaintiffs' free speech claim – the desire to speak in coordination with the FTOs – are identical to their right of association claim. If, as we contend, there is no right to 'coordinate' or otherwise associate with a terrorist organization, then a free speech claim based on identical elements should arguably be foreclosed. Arguing against this position is that in other areas of constitutional law the court has allowed independent claims based on the same factual elements; it has done so, for instance, in some cases involving free speech and freedom of religion claims.[47] But in those cases, although the activity claimed to be protected might be identical, *the interests* underlying each claim are distinct. In contrast, the free speech and freedom of association claims at issue in *Humanitarian Law Project* would, unlike a case asserting free speech and freedom of religion claims, seem to involve basically the same interests. However, for the sake of analysis, we will assume that the plaintiffs have a free speech claim distinct from their right of association claim. But, as we now discuss, the free speech interests implicated by the ban on the activity in which the plaintiffs wanted to engage are fairly modest. This restriction should, accordingly, have been subjected to a correspondingly modest level of scrutiny.

Individuals have an exceedingly strong free speech interest in advocating in favour of political organizations, even terrorist ones. Engaging in public discourse to try to persuade our fellow citizens 'that groups that the government says are bad guys are actually good guys'[48] is a 'core political expression' and entitled to the 'strongest protection' under the First Amendment. But, as the majority in *Humanitarian Law Project* properly emphasized, the material support provision does not restrict advocacy in favour of FTOs except to the extent that the advocacy is under 'the control and direction' of the FTO. The pertinent question, then, is precisely what free speech interests the plaintiffs have in such coordinated advocacy.

Key to analysing the free speech interests at stake is recognizing that, although the plaintiffs may share many of the views of the FTO, their interest in engaging in advocacy under 'the control and direction' of the FTO is not primarily in expressing the plaintiffs *own views*. Rather, it is in helping the FTO effectively express *its* views. Similarly, the plaintiffs' interests in training members of an FTO on how to use the law to peacefully resolve disputes, or teaching them how to petition international bodies for relief, does not primarily advance the plaintiffs' own expressive interest, but rather those of the FTO and its members. If these derivative, instrumental interests have any First Amendment salience distinct from a right of association claim, they are manifestly not of the same magnitude as the interest of individuals in expressing their own views on matters of public concern,[49] an interest in no way burdened by the material support prohibition so long as the plaintiffs act independently of the FTO.[50] Accordingly, the dissent was wrong to apply strict scrutiny, the standard applicable to content-based restrictions on public discourse, just as the majority was wrong to insist that the applicable standard required the government to show that the ban on the plaintiffs' speech was 'necessary to further' the interest in combatting terrorism.

What, then, was the level of scrutiny that the court should have found applicable to ban the plaintiffs' speech? In answering this question, it is instructive to compare the plaintiffs' free speech on behalf of FTOs to lawyers speaking on behalf of their client.[51] There are, of course, important differences between these two types of speech. It is telling, however, that these differences lie mostly in *the reasons* the government might have to regulate the speech at issue, for instance, in combatting terrorism as compared to protecting clients or the administration of justice. With regard to the speaker's free speech interests, in contrast, there is considerable similarity in that with respect to both types of speech, the interests are largely, if not exclusively, instrumental to, and derivative of, those on whose behalf they are speaking.[52]

Unlike the rigorous scrutiny applicable to content-based restriction on public discourse, restrictions on lawyers speaking *on behalf of a client* are generally subject to only modest scrutiny, even when the lawyer is speaking to the public on a matter of public concern.[53] This suggests that the majority in *Humanitarian Law Project* was, despite its talk about the government having the burden to show that the restriction was 'necessary to advance' the government's interest in combatting terrorism, right to actually apply a similarly modest level of scrutiny. In particular, similar to the scrutiny applicable in cases involving restrictions on speech by lawyers on behalf of their clients, the court was correct in allowing the government to fulfil its evidentiary burden by relying on what Justice Breyer aptly referred to as 'informed speculation' that the restriction would advance the government's interest.

Under this lenient level of scrutiny, the court could have accepted as sufficient to meet the government's evidentiary burden the congressional findings and the executive branch affidavit stating that the help the plaintiffs' speech provided to FTOs would free up resources, which then could be devoted to the organization's terrorism. With no need to bolster this argument to meet a 'more demanding' level of the scrutiny, the court could have pretermitted the dangerous legitimation rationale. Finally, because the standard was already deferential, the court could have also avoided the problematic discussion of the need for specific deference to the political branches in areas of national security and foreign affairs. In sum, by treating this case primarily as the right of association case that it was, the modest nature of any independent free interests at stake would have become apparent. The court could have then disposed of the free speech claim without destabilizing free speech doctrine.[54]

## Conclusion

It would be most unfortunate if terrorism were to claim among its victims the rigorous protection of dissent currently provided by American free speech doctrine. Regrettably, the Supreme Court's decision in *Humanitarian Law Project* v. *Holder* portends such an untoward consequence. It is understandable that the court was loath to strike down a law that the United States Government claimed was necessary to combat terrorism. But this was no excuse for the court's failure to realize that at the heart of this case was really an unmeritorious freedom of association claim and that, consequently, the free speech interests at issue were, at most, modest. If the court had properly conceptualized this case, and had not previously imprisoned itself with an untenably broad rule against content discrimination, it could have upheld the law without weakening the protective structure of American free speech doctrine. Let us hope for a better technical performance the next time the court is faced with a free speech challenge to an anti-terrorism law.

*We would like to thank Professors Robert Post and Eugene Volokh for their help. We would also like to acknowledge that portions of Part I of this Chapter were previously published in the Emory Law Journal as Ashutosh Bhagwat, *Terrorism and Associations*, 63 Emory L.J. 581 (2014).

## Notes

1 561 U.S. 1 (2010). The adage can be traced back to the Nineteenth Century. *See Winterbottom* v. *Wright*, 152 Eng. Rep. 402, 406 (Exch. 1842); *East India Co.* v. *Paul*, 13 Eng. Rep. 811, 821 (P.C. 1849); *United States* v. *Clark*, 96 U.S. 37, 49 (1877) (Harlan, J., dissenting) (*quoting East India Co.*, 13 Eng. Rep. at 811); *Northern Sec. Co.* v. *United States*, 193 U.S. 197, 400-01 (1904) (Holmes, J., dissenting).
2 *Id.* at 8 (quoting 18 U.S.C. §2339A(b)(1) (2006)) (internal quotation marks omitted).
3 18 U.S.C. §2339B(g)(6) (2012).
4 See 8 U.S.C. §1189(a)(1) (2012).
5 *Humanitarian Law Project*, 561 U.S. at 9–10, 15.
6 *Id.* at 14–15.
7 (1) 'train[ing] members of [the] LTTE to present claims for tsunami-related aid to mediators and international bodies'; and (2) 'offer[ing] their legal expertise in negotiating peace agreements between the LTTE and the Sri Lankan government'. *Id.* at 15.
8 *Id.*
9 *Id.* at 6. In addition, the court rejected the claim that when applied to speech the material support statute should be interpreted to require that a defendant intended to further an FTO's illegal activities. *Id.* at 16–18. It also rebuffed the claim that as applied to the plaintiffs the statute was impermissibly vague in violation of the Due Process Clause of the Fifth Amendment. *Id.* at 18–25.
10 *Id.* at 26.
11 391 U.S. 367 (1968).
12 *Humanitarian Law Project*, 561 U.S. at 27.
13 *Id.*
14 *Id.* at 27–28.
15 In holding that a more 'a more demanding standard' standard than the intermediate scrutiny urged by the government was appropriate, the court cites *Texas* v. *Johnson*, 491 U.S. 397, 403 (1989). *Humanitarian Law Project*, 561 U.S. at 28. *Johnson*, in turn, expressly equates this 'more demanding standard' with 'the most exacting scrutiny,' 491 U.S. at 412, a synonym for strict scrutiny. In its usual formulation, strict scrutiny requires the government to show that 'the "regulation is necessary to serve a compelling state interest and that it is narrowly drawn to achieve that end."' *Boos* v. *Barry*, 485 U.S. 312, 331 (1988), quoting *Perry Education Assn.* v. *Perry Local Educators Assn.*, 460 U. S. 37, 45 (1983). See also *Simon & Schuster, Inc.* v. *Members of the N.Y. State Crime Victims Bd.*, 502 U.S. 105, 117 (1992). As discussed in text, the court found that the asserted government interest was 'an urgent objective of the highest order', which would seem to be equivalent to a 'compelling state interest'; it then inquired as to whether the application of the material support law to the speech that the plaintiffs want to engage in was 'necessary to further that interest'. See text accompanying note 17 to 18, below. Differing, however, from the usual formulation of the strict scrutiny standard is the omission of any reference to the requirement that the law be 'narrowly drawn'.
16 *Humanitarian Law Project*, 561 U.S. at 28.
17 *Id.*
18 *Id.* at 30–31.
19 *Id.* at 28, 33, 38.
20 *Id.* at 39.
21 *Id.* at 39–40.
22 *Id.* at 40 (Breyer, J., dissenting).
23 *Id.* at 42.
24 *Id.* at 41, 42, 43, 44, 48, 49, 56, 58.
25 *Id.* at 43 (citing *NAACP* v. *Claiborne Hardware Co.*, 458 U.S. 886, 911 (1982); *De Jonge* v. *Oregon*, 299 U.S. 353, 364 (1937)).

26 *Id.* at 44 (citing *Claiborne*, 458 U.S. at 908; *Scales* v. *United States*, 367 U.S. 203, 229 (1961)). We agree with Justice Breyer to the extent that he means by this statement that some limited use of 'unlawful means' by an organization, such as was the case in *Claiborne Hardware*, is not sufficient to forfeit an individual's right to associate with the organization. As Chapter 4 discusses in more detail, however, Breyer is incorrect that one has a First Amendment right to associate with organizations, such as the FTOs in this case, that regularly and systematically engage in terrorism or other forms of violence, provided that the association is limited to advancing the organizations' peaceful activities. See *id.* at 56.

27 *Id.* at 47–55.

28 *Id.* at 56.

29 *Id.* at 47.

30 *Id.* at 35 (majority opinion).

31 Perhaps it was an attempt to avoid diluting strict scrutiny in these ways that led the court to avoid explicitly referring to the 'more demanding standard' as strict scrutiny. But any such anti-dilution strategy was largely rendered ineffective by the court's adopting as part of this unnamed test the key requirement of strict scrutiny that the government prove that the speech restriction was 'necessary to further' (*id.* at 28) the government's interest, but then holding that speculation rather than solid proof was sufficient to carry this burden. In contrast, the court's pretermitting any discussion of strict scrutiny's 'narrow tailoring' component may have been more effective as an anti-dilution device. Under a strict scrutiny analysis, the requirement that the restriction be narrowly drawn requires the government to show that there is no less speech-restrictive means available that will as effectively serve the government's interest. See, for example, *Boos* v. *Barry*, 485 U.S. 312, 329 (1988). Accordingly, if there was in fact a less speech-restrictive alternative available, avoiding discussion of the narrow tailoring requirement might have been an effective strategy to prevent dilution of the strength of this aspect of strict scrutiny.

32 *Humanitarian Law Project*, 561 U.S. at 33. The court's deference is consistent with other cases implicating national security and/or foreign affairs, in which it has deferred to the political branches. See, for example, *Trump* v. *Hawaii*, 138 S. Ct. 2392, 2419–20; *Korematsu* v. *United States*, 323 U.S. 214, 218–19 (1944).

33 See James Weinstein, *Extreme Speech, Public Order, and Democracy: Lessons from the Masses*, in Extreme Speech and Democracy 23, 40–2 (Ivan Hare and James Weinstein eds. 2009).

34 323 U.S. 214, 217–18 (1944) (determining it was within 'the war power of Congress and the Executive to exclude those of Japanese ancestry from the West Coast war area'). In *Trump* v. *Hawaii*, 2018 U.S. LEXIS 4026, the court at long last formally repudiated *Korematsu*, stating, '*Korematsu* was gravely wrong the day it was decided, has been overruled in the court of history, and – to be clear – has no place in law under the Constitution'. (internal quotation marks omitted).

35 341 U.S. 494, 516–17 (1951) (upholding prosecution of Communist Party leadership as consistent with the First Amendment).

36 *Humanitarian Law Project*, 561 U.S. at 30.

37 *Id.* at 49, 52 (Breyer, J., dissenting).

38 *Id.* at 39 (majority opinion).

39 Instead, the Chief Justice mischaracterizes Breyer's argument in order to avoid it. In criticizing the legitimation rationale, Breyer asserts that '[o]nce one accepts this argument, there is no natural stopping place. The argument applies as strongly to "independent" as to "coordinated" advocacy.' *Id.* at 49–50 (Breyer, J., dissenting). Roberts responds that 'Congress has settled on just such a natural stopping place: …material support coordinated with or under the direction of a designated foreign terrorist organization. Independent advocacy … is not covered.' *Id.* at 31–2 (majority opinion). In speaking of 'no natural stopping point', Breyer was obviously not suggesting that a legislative body might not decide to prohibit only coordinated speech. Rather, he was

warning that once adopted by the court as rationale for suppressing speech, there was no principled basis for limiting constitutional protection to coordinated as opposed to independent speech. That this was the point of Breyer's reference to 'no natural stopping point' is underscored by his observation that 'were the law to accept a "legitimating" effect [as grounds for suppressing speech], the First Amendment battle would be lost in untold instances where it should be won.' *Id.* at 49 (Breyer, J., dissenting).

40 *Brandenburg v. Ohio*, 395 U.S. 444, 447 (1969).

41 *Humanitarian Law Project*, 561 U.S. at 51 (Breyer, J., dissenting).

42 341 U.S. at 516–17.

43 *Korematsu* v. *United States*, 323 U.S. 214, 246 (1944) (Jackson, J., dissenting) (arguing that judicial statements sanctioning a racially discriminatory order could be used for harmful ends in future proceedings).

44 A similar problem exists with another rationale that the court employed to uphold the ban on the plaintiffs' speech. 'Providing foreign terrorist groups with material support in any form,' the court wrote, 'also furthers terrorism by straining the United States' relationships with its allies and undermining cooperative efforts between nations to prevent terrorist attacks'. *Humanitarian Law Project*, 561 U.S. at 32. As with the legitimation rationale, there seems to be no principled way to confine this justification to coordinated as opposed to independent advocacy. Independent advocacy of the legal goals of FTOs by American citizens or organizations, particularly prominent ones, would seem just as likely, arguably even more so, to upset foreign governments subject to attacks by these FTOS; such independent speech would thus strain relationships with allies engaged in cooperative efforts to combat terrorism. Indeed, this rationale is even broader than the legitimation rationale. Not only does it include speech supporting FTO but also encompasses any speech by an American, including blasphemous depictions of Mohammed or burning of a Koran, that deeply offends a foreign government with whom we are engaged in cooperative efforts to combat terrorism or, for that matter, any other cooperative venture of overriding national interest. Accordingly, this rationale would seem to justify suppressing such offensive speech.

45 See, for example, *Brown* v. *Entertainment Merchants Assoc*., 564 U.S. 786, 799–801 (2011). Even under the intermediate scrutiny applicable to commercial speech, speculative assertions that the speech regulation will combat the asserted harm are insufficient. See, for example, *Edenfield* v. *Fane*, 507 U.S. 761, 770–1 (1993).

46 *Humanitarian Law Project*, 561 U.S. at 42 (Breyer, J., dissenting).

47 See, for example, *West Virginia Bd. of Ed.* v. *Barnette*, 319 US 624 (1943).

48 Eugene Volokh, *Speech That Aids Foreign Terrorist Organizations, and Strict Scrutiny*, The Volokh Conspiracy, June 21, 2010 http://volokh.com/2010/06/21/speech-that-aids-foreign-terrorist-organizations-and-strict-scrutiny/.

49 We assume here, consistently with numerous statements and decisions by the United States Supreme Court, that the First Amendment values contributions to democratic self-governance far above other goals such as a lawyer's commercial interest in speaking on behalf of her clients. For more extended explications and defences of this position, *see* Ashutosh Bhagwat, 'Associational Speech', 120 *Yale L.J.* (2011): 979, 991–4; James Weinstein, 'Participatory Democracy as the Central Value of the American Free Speech Doctrine', 97 *Va. L. Rev.* (2011): 491.

50 In this regard it is interesting to note a parallel in the area of court's campaign finance jurisprudence. While it is unconstitutional for government to limit the amount one can spend on independent expenditures in favour of a candidate, expenditures coordinated with a candidate's campaign are considered campaign contributions, which can be strictly limited in amount. See *Buckley* v. *Valeo*, 424 U.S. 1, 46–7 (1976).

51 For another argument analogizing the *Humanitarian Law Project* court's scrutiny to scrutiny of regulations of speech by lawyers, *see* Peter Margulies, 'Advising Terrorism: Material Support, Safe Harbors, and Freedom of Speech', 63 *Hastings L.J.*

(2011): 455. Our reasons for adopting this analogy, however, are quite different from Margulies's: Margulies argues that the analogy between regulating lawyer speech and material support to FTOs is based on the fact that both regulatory schemes target 'information asymmetries'. Margulies, supra note 2348, at 458–9. In contrast, we focus on the similarity in free speech interests between lawyers advocating for their clients and the *Humanitarian Law Project* plaintiffs desire to advocate on behalf of the FTOs in that case.

52 A difference supporting the view that a lawyer has a greater free speech interest to advocate on behalf of clients is that a lawyer's client has an underlying constitutional right (albeit not a First Amendment one) to have her position advocated, either by herself or someone doing so on her behalf. In contrast, it is not at all clear that FTOs, as foreign organizations operating primarily outside of the United States, themselves have any First Amendment rights to advocate even their peaceful, legal goals. See for example, *United States* v. *Verdugo-Urquidez*, 494 U.S. 259, 265–71 (1990) (Fourth Amendment does not protect non-citizens outside the United States); *Kleindienst* v. *Mandel*, 408 U.S. 753, 762 (1972) (unadmitted, non-resident alien has no constitutional right of entry into the United States, and may be excluded because of his political views); *cf. Reno* v. *American-Arab Anti-Discrimination Committee*, 525 U.S. 471, 490–2 (1999) (aliens subject to deportation on other grounds may not challenge their deportation on the grounds that they were targeted because of their speech and political views in violation of the First Amendment). Moreover, to the extent the First Amendment restricts the government from regulating speech by foreign entities outside of the United States, it is to vindicate audience interest of those in the United States, not speaker interests of foreigners wishing to communicate with this audience. See *Lamont* v. *Postmaster Gen.*, 381 U.S. 301, 307 (1965). If foreign entities outside of the United States do not have any cognizable First Amendment interests of their own, which would seem to be the strong implication of the majority opinion in *Humanitarian Law Project*, then the plaintiffs would have significantly less of a free speech interest than lawyers have in advocating on behalf of their domestic clients.

53 See *Gentile* v. *State Bar of Nevada*, 501 U.S. 1030, 1074 (1991) ('the speech of lawyers representing clients in pending cases may be regulated under a less demanding standard'); Margulies, *supra* note 23, at 468.

54 Standing in the way of this solution, however, was the court's view that except for a few categories of speech traditionally unprotected by the First Amendment, such as obscenity and fighting words, all content-based restrictions on speech are subject to strict scrutiny. *United States* v. *Stevens*, 559 U.S. 460, 470–2; *Brown* v. *Entertainment Merchants Assn.*, 564 U.S. 786, 805 (2011). Indeed, it is likely that this approach in part led the court in *Humanitarian Law Project* to hold that some unnamed variant of strict scrutiny was the applicable standard. For criticism of court's extremely capacious view of the rule against content discrimination, see Ashutosh Bhagwat, '*When* "Speech" is not Speech', 78 *Ohio St. L. J.* (2017): 839; James Weinstein, 'Participatory Democracy as The Central Value of American Free Speech Doctrine', 97 *Va. L. Rev.* (2011): 491, 491–7, 508–14; Robert Post, 'Recuperating Free Speech Doctrine', 47 *Stan. L. Rev.* (1995): 1249.

# 9 Free speech and counter-terrorism in Australia

*Keiran Hardy and George Williams*

## I Introduction

Only one democratic nation fails to expressly protect freedom of speech in its constitution or other enforceable national human rights instrument. That nation is Australia. Free speech is readily accepted as an important human right in Australia, as evidenced by ongoing public debate about legal restrictions on offensive speech.[1] But national protection of free speech is confined to constitutional implications and techniques of statutory interpretation. This contrasts with the formal protection afforded through the First Amendment to the United States Constitution, section 2 of the *Canadian Charter of Rights and Freedoms*, and Article 10 of the European Convention on Human Rights, as ratified in the United Kingdom (UK) through the *Human Rights Act 1998* (UK).

The lack of formal protection for free speech and other human rights has allowed Australia's federal parliament to enact many laws in response to terrorism that would be unthinkable in these other countries. This is particularly the case with respect to the intelligence gathering powers of the Australian Security Intelligence Organisation (ASIO), Australia's domestic security service. Australia's counter-terrorism laws impact on free speech through broad criminal offences, strict requirements around operational secrecy, and a lack of protection for intelligence whistle-blowers. In particular, Australia's legal responses to terrorism severely restrict the ability of journalists to report freely on national security matters in the public interest.

In this chapter, we assess the impact of Australia's counter-terrorism laws on freedom of speech. We adopt the meaning given to freedom of expression in Article 19(2) of the *International Covenant on Civil and Political Rights* ('ICCPR'), which states:

> Everyone shall have the right to freedom of expression; this right shall include freedom to seek, receive and impart information and ideas of all kinds, regardless of frontiers, either orally, in writing or in print, in the form of art, or through any other media of his choice.

Australia has ratified the ICCPR and indicated its ongoing support for the instrument,[2] but has not incorporated this or other rights by way of statute.

This inconsistency between the ideals of human rights and their actual protection in domestic law characterizes Australia's unique approach to rights protection.

In Part Two, we explain the extent to which free speech is protected by Australian law, covering its constitutional, common law, and statutory basis. In Part Three, we identify Australia's legal responses to terrorism that impact on free speech, including restrictions on 'advocating' terrorism,[3] and assess that impact. Here, we also address policy programs for countering violent extremism, though these remain underdeveloped in Australia compared to the UK and Western Europe. Such programs can impact on free speech by discouraging forms of expression that are contrary to a country's 'fundamental values'.[4] As addressed by other authors in this collection,[5] the UK's *Prevent* strategy in particular has raised debates about free speech in schools and universities.[6]

In Part Four, we draw lessons and observations from Australia's experience of using counter-terrorism laws to regulate speech. A key theme is that the Australian government has used recurring threats of terrorism to justify increased surveillance powers and a crackdown on intelligence whistle-blowing, which poses significant risks to freedom of the press.

## II Free speech in Australian law

The Australian *Constitution* contains only a few express rights, including the right to trial by jury and freedom of religion.[7] Free speech is protected by the *Constitution* only in a limited way through textual implication. The Constitution states, in ss.7 and 24, that members of the federal parliament must be 'directly chosen by the people'. In two cases, in 1992,[8] the Australian High Court derived from these words an implied freedom of political communication. The court reasoned that the *Constitution* creates a system of representative government, and this necessarily implies that Australians must be free to communicate about political matters, such as the policies of those seeking election to the federal parliament. In *Lange* v. *Australian Broadcasting Corporation*,[9] the High Court set out two questions for determining whether a law is invalid due to the implied freedom:

1. First, does the law effectively burden freedom of communication about government or political matters either in its terms, operation of effect?
2. Second, if the law effectively burdens that freedom, is the law reasonably appropriate and adapted to serve a legitimate end in a manner which is compatible with the maintenance of the constitutionally prescribed system of representative and responsible government?[10]

The first limb demonstrates that this freedom is limited to speech about political matters; it is not a general right to freedom of expression. It does not protect artistic, commercial, personal or academic expression, except where those relate in some way to the government or the election of members of parliament. The second limb is essentially a proportionality test.[11] Neither of these limbs protects an individual right or freedom; rather, they establish a constraint on the federal parliament's lawmaking powers to serve systemic interests in the *Constitution.*

Since those earlier cases, the implied freedom has only been used twice to strike down a law. In 2013, it was used to invalidate a New South Wales law which banned the making of donations to political parties by corporations, unions, and individuals not on the electoral role.[12] In 2017, it was used to invalidate Tasmanian legislation which banned participation in protest activities on business premises.[13] In *Monis* v. *The Queen*, a challenge to the federal offence of using a postal service to menace, harass or offend was unsuccessful after the High Court judges reached a 3:3 split.[14] The accused, later called the Sydney Siege gunman, who held 16 hostages in the Lindt café, had been charged with 13 counts of that offence after writing denigrating letters to the relatives of soldiers killed on active service in Afghanistan.

Limited national protection for free speech is also provided by the principle of legality, a common law rule which guides judicial interpretation of statutes. In a series of cases dating back to *Potter* v. *Minahan*,[15] the High Court recognized a judicial presumption that the legislature does not intend to interfere with fundamental rights and freedoms. This rule of statutory interpretation is considered an aspect of the rule of law.[16] More recently, in *Momcilovic* v. *The Queen*, the court expressed the principle in the following terms:

> It is expressed as a presumption that Parliament does not intend to interfere with common law rights and freedoms except by clear and unequivocal language for which Parliament may be accountable to the electorate. It requires that statutes be construed, where constructional choices are open, to avoid or minimise their encroachment upon rights and freedoms at common law.[17]

The full extent of common law rights protected by the principle of legality is unclear, but free speech is among those typically recognized.[18] The problem comes when parliaments restrict speech or other human rights through 'clear and unequivocal language'. In such a case, where no 'constructional choices are open', the presumption cannot be relied upon.

Statutory protection for human rights exists at the state level in Victoria and the Australian Capital Territory.[19] These include the right to freedom of expression.[20] They provide for weak-form of judicial review, allowing the relevant Supreme Court to issue a declaration of incompatibility or inconsistent interpretation.[21] However, these laws only operate within their own jurisdiction, and so have no impact on legislation enacted by the federal parliament. While crime control is typically a state responsibility, most of Australia's counter-terrorism laws have been enacted by the federal parliament. This was made possible once the states 'referred' their powers in this area to the Commonwealth following the 9/11 attacks.[22]

There is no general statutory protection of free speech at the national level. This contrasts with the statutory protection of other human rights, like those to privacy and freedom from discrimination.[23] In 2011, the federal parliament created a Parliamentary Joint Committee on Human Rights, which allows for pre-enactment scrutiny of bills on human rights grounds.[24] This process has little impact, particularly in the face of political and community pressure to respond strongly to the threat of terrorism.[25] The Parliamentary Joint Committee did not exist at the time when the majority of Australia's counter-terrorism laws were enacted.[26]

The limited protection offered to human rights under Australian law means there may be no remedy even for significant violations. For example, in *Al-Kateb* v. *Godwin*,[27] a majority of the High Court held that there was no constitutional prohibition on legislation permitting the indefinite detention of asylum seekers. One judge described that result as 'tragic', but acknowledged that it was not for the court 'to determine whether the course taken by parliament is unjust or contrary to basic human rights'.

The influence of human rights on Australian law remains very limited. There is no domestic reference point for gauging the impact of counter-terrorism laws on free speech or for post-enactment judicial review. Where legislation violating human rights is challenged, complainants are often forced to rely upon other features of the *Constitution* to argue their case. This can transform concerns over human rights into debates about federalism or judicial power, leaving little or no room for an effective human rights discourse. As Walker notes, this disappointing approach is characteristic of the Australian experience:

> The contrasting emphasis in Australia on the appropriate constitutional capacities of institutions of state, rather than the rights of individuals, certainly produces different, and sometimes (to British perspectives at least) disappointingly solipsistic and positivistic forms of reasoning.[28]

Ultimately, Australia (like other United Nations member states) remains subject to oversight by the United Nations Human Rights Committee ('UN Committee'). This requires the production of five-yearly reports on Australia's implementation of the ICCPR,[29] but this process also has little direct impact. The UN Committee has reported on recurring human rights violations by the Australian government, but only a small percentage of these have been remedied.[30] At times, the process has also been treated with disdain. While in office, former Prime Minister Tony Abbott claimed, in response to UN Committee findings, that Australians were 'sick of being lectured to' by the United Nations.[31]

## III Regulating speech in counter-terrorism

Since 2002, the federal parliament has enacted 70 laws in response to terrorism.[32] Most of these were passed in response to 9/11 and the London bombings, but many new laws (nine tranches of legislation) have also been enacted in response to the threat of Islamic State.[33] These recent laws have introduced some of Australia's most controversial measures, including the stripping of citizenship for dual nationals involved in terrorism.[34] Kent Roach has described this extensive lawmaking as a form of 'hyper-legislation'.[35]

Many of these controversial laws have been made possible because Australia lacks national protection for human rights. In this section, we identify Australia's legal responses to terrorism that impact on freedom of speech and assess that impact. We also address policy programs for countering violent extremism, although these have received far less attention and investment in Australia compared to the UK and Western Europe. Australia's approach to counter-terrorism is characterized by an almost exclusive focus on coercive legal measures, at the expense of longer-term approaches that would address the underlying causes of terrorism.

### *A Advocating terrorism*

In 2014, in response to the threat from foreign fighters, the federal parliament enacted a new offence for advocating terrorism. This came relatively late compared to the UK's offence for encouraging and glorifying terrorism, which was enacted after the 2005 London bombings.[36] The Australian offence has yet to be prosecuted or tested in court.

Section 80.2C of the *Criminal Code Act 1995* (Cth) ('Criminal Code') makes it an offence punishable by five years' imprisonment to advocate the doing of a terrorist act or terrorism offence where the person is reckless as to whether another person will engage in that conduct as a result.[37] A person advocates terrorism if he or she 'counsels, promotes, encourages or urges the doing of a terrorist act or the commission of a terrorism offence'.[38]

This offence goes beyond the law of incitement; it extends to reckless encouragement and the 'promotion' of terrorism. The offence could apply to reckless statements of support for terrorism posted online, even where the person has no intention to commit a terrorist act or to encourage others to do so. The idea of 'promotion' could even plausibly extend to a 'retweet' or Facebook 'like' of another person's words, meaning that an individual could be prosecuted for words they did not say, but simply repeated or agreed with. While the actions of Islamic State and other terrorist organizations cannot be morally justified, it does not follow that criminal liability should attach to speech acts which fall below the level of intentionally inciting violence.

Advocating terrorism also provides a basis for proscribing terrorist organizations. Under div 102 of the Criminal Code, an organization may be declared a terrorist organization in regulations made by the Governor-General.[39] Once this occurs, a number of serious offences apply to the organization's members (including membership, recruitment, and training).[40] For the purposes of div 102, advocating terrorism includes situations where:

> the organisation directly praises the doing of a terrorist act in circumstances where there is a substantial risk that such praise might have the effect of leading a person (regardless of his or her age or any mental impairment that the person might suffer) to engage in a terrorist act.[41]

This is especially problematic because it criminalizes speech based upon the reaction of someone who suffers from a mental impairment. A person could be imprisoned for membership of a terrorist organization because the leader of that organization praised terrorism in circumstances where there was a risk that somebody with a severe mental disability or illness might act on their words. It also means that a person could be imprisoned for words said by the leader of an organization which they do not even agree with.

Since 2007, advocacy of terrorism has also provided the basis for refusing classification of publications. The *Classification (Publication, Films and Computer Games) Act 1995* (Cth) ('Classification Act') sets out Australia's classification scheme, allowing for the regulation of dangerous and obscene publications. Section 9A of that Act provides that a publication, film or computer game must be refused classification if it advocates terrorism. The Classification Act relies on the same definition of advocacy as div 102, meaning that a publication can be refused classification on the grounds that somebody with an intellectual disability or mental illness might act on words or images that praise terrorism. These provisions have the capacity to censor a broad range of publications.[42] Few potential audience members are excluded from an assessment of whether a publication creates a risk of terrorism.

### *B Urging violence*

A series of offences in the Criminal Code criminalizes speech acts that 'urge violence'. These provide penalties of up to seven years' imprisonment where a person urges another person to overthrow the constitution or the government, interfere with parliamentary elections or a referendum or use force or violence against a group on the grounds of 'race, religion, nationality, national or ethnic origin or political opinion'.[43] There is a defence for acts done in good faith, such as encouraging someone to lawfully bring about a change to the law.

These offences are an amended version of sedition laws that were enacted in 2005 in response to the London bombings. Those earlier laws were rushed through parliament over the course of a few weeks, with little opportunity for scrutiny or debate. Indeed, at the time of their passage, it was widely regarded that the sedition offences were flawed and significantly impacted on free speech. The offences required only 'reckless' rather than intentional encouragement, they were not linked to the use of force or violence, and there was no consideration given to genuine academic, scientific or artistic work. Despite this, the laws were enacted on the understanding that they would soon be reviewed by the Australian Law Reform Commission ('ALRC'). Unsurprisingly, the ALRC identified extensive problems with the laws,[44] but it was not until 2010 that they were amended into their current form.[45]

### *C Operational secrecy*

Many of Australia's counter-terrorism powers have strict legal requirements around operational secrecy. A key example is section 35P of the *Australian*

*Security Intelligence Organisation Act 1979* (Cth) ('ASIO Act'), which criminalizes the disclosure of information relating to 'Special Intelligence Operations' (SIOs). An SIO is an undercover operation approved by the Attorney-General in which ASIO officers are granted immunity from civil and criminal liability.[46] However, immunity is not granted for acts that cause death or serious bodily injury, involve a sexual offence, cause serious property damage or constitute torture.[47]

Section 35P provides a penalty of five years' imprisonment where a person discloses any information relating to an SIO and the effect of that disclosure 'will endanger the health or safety of any person or prejudice the effective conduct of a special intelligence operation'.[48] The person need only be reckless as to whether the disclosure will cause such harm, and the penalty is doubled to 10 years if the person intends or knows that such harm will result.[49]

The original wording of this offence did not include any requirement as to the harm caused by disclosing the information. It would have applied to any person who disclosed information relating to an SIO. This caused a significant backlash from media organizations, as it exposed journalists to significant criminal penalties. A journalist would face five years in prison if they happened to reveal information that related to one of ASIO's special undercover operations, provided they were aware of a substantial risk that the information could relate to an SIO. This would have had a significant chilling effect on the ability of journalists to report on dawn raids, terrorism prosecutions, misconduct by intelligence agencies, and other national security matters in the public interest. The offence was amended to its current form after an inquiry and a report made by the Independent National Security Legislation Monitor (INSLM).[50] Even as amended, the offence may continue to have a chilling effect on media reporting since it includes no exemption for information disclosed in the public interest. The offence has been criticized by the Media, Entertainment and Arts Alliance as an 'outrageous attack on press freedom' and 'not worthy of a healthy, functioning democracy'.[51]

Similar offences apply to other counter-terrorism powers. Part III, div 3 of the ASIO Act allows the Attorney-General to issue 'questioning and detention warrants'. These allow ASIO to question a person for up to 24 hours in eight-hour blocks, and to detain them for up to a week for that purpose.[52] The powers are for intelligence gathering rather than investigation, which allows non-suspects – including family members or even members of the public – to be detained. While the warrant is in force, and for a period of two years after their detention, the person faces five years in prison for disclosing any information about the warrant.[53]

The power to issue 'Preventative Detention Orders' (PDOs) is another extraordinary Australian invention. Under div 105 of the Criminal Code, the Australian Federal Police may detain a person for up to 48 hours to prevent an imminent terrorist attack or preserve evidence in relation to a recent attack.[54] The period of detention can be extended to 14 days under state legislation.[55] During that time, a detainee may call a family member, employer or roommate, but they are not permitted to reveal anything about their detention, except to say they are 'safe but … not able to be contacted for the time being'.[56] If they disclose any information about their detention – including the bare fact that they are being detained – they can be imprisoned for up to five years.[57] It is even an offence for one parent to tell the other parent about their child's detention if the detainee has not separately contacted the second parent.[58] These extraordinary powers led the Council of Australian Governments Counter-Terrorism Review Committee ('COAG Review') to describe PDOs in the following terms:

> [T]he concept of police officers detaining persons 'incommunicado' without charge for up to 14 days, in other than the most extreme circumstances, might be thought to be unacceptable in a liberal democracy. There are many in the community who would regard detention of this kind as quite inappropriate. To some, it might call to mind the sudden and unexplained 'disappearances' of citizens last century during the fearful rule of discredited totalitarian regimes.[59]

The PDO powers and ASIO's questioning and detention powers were set to expire under a sunset clause in 2015. Before this time, the COAG Review and the INSLM recommended the repeal of PDOs, and the INSLM recommended the repeal of ASIO's detention powers.[60] However, both sets of powers were extended in response to the threat of foreign fighters.

### *D Intelligence disclosures*

The first of the Australian government's responses to foreign fighters included wide-ranging reforms on ASIO's surveillance powers and offences for disclosing intelligence information.[61] These laws did not relate directly to foreign fighters or Islamic State, but were framed as being urgently needed in response to that threat.[62] It is now an offence punishable by 10 years' imprisonment for the employee of an intelligence agency to reveal information obtained in the course of their duties.[63] It is an offence punishable by three years' imprisonment to copy or record information outside the terms of the person's employment.[64]

Intelligence officers should be punished for leaking information to foreign agents or intentionally harming Australia's national security. However, these offences should also be viewed in light of the lack of legal protections for intelligence whistle-blowers. The *Public Interest Disclosure Act 2013* (Cth) effectively provides no protection for genuine whistle-blowers who reveal intelligence information in the public interest.[65] There is no legal mechanism for an intelligence officer to reveal, for example, that ASIO officers had tortured a suspect or embezzled money from an undercover operation. Disclosures about misconduct must be made internally to the organization in the first instance or to the Inspector-General of Intelligence and Security (IGIS).[66] These mechanisms may be appropriate in many cases, but there is no separate protection for intelligence whistle-blowers where these alternatives prove inadequate and it is in the public interest for serious misconduct or corruption to be revealed.

### *E Metadata*

Journalists are also at risk from Australia's data retention laws, which require communications service providers to retain customers' metadata for a period of two years.[67] Metadata includes information other than the substance or contents of a communication – such as the time, date, and location of a phone call, email or SMS. This data may be obtained by ASIO, state and federal police, and other 'enforcement agencies' without a warrant.[68]

Access to journalists' metadata could expose their sources, including government officials and intelligence whistle-blowers. After media organizations raised these concerns, a 'journalist information warrant' process was introduced. Access to journalists' metadata is now restricted unless 'the public interest in issuing the warrant outweighs the public interest in protecting the confidentiality of the identity of the source'.[69] However, journalists are not able to contest these warrants (including because the journalist need not be notified of the warrant's existence), and the regime will not prevent journalists' metadata from being collected in connection with criminal offences like section 35P of the ASIO Act.[70]

### *F Foreign interference*

In 2017, the Turnbull government introduced a bill to combat foreign interference in Australia's political system.[71] The laws are widely regarded as targeting the influence of the Chinese Communist Party in Australia.[72] (At the time of writing, the laws are under review by the Parliamentary Joint Committee on Intelligence and Security).

Among other changes, the new laws will significantly increase the scope of existing espionage offences.[73] That offence will now apply where a person 'deals' with information concerning Australia's 'national security' and the information is or will be made available to a foreign interest.[74] 'Dealing' with information includes not only communicating information, but also copying, possessing or receiving it.[75] National security is defined to include not only security and defence but also anything relating to Australia's 'political, military or economic relations' with other countries.[76] A maximum penalty of life imprisonment will apply where the person *intends* to prejudice Australia's national security. A maximum of term of 25 years' imprisonment will apply where the person is *reckless* as to whether such harm will be caused. Penalties of 25 years' imprisonment can also be imposed even where the information does not of itself relate to national security.[77]

This means that a journalist could face 25 years in prison for receiving information leaked from a government official, even if that information is not sensitive for national security reasons. The offences would apply where the journalist intends to publish the information in the public domain, and is reckless as to whether disclosing the information would harm Australia's national security or advantage a foreign government. Indeed, the offences would be triggered before the journalist decided to publish the information. This is an extraordinary expansion of the existing espionage offences, which apply to recording or communicating sensitive national security information with an intent to harm Australia's security or defence.[78] If enacted in their current form, the amendments are likely to have a significant chilling effect on the ability of media organizations to report freely on Australia's foreign relations, including on political and economic matters.

### *G Countering violent extremism*

In contrast to the UK and Western Europe, programs for countering violent extremism (CVE) have received far less attention and investment in Australia. Australia's counter-terrorism laws are framed by broader strategy documents relating to CVE,[79] but these have attracted little national attention. When the Abbott government came to office in 2013, it initially dropped the $9.7 million in funding that the prior Labor government had allocated to a grants program for 'building resilient communities'. Rather than encouraging communities to work together, Prime Minister Abbott employed the divisive rhetoric of joining 'team Australia'.[80]

The Abbott government later allocated $64 million for CVE, though the majority of these funds are to be spent on policing activities. Aside from a small community-based grants program,[81] similar to that introduced under Labor, the coalition government's CVE strategy remains unclear and undeveloped. Prime Minister Malcolm Turnbull has, instead, focused on strengthening an already extensive legal framework. He has signalled a strong stance on terrorism, announcing new laws at press conferences in front of Special Forces soldiers and tactical police units.[82]

The lack of investment in CVE means that Australia has not experienced the same controversies as the UK over the impact of CVE strategies on free speech in schools and universities.[83] However, this does not signal any positive aspects of the Australian experience, but rather a lack of commitment to addressing the underlying causes of terrorism.

## IV Trends and lessons

This section identifies several trends and lessons from Australia's experience of using counter-terrorism laws to regulate speech. The lack of national protection for human rights has allowed the federal parliament to make extraordinary incursions into free speech and other human rights in ways that would not be possible in other countries. This has impacted most significantly on the freedom of journalists to report on national security matters.

### *A Inadequate parliamentary process*

A recurring theme in Australian counter-terrorism is the lack of appropriate scrutiny given to laws passed by the federal parliament. The 2014 legislation that introduced the offence of advocating terrorism provides a key example. The bill was 160 pages long and introduced some of the most controversial changes to Australian counter-terrorism law in nearly a decade.[84] And yet, interested parties were given just eight days to make submissions to the Parliamentary Joint Committee on Intelligence and Security. Following that, the bill was given just three days' scrutiny in parliament, with debate in the House lasting just two days.

For laws impacting on free speech, a concerning practice has been to enact offences recognized as problematic, and then later seek to have them remedied. This was first seen with the Howard government's sedition offences in 2005. Those laws passed through parliament on the understanding that they would be reviewed by the ALRC after their enactment. It was not until five years later that many of the problems with those laws were remedied. During that time, the law continued to provide for lengthy jail terms.

A similar process occurred with section 35P of the ASIO Act. It was only after the legislation was enacted that sections of the media became aware of the substantial impact that section 35P was likely to have on journalists by criminalizing the disclosure of information relating to SIOs. A vocal media and community reaction led Opposition Leader Bill Shorten to write to the Prime Minister to request that section 35P be referred to the INSLM. After the INSLM's report, the offence was finally amended. The media's slow reaction to the danger was lamented by Laurie Oakes, a prominent Australian political journalist, in his 2015 Melbourne Press Freedom Dinner. Oakes conceded that journalists 'didn't take up the issue at the start, and once the law is on the statute books winding it back becomes a very difficult proposition'.[85] However, that delayed reaction was in large part due to the speedy passage of the legislation through parliament.

Pre-enactment scrutiny of legislation by the Parliamentary Joint Committee on Human Rights has also proven ineffective in protecting free speech. In examining the 2014 foreign fighters legislation, the committee reported that the offence of advocating terrorism impacted unduly on free speech, and that the government had failed to offer a legitimate objective behind the legislation.[86] It identified a range of existing criminal offences, including incitement, that would perform a similar function without impacting on free speech to the same degree. It concluded that 'the advocating terrorism offence provision, as currently drafted, is likely to be incompatible with the right to freedom of opinion and expression'.[87] However, the legislation was enacted in its original form.

Even where significant violations of free speech are identified in legislation, little is done to remedy this in parliament. This is a significant failing, as the legislation cannot be challenged in the court's, post-enactment, on the grounds of free speech or other human rights.

### *B Promoting terrorism*

Intentionally encouraging criminal acts has long been criminalized through the law of incitement. An important feature of Australia's new advocacy offence is that it criminalizes the broader notion of 'promoting' terrorism. An organization can also be listed as a terrorist organization if it 'praises' terrorism where there is a substantial risk that the words will lead another person, even one with a severe mental illness, to engage in terrorism. These standards are similar to those of the UK's offence of encouraging terrorism, which includes reckless encouragement and statements which glorify the commission or preparation of terrorist acts.[88]

The precise meaning of 'promoting' terrorism is yet to be determined by an Australian court, but the wording is certainly broader than incitement, which requires intentional encouragement to commit a crime. In that respect, the Australian law (like the UK offence) goes beyond United Nations Security Council Resolutions 1624 and 2178, which called on member states to criminalize the incitement of terrorism.[89] The Australian government has not given sufficient justification as to why free speech should be undermined by a broader offence for 'advocating' terrorism when this is not mandated internationally.

In counter-terrorism, the Australian and the UK governments have moved beyond criminalizing speech acts that would lead directly to harm being caused to others. Rather, any speech acts which create a *risk* of terrorism – including promoting, praising, and glorifying terrorism – are now considered fair game for the criminal law. This is an unacceptable widening of the state's power to criminalize speech in a modern democracy. For speech to attract criminal sanction, the person uttering the words should intend that harm be caused.

### *C Preventing speech*

A similar widening of the criminal law on speech can be seen in expanded offences for intelligence disclosures and espionage. The penalties for these offences have been dramatically increased. Previously, an intelligence officer who disclosed classified information would face two years in prison – now they can face up to 10 years in prison.[90] The offence of espionage currently attracts a maximum penalty of 25 years' imprisonment.[91] If the current foreign interference bill is passed, the maximum penalty will be life imprisonment.

More importantly, amendments to these offences signal a focus on preventing disclosures from happening in the first place, rather than punishing a person for disclosing information. In addition to increased penalties, intelligence officers now face three years in prison for 'unauthorised dealing with records'.[92] This includes any copying or recording of information outside the terms of the person's employment. If the current foreign interference bill is passed, it will be a criminal offence merely to *receive* or *possess* information that could harm national security, where that information will be disclosed to a foreign principal.[93] There will also be a separate offence, punishable by 15 years' imprisonment, for preparing an act of espionage.[94] This will apply to *any* conduct that a person does in preparation for espionage.

This move towards preventing rather than punishing speech acts parallels that seen earlier in the development of preparatory terrorism offences. Whereas the criminal law has traditionally punished people for engaging in harmful conduct, counter-terrorism laws have consistently targeted early preparatory activities for terrorism, including training, membership of organizations, and collecting terrorist documents. This has been conceived as a form of 'pre-crime' based on notions of risk and actuarial justice.[95] Recent amendments to Australia's national security laws suggest a similar trend in the criminal law on speech.

### *D Freedom of the press*

Recent additions to Australia's counter-terrorism laws have a substantial impact on freedom of the press. These include section 35P of the ASIO Act, the mandatory data retention scheme, and the current foreign interference bill. Other offences ensure strict operational secrecy of PDOs and ASIO's questioning and detention warrant powers.[96] Each of these laws restricts the ability of journalists to report on national security matters. There are no exemptions for information disclosed in the public interest. National whistle-blower protections in the *Public Interest Disclosure Act 2013* (Cth) apply only to public employees; not to journalists, private citizens or other employees of private companies.

These laws are not necessarily an intentional crackdown on journalists. Rather, they reflect a crackdown on intelligence whistle-blowing in the wake of the WikiLeaks and Snowden revelations. The Australian government's approach has been opportunistic, framing these secrecy laws as a response to terrorism when, otherwise, there would not necessarily be the same public appetite for criminalizing leaks from government agencies. Another important factor is growing concern over Chinese influence in Australia.[97]

The Australian government has maintained that it will not use these laws to prosecute a journalist for 'doing their job', but such assurances are not sufficient to protect a free press. Instead, they make journalists dependent upon a government decision not to prosecute them, including in respect of information that may be damaging or embarrassing to the government. The effect is to make journalists think twice about whether to report on national security matters. Instead, the law itself must be crafted so that prosecuting journalists for official reporting in the public interest is not possible.

Similar issues around press freedom have been debated in the UK,[98] but these tensions are characteristic of Australia's responses to terrorism in a way not fully replicated elsewhere. One commentator has argued that foreign interference laws will make Australia the 'worst in the free world for criminalising journalism'.[99] A coalition of Australia's largest media organizations believe that 'fair scrutiny and public interest reporting is increasingly difficult and there is a real risk that journalists could go to jail for doing their jobs'.[100]

## V Conclusion

Australia's record of enacting counter-terrorism laws reveals a disturbing lack of sensitivity to the importance of freedom of speech. Laws have been enacted that enable people to be jailed for expressing opinions and for conduct that falls well short of an incitement to violence. The impact upon freedom of speech is particularly evident in the case of media freedom. Australia's laws in this regard sit uneasily with the recognition of the United Nations Human Rights Committee that an uncensored press remains 'one of the cornerstones of a liberal democracy'.[101]

Freedom of the press remains a core aspect of free speech more generally, which needs to be protected for a democracy to function effectively. Press freedom is a measure of how much a society values the rights to freedom of opinion and expression. It is necessary to ensure the enjoyment of other human rights, as an uncensored press allows information and ideas about public policy, including on national security matters, to be communicated freely between citizens and their elected representatives. A free press is necessary to maintain both an informed public and an accountable government.

Australia's legal responses to terrorism signal a distinct lack of concern for these values. Disclosure offences, with significant penalties, restrict the publishing of information which relates to operational matters, even if revealing that information would be in the public interest. It would take a brave journalist in Australia to reveal significant wrongdoing by employees of ASIO or another intelligence agency – even if it involved seriously harming suspects, large-scale fraud, systemic corruption or other misconduct.

Recent amendments and proposals also reveal that Australia, like the UK, now treats speech acts, which create a risk of harm, to be worthy of criminal sanction. A series of offences now criminalizes acts preparatory to some predicted future disclosure – including the copying, recording, receiving, and possessing of national security information. This parallels the previous development of other counter-terrorism laws that criminalize preparatory action.

Many of these laws are possible because Australia is unique amongst democratic nations in lacking anything akin to a national Bill of Rights. This has enabled the enactment of 70 counter-terrorism laws, which include wide-ranging powers and offences not found elsewhere. Australia faces a serious ongoing threat of terrorism and has experienced some recent attacks.[102] However, it is notable that Australia has not experienced the same number of recurring attacks or fatalities as other countries, and yet continues to develop some of the world's most extraordinary legal responses to terrorism.

## Notes

1 See, for example, Katherine Gelber, 'Free speech is at risk in Australia, and it's not from section 18C', *The Conversation*, 13 September 2016; David Leyonhjelm, '18C debate highlights the ethnic threat to free speech', *Australian Financial Review*, 30 March 2017; Andrew P Street, 'The 18C battle is about making hate speech acceptable, not protecting free speech', *Sydney Morning Herald*, 1 March 2017.

2 See Australian Government, *International Covenant on Civil and Political Rights: Australia's Sixth Report to the United Nations Human Rights Committee* (2016).

3 *Criminal Code Act 1995* (Cth), s80.2C.

4 Home Office, *Prevent Strategy* (Cm 8092, June 2011) 107.

5 See, respectively, chapters by Cram, Fenwick and Fenwick, and Neal in this collection.

6 See, for example, Chris Kyriacou *et al.*, 'British Muslim University Students' Perceptions of Prevent and its impact on their sense of identity' *Education, Citizenship and Social Justice* 12, no. 2 (2017); Sue Hubble, 'Freedom of Speech and Preventing Extremism in UK Higher Education Institutions (House of Commons Briefing Paper CBP 7199, 20 May 2015).

7 *Australian Constitution*, ss80, 116. See generally George Williams and David Hume *Human Rights under the Australian Constitution* (Oxford University Press, 2nd edition, 2013).

8 *Nationwide News Pty Ltd* v. *Wills* (1992) 177 CLR 1; *Australian Capital Television Pty Ltd* v. *Commonwealth* (1992) 177 CLR 106.

9 *Lange* v. *Australian Broadcasting Corporation* (1997) 189 CLR 520.

10 The words 'in the manner which' were added by *Coleman* v. *Power* (2004) 220 CLR 1.

11 In *McCloy* v. *New South Wales* (2015) 257 CLR 178, the court applied a proportionality test more directly, holding that the second limb should assess whether the burden on political speech is suitable, necessary, and adequate in its balance of competing objectives.

12 *McCloy* v. *New South Wales* (2015) 257 CLR 178.

13 *Brown* v. *Tasmania* [2017] HCA 43.

14 *Monis* v. *The Queen* (2013) 249 CLR 92.

15 *Potter* v. *Minahan* (1908) 7 CLR 277. See particularly *Coco* v. *R* (1994) 179 CLR 427.

16 *Electrolux Home Products Pty Ltd* v. *Australian Workers Union* (2004) 221 CLR 309.

17 *Momcilovic* v. *The Queen* (2011) 245 CLR 1.

18 See James Spigelman, 'The Common Law Bill of Rights: First Lecture in the 2008 McPherson Lectures – Statutory Interpretation and Human Rights' (Speech delivered at the University of Queensland, Brisbane, 10 March 2008) 23.

19 *Charter of Human Rights and Responsibilities Act 2006* (Vic); *Human Rights Act 2004* (ACT).

20 *Charter of Human Rights and Responsibilities Act 2006* (Vic), s15; *Human Rights Act 2004* (ACT), s16.

21 *Charter of Human Rights and Responsibilities Act 2006* (Vic), s36; *Human Rights Act 2004* (ACT), s32.

22 *Australian Constitution*, s51(xxxvii).

23 *Privacy Act 1988* (Cth); *Racial Discrimination Act 1975* (Cth); Sex Discrimination Act 1984 (Cth).

24 *Human Rights (Parliamentary Scrutiny) Act 2011* (Cth), s7.

25 See G Williams and D Reynolds, 'The Operation and Impact of Australia's Parliamentary Scrutiny Regime for Human Rights' *Monash Law Review* 41, no. 2 (2015): 469.

26 See George Williams, 'The Legal Legacy of the War on Terror' *Macquarie Law Journal* 12 (2013): 3, 7; George Williams, 'A Decade of Australian Anti-Terror Laws' *Melbourne University Law Review* 35, no. 3 (2011): 1136.

27 *Al-Kateb* v. *Godwin* (2004) 219 CLR 562.

28 Clive Walker, 'The Reshaping of Control Orders in the United Kingdom: Time for a Fairer Go, Australia!' *Melbourne University Law Review* 37, no. 1 (2013): 143, 147.

29 Australian Government, *International Covenant on Civil and Political Rights*, above n. 2.

30 See, for example, Anna Cody and Maria Nawaz, 'UN slams human rights record: what this means for Australia', *SBS News*, 10 November 2017; Ben Doherty, '"Unacceptable": UN Committee damns Australia's record on human rights', *Guardian*, 19 October 2017.

31 Lisa Cox, 'Tony Abbott: Australians "sick of being lectured to" by United Nations, after report finds anti-torture breach', *Sydney Morning Herald*, 10 March 2015.
32 By 2013, the federal Parliament had enacted 61 counter-terrorism laws: see Williams, 'The Legal Legacy of the War on Terror', above n. 26; Williams, 'A Decade of Australian Anti-Terror Laws', above n. 28. A further nine pieces of legislation have been enacted in response to the recent threat of foreign fighters and related homegrown terrorism: *National Security Legislation Amendment Act (No 1) 2014* (Cth), *Counter-Terrorism Legislation Amendment (Foreign Fighters) Act 2014* (Cth), *Telecommunications (Interception and Access) Amendment (Data Retention) Act 2015* (Cth), *Australian Citizenship Amendment (Allegiance to Australia) Act* 2015 (Cth), *Counter-Terrorism Legislation Amendment Act (No 1) 2016* (Cth), *Criminal Code Amendment (High Risk Terrorist Offenders) Act 2016* (Cth), *Anti-Money Laundering and Counter-Terrorism Financing Amendment Act 2017* (Cth), *Transport Security Legislation Amendment Act* 2017 (Cth), *Telecommunications and Other Legislation Amendment Act 2017* (Cth).
33 Ibid.
34 *Australian Citizenship Amendment (Allegiance to Australia) Act* 2015 (Cth).
35 Kent Roach, *The 9/11 Effect* (Cambridge, Cambridge University Press, 2011), 309.
36 *Terrorism Act 2006* (UK), s1.
37 *Criminal Code Act 1995* (Cth), s80.2C(1).
38 *Criminal Code Act 1995* (Cth), s80.2C(3).
39 *Criminal Code Act 1995* (Cth), s102.1(1).
40 See *Criminal Code Act 1995* (Cth), s102.2–102.8.
41 *Criminal Code Act 1995* (Cth), s102.1(1A)(c).
42 See further David Hume and George Williams, 'Advocating Terrorist Acts and Australian Censorship Law' *Public Law Review* 20 (2009): 37; David Hume and George Williams, 'Australian Censorship Policy and the Advocacy of Terrorism' *Sydney Law Review* 31 (2009): 381.
43 *Criminal Code Act 1995* (Cth), ss80.2–80.2D.
44 Australian Law Reform Commission, *Fighting Words: A Review of Sedition Laws in Australia* (2006).
45 *National Security Legislation Amendment Act 2010* (Cth).
46 *Australian Security Intelligence Organisation Act 1979* (Cth), s35K.
47 *Australian Security Intelligence Organisation Act 1979* (Cth), s35K(e).
48 *Australian Security Intelligence Organisation Act 1979* (Cth), s35P(1).
49 *Australian Security Intelligence Organisation Act 1979* (Cth), s35P(2).
50 Independent National Security Legislation Monitor, *Report on the Impact on Journalists of Section 35P of the ASIO Act* (Australian Government, 2015).
51 Media, Entertainment and Arts Alliance, *MEAA Says National Security Law an Outrageous Attack on Press Freedom in Australia* (26 September 2014) Media, Entertainment and Arts Alliance Media Room www.meaa.org/mediaroom/meaa-says-national-security-law-an-outrageous-attack-on-press-freedom-in-australia; Christopher Warren and Mike Dobbie, *Surveillance State Seizes Its Chance*, (24 October 2014) Walkley Foundation http://walkleys.com/surveillance-state-seizes-its-chance
52 See *Australian Security Intelligence Organisation Act 1979* (Cth), ss34E, 34G.
53 *Australian Security Intelligence Organisation Act 1979* (Cth), s34ZS.
54 *Criminal Code Act 1995* (Cth), 105.4.
55 See, for example, *Terrorism (Police Powers) Act 2002* (NSW), s26K(2); *Terrorism (Preventative Detention) Act 2005* (Qld) s12(2).
56 *Criminal Code Act 1995* (Cth), s105.35.
57 *Criminal Code Act 1995* (Cth), s105.41(1).
58 *Criminal Code Act 1995* (Cth), s105.41(4A).
59 Council of Australian Governments, *Council of Australian Governments Review of Counter-Terrorism Legislation* (Australian Government, 2013) 68.

60 Ibid., Bret Walker SC, *Declassified Annual Report: 20 December 2012* (Australian Government, 2013) 67, 106. The Parliamentary Joint Committee on Intelligence and Security, *ASIO's Questioning and Detention Powers* (March 2018) has also since recommended the repeal of this power.
61 *National Security Legislation Amendment Act (No 1) 2014* (Cth).
62 See Keiran Hardy and George Williams, 'Australian Legal Responses to Foreign Fighters' *Criminal Law Journal* 40, no. 4 (2016): 196, 204.
63 *Intelligence Services Act 2001* (Cth), ss39–40B.
64 *Intelligence Services Act 2001* (Cth), ss40C–40M.
65 See Keiran Hardy and George Williams, 'Terrorist, Traitor or Whistleblower? Offences and Protections for Disclosing National Security Information in Australia', *University of New South Wales Law Journal* 37, no. 2 (2014): 784.
66 *Public Interest Disclosure Act 2013* (Cth), s34.
67 *Telecommunications (Interception and Access) Act 1979* (Cth), s187A.
68 *Telecommunications (Interception and Access) Act 1979* (Cth), ss175, 178.
69 *Telecommunications (Interception and Access) Act 1979* (Cth), ss180L, 180T(2)(b).
70 *Telecommunications (Interception and Access) Act 1979* (Cth), s176A(3B).
71 National Security Legislation Amendment (Espionage and Foreign Interference) Bill 2017 (Cth).
72 See, for example, Andrew Greene, 'China blasts Australia over Turnbull government's foreign interference laws', *ABC News*, 6 December 2017; 'Turnbull admits China "tensions" over foreign interference laws', *SBS News*, 12 April 2018.
73 *Criminal Code Act 1995* (Cth), s91.1.
74 *National* Security Legislation Amendment (Espionage and Foreign Interference) Bill 2017 (Cth), cl 17.
75 National Security Legislation Amendment (Espionage and Foreign Interference) Bill 2017 (Cth), cl 10.
76 National Security Legislation Amendment (Espionage and Foreign Interference) Bill 2017 (Cth), cl 16.
77 National Security Legislation Amendment (Espionage and Foreign Interference) Bill 2017 (Cth), cl 17.
78 *Criminal Code Act 1995* (Cth), s91.1.
79 Council of Australian Governments, *Australia's Counter-Terrorism Strategy: Strengthening Our Resilience* (Australian Government, 2015); Australian Government, *Preventing Violent Extremism and Radicalisation in Australia* (2015).
80 See L Cox, '"You don't migrate to this country unless you want to join our team": Tony Abbott renews push on national security laws' *Sydney Morning Herald* (18 August 2014).
81 Australian Government, *Living Safe Together* (2017) Available at: www.livingsafe-together.gov.au/aboutus/Pages/current-activities.aspx (last accessed 14 May 2018).
82 See Keiran Hardy, 'Caution needed as the government expands the military's role in counter-terrorism', *The Conversation*, 18 July 2017.
83 See Kyriacou, above n. 6; Hubble, above n. 6.
84 See Hardy and Williams, above n. 62, 202.
85 Laurie Oakes, 'These Things Can't Just Be Left to Government' (Speech delivered at the Melbourne Press Freedom Dinner, 25 September 2015).
86 Parliamentary Joint Committee on Human Rights, *Examination of Legislation in Accordance with the Human Rights (Parliamentary Scrutiny) Act 2011 (2014) – Fourteenth Report of the 44th Parliament* (2014), 51.
87 Ibid. 52.
88 *Terrorism Act 2006* (UK), s1.
89 SC Res 1624, UN SCOR, 60th sess, 5251st mtg, UN Doc S/RES/1624 (14 September 2005); SC Res 2178, UN SCOR, 69th sess, 7272nd mtg, UN Doc S/RES/2178 (24 September 2014).

90 *Intelligence Services Act 2001* (Cth), ss39–40B.
91 *Criminal Code Act 1995* (Cth), s91.1.
92 *Intelligence Services Act 2001* (Cth), ss40C–40M.
93 National Security Legislation Amendment (Espionage and Foreign Interference) Bill 2017 (Cth), cl 17.
94 Ibid.
95 See, for example, Lucia Zedner, 'Pre-Crime and Post-Criminology?' *Theoretical Criminology* 11, no. 2 (2007): 261; Jude McCulloch and Sharon Pickering, 'Pre-Crime and Counter-Terrorism: Imagining Future Crime in the "War on Terror"' *British Journal of Criminology* 49, no. 5 (2009): 628.
96 *Criminal Code Act 1995* (Cth), s105.41; *Australian Security Intelligence Organisation Act 1979* (Cth), s34ZS.
97 See, e.g., Greene, above n. 72.
98 See, for example, Roy Greenslade, 'The data protection bill is yet another legal threat to UK press freedom', *Guardian*, 4 December 2017.
99 Johan Lidberg, 'New bill would make Australia worst in the free world for criminalising journalism', *The Conversation*, 1 February 2018.
100 Media, Entertainment & Arts Alliance, *Joint Media Organisations Submission on National Security Legislation Amendment (Espionage and Foreign Interference) Bill 2017* (2017) Available at: www.meaa.org/mediaroom/joint-media-organisations-submission-on-national-security-legislation-amendment-espionage-and-foreign-interference-bill-2017/
101 Human Rights Committee, General Comment No 34: Article 19: Freedoms of Opinion and Expression, 102nd sess, UN Doc CCPR/C/GC/34 (12 September 2011) 3.
102 Australian National Security, *National Terrorism Threat Advisory System* (2017) Available at: www.nationalsecurity.gov.au/securityandyourcommunity/pages/national-terrorism-threat-advisory-system.aspx. See, for example, Michael Safi and Shalailah Medhora, 'Sydney CBD Siege: Hostages Forced to Hold Black and White Islamic Flag', *Guardian* (Sydney), 15 December 2014; Nick Ralston, 'Parramatta Shooting: Curtis Cheng Was on His Way Home When Shot Dead', *Sydney Morning Herald*, 3 October 2015.

# 10 Addressing terrorism in New Zealand's low threat environment

*Andrew Geddis and Elana Geddis*

## Introduction

New Zealand is fortunate that terrorism represents more of a latent threat than a lived reality. Its government currently assesses the risk of a terrorist incident as 'low' (meaning, 'possible, but not expected'), with that assessment only changing from 'very low' in 2014. The country's last experience of a terrorist act causing injury or death was the 1985 bombing of Greenpeace's flagship 'The Rainbow Warrior' by agents of the French secret services. And while New Zealand's Security Intelligence Service (SIS) maintains a 'counter terrorism risk register' of some 30 to 40 individuals who are 'assessed to represent a potential threat to New Zealand, related to terrorism',[1] the number on this list remains relatively static. Nor are all of these individuals considered likely to carry out an act of terrorism within New Zealand; instead, some are potential supporters of off-shore terrorist activities. Therefore, while no society can today be considered totally immune, terrorism poses much less of a perceived risk in New Zealand rather than in the other countries included in this collection.

A number of factors may account for this state of affairs. New Zealand is a comparatively peaceful society[2] where domestic social schisms have, by-and-large, been managed without escalating to the level of armed violence. And as a committed supporter of the international rule of law and the role of the United Nations, New Zealand has, largely, stood apart from those military actions in the Middle East not specifically authorized by the UN Security Council. Where New Zealand has contributed armed forces to deployments, such as the United Nations Assistance Mission in Afghanistan, these have been portrayed primarily as non-combat training and infrastructure development exercises.[3] Finally, New Zealand does not harbour significant numbers of individuals in thrall to the sorts of extreme ideologies that have fuelled recent terrorist actions globally. Only a scattering of micro-groups espouse the far-right beliefs that have motivated many domestic terror attacks in the USA and Europe, while the country's relatively small Muslim population[4] contains few adherents to the more radical Salafi-jihadism interpretation of that faith. Deliberate immigration and refugee policy – which then can be enforced due to New Zealand's geographic isolation and corresponding difficulty to physically access – has sought to prevent individuals harbouring such ideologies from entering into or remaining in the country.[5]

Consequently, there has not been a strong felt need for new laws and practices to combat the threat of terrorism; nothing akin to the United Kingdom's Prevent and Channel programmes has been publicly suggested or discussed in the New Zealand context. While individual institutions have adopted strategies to counter violent extremism[6] there is no publicly declared centralized approach to identifying and combatting radicalization. Those very few occasions where terrorist-related activities have taken place within New Zealand have been addressed through the individual application of long-standing criminal law provisions rather than specific terror-related offences.

However, internal and external factors have conspired to produce some limited legal changes;[7] the nation's media regularly reports on overseas attacks while its intelligence and law enforcement services (coordinated through the 'Combined Threat Assessment Group') emphasize that, despite its remoteness, New Zealand can never consider itself to be immune from such incidents. Wanting to be seen to be keeping the population safe from even a remote risk of terrorist harm provides a strong political motivation to act. Additionally, and as already noted, New Zealand is assiduous in meeting its international obligations and expectations.[8] Where the global community has called for its members to take action to combat terrorism the government responded quickly by amending the law. New Zealand may thus be described as a fast follower in responding to international terrorism.

Against this background, the current chapter recounts those changes to New Zealand's legislative framework, judicial processes, and intelligence agencies that have occurred during the 'war on terror' era. In the immediate wake of 9/11, New Zealand enacted the Terrorism Suppression Act 2002. Despite an ever-growing list of organizations designated as 'terrorist entities' under its provisions, this legislation has had virtually no practical effect, as its wording has been found seriously wanting. Of more importance was the enactment in 2014 of 'terrorist fighters' legislation, designed to prevent New Zealand's citizens from participating in acts of international terrorism. Not only has this legislation actually been applied to individual New Zealand passport holders, its provisions have also contributed to a creeping development of secret court proceedings within the New Zealand legal system. Finally, the increasing visibility of terrorism as a potential threat to national security has also contributed to the reorganization and progressive empowerment of New Zealand's security services, the SIS, and the Government Communications Security Bureau. While these combined changes are comparatively limited, they have raised important questions relating to freedom of association, rights to justice, and appropriate limits for state action in the name of security.

## Terrorism and New Zealand's general law

The challenge of terrorism primarily has been managed within New Zealand's existing legal framework. Its criminal law has long proscribed virtually all forms of 'terrorist' activity. Causing physical harm to others, much less death, provides for a myriad of possible offences. Likewise, intentional damage to property is an offence.[9] Issuing any threat to kill or harm another[10] or a written threat to destroy property[11] is an offence irrespective of the motive for doing so.[12] And various forms of terrorist propaganda may constitute an incitement to commit these offences[13] or, as shall be seen, are rendered unlawful by New Zealand's general prohibition on possessing or distributing 'objectionable' publications.[14]

These criminal law prohibitions are applied in light of the New Zealand Bill of Rights Act 1990 (NZBORA), which guarantees civil and political rights, such as freedom of expression, freedom of association, and freedom of religion. The executive branch of government may only impose such reasonable limits upon these rights as can demonstrably be justified in a free and democratic society.[15] While parliament still retains the sovereign lawmaking power to legislate inconsistently with the NZBORA,[16] the courts are instructed to interpret all legislation in a 'rights friendly' manner where they can do so.[17] Not only does this matrix require an explicit balancing exercise between individual rights and societal harms when applying existing laws, it also informs decisions on whether that law is adequate or desirable. For example, in 2007 New Zealand repealed the Crimes Act 1961 provisions relating to sedition,[18] which criminalized various actions carried out with 'an intention to incite violence or create public disorder, for the purpose of resisting or disturbing constituted authority'.[19] This repeal took place in the wake of a successful prosecution for seditious conspiracy of an individual who smashed an axe through the window of the Prime Minister's electorate office in protest against recently enacted legislation and left a leaflet calling for others 'to take similar action'.[20] The New Zealand Law Commission subsequently recommended the sedition offences be removed from the statute books as they represented too great a threat to the exercise of NZBORA protected rights, recognising that:[21]

> … in these days of terrorism, while it might be tempting to look to sedition to contribute to the suppression of terrorism, in our view, the seditious offences in the Crimes Act 1961 are not an appropriate response to the threat of terrorism. There are other ways of dealing with such conduct.

The government subsequently agreed, and parliament voted for repeal by a 114–7 margin.

Consequently, increased concerns regarding terror attacks did not require a fundamental rethink of New Zealand's legal order, nor have they been treated as a trumping argument that overrides competing rights concerns in policy discourse. Instead, those very few terror-related activities that have occurred in New Zealand have been addressed through the application of general criminal law provisions. In particular, the last couple of years have seen the courts deal with individuals possessing terrorist propaganda and a curtailed attempt at launching a copycat 'lone wolf' terrorist attack.

### *Prosecutions for possessing and distributing terrorist propaganda*

As noted, New Zealand's geographic isolation enables it to maintain tight and effective controls over who may physically enter the country. However, the internet's distribution of information poses obvious problems when combatting terrorist propaganda. The increasing sophistication of on-line material produced by terrorist groups also increases the risk that it will radicalize individuals already in the country, leading them to conduct a lone wolf attack (as discussed below). Nevertheless, New Zealand has no specific legislation dealing with the simple possession or distribution of terrorist propaganda. Rather, this issue has been dealt with under the country's general censorship regime.[22]

In particular, the Films, Videos, and Publications Classification Act 1993 deems a publication (including a computer file) to be 'objectionable' if it 'promotes or supports, or tends to promote or support ... acts of torture or the infliction of extreme violence or extreme cruelty'.[23] In making this judgment, the extent to which a publication 'promotes or encourages criminal acts or acts of terrorism' must be considered.[24] Consequently, material such as an Islamic State (IS) video praising the depicted execution of captured troops will be classified differently to a documentary film containing the same images. Where a publication is deemed objectionable, it is an offence to have made, possessed, distributed or exhibited it, whether or not the person concerned knew or had reasonable cause to believe it was objectionable.[25] This legal framework has been applied three times in the last two years to individuals found to be in possession of objectionable images and video recordings produced by IS depicting graphic acts of torture and murder. Two of these cases involved simple possession of a small amount of IS-sourced material, for which a home detention sentence was given. The third, however, related to a man who had downloaded and stored a large number of electronic files before attempting to distribute them to others. This offending resulted in a jail term of three years and nine months.[26]

The Court of Appeal subsequently upheld this sentence.[27] In the course of doing so, it rejected the Crown's invitation to apply sentencing decisions under the Terrorism Act 2006 (UK) for the offence of dissemination of a terrorist publication, holding the elements of that offence to be too different to be of assistance.[28] However, the court did find that 'the purpose of communicating or encouraging support [for terrorist activities], even if relatively passive support, nevertheless significantly aggravates th[e] offending';[29] 'especially troubling is that the distribution might have created support for an organization that promotes and encourages criminal acts or acts of terrorism'.[30] Those factors justified a strong deterrent response. Consequently, not only is terrorist propaganda more likely to be classified as objectionable under New Zealand's censorship regime, but its intended effect is then treated as an aggravating factor at sentencing.

### *Rehabilitating a radicalized 'lone wolf'*

In the 17 years since 9/11, only one person has appeared before New Zealand's courts for embarking on what can be classified a terrorist action. While many details of the case are suppressed to protect the offender's identity, media reports recount that a teenager radicalized by online material intended to use a car and a knife to inflict civilian casualties in a now unfortunately familiar manner.[31] However, he aborted his actions without inflicting any injuries, reportedly 'because he did not have the means to kill enough people'. After his arrest and guilty plea to eight general criminal charges, the sentencing judge deliberately chose a rehabilitative sentence rather than one primarily aimed at deterrence. Consequently, a two-year term of intensive community supervision under judicial monitoring was imposed, with conditions that the teenager be subject to GPS monitoring and live at a specified address. A further condition required him to undergo regular counselling by a member of the local Muslim community. Subsequent reports indicate that this rehabilitative focus has been successful; in particular, the offender has developed an enthusiasm for golf.[32] Importantly, this response was a matter of individual judicial discretion under general sentencing law, rather than part of any formal, societal-wide policy on combatting radicalization.

### *Expanding New Zealand's legal responses to terrorism*

Despite New Zealand's general laws proving flexible enough to capture and respond to terrorism related activities, domestic and external pressures have resulted in changes to New Zealand's legislative framework, its judicial processes, and the operations of its security agencies. The rest of the chapter considers these particular matters.

## The Terrorism Suppression Act 2002 (and its discontents)

Prior to 2001, New Zealand already had adopted a range of terror-related legislative measures as a result of its commitment to various international treaties.[33] It had also enacted the International Terrorism (Emergency Powers) Act 1987 in the wake of the Rainbow Warrior sinking, granting the police special powers in the event of an 'international terrorist emergency'. And in May of 2001, the government had introduced the Terrorism (Bombing and Financing) Bill in parliament to implement its obligations under the International Convention for the Suppression of Terrorist Bombings and the International Convention for the Suppression of Financing of Terrorism. This bill took on new importance following the 9/11 attacks and the subsequent issuance of United Nations Security Council Resolution 1373, which mandated broad-ranging state action against the financing of terrorism, and required all United Nations member states to report within 90 days on steps taken to implement the resolution. In response, the bill was hastily and significantly amended before its final enactment as the renamed Terrorism Suppression Act 2002.

This legislation has a twofold focus. First, it introduces a number of specific terrorism-related offences. Second, it sets out a process whereby individuals, groups, and organizations may be designated as terrorist entities or associated entities, and imposes legal prohibitions on taking actions that support such entities. Common to both legislative objectives is the concept of a 'terrorist act', which the legislation defines in terms of its aim, purpose, and intent.[34] In short, a terrorist act is defined as follows: Any action aimed at inflicting certain specified serious harms carried out 'for the purpose of advancing an ideological, political, or religious cause' and intended to either 'induce terror in a civilian population' or 'unduly compel or force a government or an international organization to do or abstain from doing any act'.

The Terrorism Suppression Act then makes it an offence to engage in a terrorist act,[35] finance a terrorist act,[36] recruit for or facilitate the actions of a group that engages in terrorist acts,[37] or harbour a person who has committed a terrorist act.[38] However, these various offence provisions are of doubtful efficacy, due to their failed application to the so-called 'Operation 8' arrests made in 2007.[39]

Operation 8 was a joint SIS and police surveillance operation, which concluded that a group of left-wing and Māori activists were engaged in armed and terrorism-related training activities. A subsequent large-scale – and, as shall be seen, somewhat flawed – police response resulted in 41 search warrants being executed and 18 arrests made. The police then sought the Solicitor General's permission to file charges against those arrested for participating actively in a group planning to commit a terrorist act. However, permission was denied because:

> … in examining the relevant provisions of the Terrorism Suppression Act I have concluded that legislation is unnecessarily complex, incoherent, and, as a result, almost impossible to apply to the domestic circumstances observed by the Police in this case.[40]

The Solicitor General further stated that the main reason for his decision was a lack of sufficient evidence to establish the 'very high standard that a group or entity was planning or preparing to commit a terrorist act as that term is defined in the legislation'.[41]

As a consequence, and in keeping with New Zealand's approach of using the general law to combat concerns about terrorism, those arrested were instead charged with unlawful possession of firearms[42] and membership of an organized criminal group.[43] Following a Supreme Court ruling that the police had obtained some surveillance evidence unlawfully,[44] charges against all but four of the accused were dropped. The remaining four defendants were then found guilty, but only on the lesser unlawful possession of firearms charges. Subsequently, the country's Independent Police Complaints Authority issued a report on the Operation 8 searches, which held that some were 'contrary to law, unjustified and unreasonable'.[45] This report led to a personal apology being made by the Police Commissioner to the communities most affected by the police action, at which he shared a cup of tea with one of the four convicted individuals.[46] The Terrorism Suppression Act has not been cited in any subsequent policing operations, while initial government proposals to amend the legislation to address the Solicitor General's concerns have not eventuated.

The legislation has been used, however, to designate a range of overseas organizations as 'terrorist entities' or 'associated entities'. Property belonging to such a designated entity may be seized;[47] financial institutions must report suspicions about property that may belong to such a designated entity;[48] and it is a criminal offence to provide financial or other help to such a designated entity.[49] It also is an offence to knowingly recruit for a group that is a designated entity,[50] or participate in a group for the purpose of enhancing its ability to carry out a terrorist act, knowing or being reckless as to whether the group is a designated entity.[51] Simple membership of a designated entity, however, is not an offence. The decision to designate an organization a terrorist entity (one suspected of planning or carrying out a terrorist act) or an associated entity (one that helps facilitate a terrorist entity in the carrying out a terrorist act) finally rests with the country's Prime Minister. She or he need only 'believe on reasonable grounds' that an entity meets the legislation's definition to make the relevant designation. While such decisions are susceptible to judicial review,[52] the legislation requires that any 'classified security material' used in making the decision be withheld from the designated entity in any such legal proceedings.[53]

In practice, entities are designated under the Terrorism Suppression Act in two ways. Any person or group that the United Nations has listed as a terrorist entity pursuant to UNSC resolutions 1267/1989/2253/1988 automatically become a designated entity.[54] New Zealand has made its own, separate determination that an additional 20 organizations are terrorist entities, reflecting its general obligation under UNSC resolution 1373 to outlaw the financing of, participation in, and recruitment to terrorist groups. These particular organizations have been selected not only because there is evidence that they have committed terrorist acts, but also because it is believed designation by New Zealand will contribute in some way to the international security environment.[55] Notably, however, none of the 20 cases for designation allege that the group in question has any presence in or support from New Zealand or that it poses any direct threat of carrying out terrorist acts within New Zealand. More significant is that they all have been designated as terrorist entities by New Zealand's closest security partners.

The consequences of designation as a terrorist entity under the Terrorism Suppression Act raise obvious potential freedom of association issues.[56] Simply contributing funds to such an entity, for instance, could attract a prison term of up to seven years. However, in practice, the designation process has had no real impact in New Zealand. No charges have been laid in relation to dealings with designated entities, and no property of such entities has been seized. Instead, the designation process serves a largely symbolic purpose; as the Prime Minister stated recently when adding two organizations to the list of designated terrorist entities, New Zealand's actions primarily operate as a signal that it 'supports international efforts to combat global terrorism'.[57]

## Countering Terrorist Fighters Legislation Bill

While the risk of terror attacks occurring in New Zealand has never been considered any greater than low, individual New Zealanders have been actively involved with designated terrorist entities in places such as Iraq and Syria.[58] Such 'terrorist fighters' raise two concerns. First, their overseas experiences may further radicalize them, resulting in their carrying out terrorist acts upon their return to New Zealand. Second, the country has an obligation under UN Security Council Resolution 2178 to prevent its citizens from participating in terrorist actions anywhere in the world. Citing these reasons, in 2014 the government introduced the Countering Terrorist Fighters Legislation Bill into parliament to provide greater powers to monitor those suspected of planning to join terrorist entities overseas, as well as to disrupt their travel. The legislation then progressed through the parliamentary lawmaking process under urgency; the usual six-month long select committee process was reduced to allow the public only two days in which to make submissions, while the bill was enacted into law some two weeks after first introduction.[59] This legislative haste was the subject of strong political criticism, with the main opposition party at the time claiming:[60]

> The process that the Government followed was appalling, pushing through legislation with intrusive powers in just over a week with only two days allowed for public submission. For a bill of this significance, this timeframe was unacceptable....

Such parliamentary disagreement over security-related legislation was unusual, as international obligations and domestic political calculation had previously combined to create a broad consensus on the need for changes to the law.

The finally enacted legislation had two main features. First, it authorized the SIS to conduct covert video surveillance on private property for the detection, investigation or prevention of any actual, potential or suspected terrorist act, or facilitation of a terrorist act. Second, it extended the powers of the Minister of Internal Affairs to suspend or cancel the passport of any individual believed on reasonable grounds to pose a danger to New Zealand's or another country's national security because of an intention to engage in or facilitate a terrorist act.[61] Such individuals are not, however, prohibited from returning to New Zealand from overseas;[62] indeed, the minister is required to issue them with an emergency travel document to permit them to do so.[63]

Public concerns were expressed about both aspects of the legislation. Conferring greater surveillance powers on the SIS was challenged as an unnecessary extension of their domestic role. However, as parliament recently had legislated to enable the police and other enforcement agencies to obtain 'visual surveillance warrants' permitting covert video recording on private property,[64] the effect of the new law was simply to enable the SIS to conduct such surveillance directly rather than relying on the police to do it for them. The issue of empowering a minister to withhold or cancel passports from suspected terrorist fighters was more contentious. In particular, there were concerns that the ministerial power might be used against individuals wanting to become involved in non-terrorist activities in places such as Syria and Iraq. The historical analogy of the International Brigade fighting on the republican side in the Spanish Civil War was raised as an argument against wide governmental powers to interfere with New Zealanders' travel.[65] However, the minister in charge of the bill reassured parliament that the bill would not have this effect:[66]

> … this bill does not go anywhere near as far as the Australian legislation, which seeks to ban Australian citizens from even travelling to certain areas unless they have lawful excuse. This legislation does not prevent New Zealanders from travelling to these areas, although obviously we would strongly advise against it. As I said, in order to have a passport cancellation occur, the Minister must be satisfied that the person intends to engage in, or facilitate, a terrorist act. That is the core concept to which all these provisions apply.

## The rise of 'secret court' procedures

An additional feature of the Countering Terrorist Fighters Legislation Bill was the extension of closed or 'secret' procedures to court proceedings challenging the legality of any decisions made under the new powers it contained.[67] These proceedings allow cases to be heard in closed court, without the complainant, the public or the media present. They raise serious questions with respect to both natural justice and the broader principle of 'open justice' – under which 'justice should not only be done, but should manifestly and undoubtedly be seen to be done'.[68] That principle has been recognized as going 'to the very existence and health of [New Zealand's] political and legal institutions'.[69] The adoption of such procedures reflects the New Zealand government's growing sensitivity to the potential disclosure of classified security information in court, particularly where such information has been obtained through relationships with foreign security agencies.

Unlike some comparable jurisdictions, New Zealand has no generally applicable procedures for closed court hearings in cases involving classified security information.[70] Where classified security information may be relevant to issues in a civil or criminal trial, it has been dealt with under established public immunity rules regarding the disclosure and admissibility of evidence[71] and the inherent jurisdiction of the court to regulate its own procedures.[72] However, beginning with the Terrorism Suppression Act 2002, a limited number of specific closed court procedures have been created by statute. These procedures require the court to hear the government's case in the absence of the affected party, his or her legal advisors or members of the public. Classified security information may be relied upon in evidence, even though it has not been disclosed to the affected party or his/her legal team. The legislative procedures seek to strike the illusory 'perfect balance' between the government's interests in protecting classified security information and an individual's right to fairness and natural justice.[73]

The New Zealand government's position has consistently been that, while closed court procedures do infringe on natural justice and fair trial rights, that infringement is necessary, justified, and proportionate in the interests of national security.[74] The New Zealand Human Rights Commission,[75] the Law Society,[76] and other critics and commentators have disagreed.[77] In 2013, the Human Rights Commission took the unusual step of drawing its concerns about a proposed new closed court procedure to the Prime Minister's attention, noting:

> Despite the opinion of the Attorney-General to the contrary (as a Court can appoint a special advocate), the Commission considers that the limitation is unjustified and a disproportionate response to the need to protect classified security information in this context [...].

### *Features of the statutory closed court procedures*

Six closed court procedures have been created by statute in New Zealand.[78] While they share a number of common elements, '[t]here are inconsistencies in approach, and new regimes have been enacted in response to particular issues rather than in a coherent and principled way.'[79]

Each of the procedures apply to court proceedings where classified security information has been involved in the decision-making process or will be relied on in court. 'Classified security information' is defined by reference both to the nature of the information and the risks that might arise from its disclosure. The threshold question of whether a particular piece of information meets the statutory definition is determined by the government. The procedures allow for classified security information to be withheld from the person affected and his or her legal advisors, to be heard by the court in their absence. A summary of the information must be provided to the person affected, but in most cases that summary is prepared by the government and must be approved by the court without modification.

In an effort to minimize the unfairness inherent in these restrictions, and drawing on practice in the United Kingdom and Canada, three of the statutory regimes provide for the appointment of special advocates.[80] Such advocates are appointed by the court at its discretion. They are authorized to prepare the affected party's case, examine and cross-examine witnesses, make submissions to the court, and assist in any settlement of the case. The special advocates are given access to classified security information but, once they have accessed it, they are prevented from communicating with the affected party or his or her lawyers, except with the approval of the court. These significant limitations on the special advocate's rôle have lead the New Zealand Law Society to conclude that the use of special advocates 'should always be a measure of last resort' and '[i]n all but the most unusual of circumstances, the Crown should be able to make its decisions and prepare its case without substantial reliance on 'national security' information'.[81]

Because of their nature, any proceedings under the closed court procedures are themselves usually confidential and are not reported. To date, there has been only one reported proceeding regarding the application of these procedures: *A* v. *Minister of Internal Affairs.*[82] The proceeding concerned A's appeal and judicial review of a decision by the minister to suspend, and later cancel, her passport on the grounds that he believed that she intended to facilitate a terrorist act in an overseas country.

A preliminary application in 2017 challenged the minister's decision not to disclose certain information to A under the closed court procedures contained in sections 29AA to 29AC of the Passports Act 1992. The High Court held that the closed procedures did apply to A's case, but noted:[83]

> A statutory provision that material and potentially decisive evidence in a court proceeding is to be presented to the Court and considered in the absence of the party adversely affected is as flagrant a breach of the fundamental right [to natural justice] recognized in s27 of [the New Zealand Bill of Rights Act 1990] as could be contemplated.

Dobson J further commented:[84]

> The whole of our common law tradition, as bolstered by the rights and protections recognised by [the New Zealand Bill of Rights Act 1990] render the procedures under s29AB an anathema to the fundamental concepts of fairness.

But, he was forced to concede:[85]

> … the reality is that Parliament has recognised the justification for the use of that procedure in defined circumstances and the Court had no option but to apply it in the present case.

### *Protection of foreign intelligence information*

One striking feature of the New Zealand closed court procedures is the extent to which they protect intelligence information gathered by foreign governments. In all of the statutory regimes, protection of foreign intelligence information is an independent ground for the non-disclosure of classified security information – which is not reliant on any separate finding of prejudice to New Zealand's national security. Foreign intelligence information can be withheld where the government that provided the information does not consent to its disclosure or where disclosure would be likely to prejudice the entrusting of such information to a future New Zealand government.[86]

This deference to what is sometimes referred to as the 'control' or 'confidentiality principle' stems from New Zealand's membership of the global intelligence-sharing alliance known as 'Five Eyes'.[87] This alliance, comprising the United States, the United Kingdom, Canada, Australia, and New Zealand, actively cooperates in collecting and sharing intelligence information. As the smallest partner within the alliance, with potentially the most to gain, it is little surprise that the New Zealand intelligence community places particular importance upon it. In reliance on a briefing from New Zealand intelligence agencies, the New Zealand Law Commission, for example, concluded that:[88]

> The notion of protecting national security must also take into account the importance of New Zealand's intelligence gathering partnerships and the confidence our allies have in us as well as the methodologies and sources used and the potential consequences of these being made public.

The High Court, in *A* v. *Minister of Internal Affairs*, at first appeared less ready to accept this conflation of New Zealand's 'national security' and the retention of 'the confidence of our allies', suggesting:[89]

> There may arguably be grounds for questioning the extent of national security concerns in cases where no issue of New Zealand's own national security arises. In those cases, including the present one, a potentially less compelling concern is likely to arise that disclosure of the information held will compromise the processes for investigation or availability of reciprocal exchange of information with security services in other countries.

Those hesitations were consistent with somewhat more trenchant concerns expressed by judges in the United Kingdom. Lord Judge CJ, in the case of *Mohamed* v. *Secretary of State for Foreign and Commonwealth Affairs*,[90] expressed considerable discomfort at the weight that was placed on the 'confidentiality principle' by the Secretary of State in that case. He rejected the suggestion that the confidentiality principle was a rule of law,[91] and laid down a clear marker to the United Kingdom government that:[92]

> … in our country, which is governed by the rule of law, upheld by an independent judiciary, the confidentiality principle is indeed subject to the clear limitation that the government and the intelligence services can never provide the country which provides intelligence with an unconditional guarantee that the confidentiality principle will never be set aside if the courts conclude that the interests of justice make it necessary and appropriate to do so.

However, in a subsequent decision, addressing the grounds for withholding information in more detail, the High Court demonstrated greater openness to the government's extended notion of national security.[93] Although asserting that the court would apply a 'rigorous test' in reviewing whether information should be withheld under the closed procedures,[94] Dobson J admitted that, under the terms of the statute,[95]

> the standard to be applied creates a low threshold for accepting the Crown's position. The court need only be satisfied that it is desirable (that is, less

> than necessary) to concur with the withholding of [classified security information] for its protection.

Dropping the threshold even further, he accepted the Crown's argument that it could be 'desirable' to protect foreign intelligence information even where the foreign source of the information had consented to its disclosure or the information was already in the public domain.[96]

Underpinning Dobson J's analysis was his resignation to the conclusion that parliament has deliberately provided a process where protection of the confidentiality of information, essentially in the interests of national security, is to prevail over the rights of affected litigants to usual standards of fair procedure, so that he had no capacity to consider the value of those rights when interpreting the statute's provisions or deciding what might be 'desirable' in a given case.[97]

## Review of the intelligence services

In response to changes in the international security landscape, a large-scale review of New Zealand's intelligence agencies[98] and their oversight mechanisms was completed in February 2016.[99] This review was the first (and only) review conducted pursuant to a statutory requirement for regular reviews of New Zealand's intelligence agencies and their governing and oversight legislation.[100] It was completed against the backdrop of a number of controversies surrounding the operation of New Zealand's intelligence agencies – including revelations in 2013 that the communications of a number of New Zealanders had been unlawfully intercepted over a period of several years.[101] These revelations of unlawful behaviour coincided with the Snowden leaks and the growing public sensitivity to the possibility of 'mass surveillance' observed across the liberal democratic world.

The reviewers placed their report in the context of a changing and increasingly complicated security environment, including a perception of growing extremism. Globalization and changing technologies meant that New Zealand could no longer consider itself to be sheltered from terrorism and other threats.[102] The fact that New Zealand had not, to date, experienced terrorist attacks or publicly disclosed serious security threats did not mean that such threats did not exist or 'may not arise in the future'.[103] The *potential risk* of a threat in the future was, therefore, equated with the existence of an *actual threat* in the present.

The starting point of the review's analysis of human rights considerations was that security and human rights were complementary rather than competing rights: 'Security is a prerequisite to a free, open and democratic society in which individuals can go about their lawful activities without undue interference with their rights.'[104] On that basis, '[s]ecurity *is* a human right, and the law that protects human rights must be flexible enough to allow a balance to be struck within it.'[105] This approach seemingly absolved the reviewers of the need to analyse human rights issues at the more granular level usually required under NZBORA, and to consider the specific incursions on rights that different intelligence gathering activities involve.[106]

A key element of the review was its analysis of the concept of 'national security' in the modern globalized environment.[107] The reviewers argued that 'national security' should be defined in a way that limited it to protecting New Zealand's interests against certain specified threats. But those threats were defined broadly to include both threats to New Zealand's 'economic security' and to 'international security'. That, in turn, 'would include contributing to efforts to promote order and protect human rights in unstable parts of the world, which can indirectly affect New Zealand's security'.[108] The lens of New Zealand's 'national' security was thus broadened to encompass even potential threats that might arise beyond New Zealand's borders.[109]

Against that context, the review's central recommendation was for the adoption of a 'single and comprehensive Act of Parliament' setting out: how the intelligence agencies were constituted; their objectives and functions; how their activities would be authorized; and appropriate oversight mechanisms.[110] It recommended that the objectives of the intelligence agencies should be to contribute to: the protection of New Zealand's national security; its international relations and well-being; and its economic well-being. Intelligence gathering activities should be permitted only where necessary to meet those objectives. The targeting of New Zealanders should be permitted for the first objective – the protection of national security only. The existing oversight mechanisms of the Inspector-General of Intelligence and Security and parliament's Intelligence and Security Committee should be retained and enhanced. Clearer procedures and controls should be put in place for access to information collected by other New Zealand agencies for other purposes. Cooperation with foreign partners should continue, but should be consistent with the agencies' objectives and functions and New Zealand law – including human rights obligations.

### *Intelligence and Security Act 2017*

The review's recommendations were largely taken up by the government and implemented through the Intelligence and Security Act 2017. The agencies' objectives have been defined as encompassing New Zealand's international relations and its economic well-being as well as their traditional objective of 'national security'.[111] Contrary to the reviewers' recommendation, 'national security' is not defined in the Act, despite a significant number of public submissions emphasising the importance of a clear statutory definition.[112] However, its meaning can be elaborated by reference to the specific 'harms' against which the agencies may act on national security grounds.[113] These include relatively concrete harms such as 'sabotage' as well as more diffuse threats such as 'terrorism or violent extremism' or threats to the 'operation of the Government of New Zealand' or its 'sovereignty'.

Lawful activities in the fulfilment of the agencies' objectives do not require authorisation.[114] But, otherwise unlawful activities must be authorized by a warrant issued by the minister, and, in some cases, a judicial commissioner.[115] Warrant decisions can be reviewed by the Inspector-General of Intelligence and

Security,[116] but cannot be overturned by that office.[117] A warrant can only be issued to target a New Zealand citizen or permanent resident on national security grounds, and not for the broader objectives of contributing to New Zealand's international relations or economic wellbeing.[118] Non-New Zealanders, by contrast, can be targeted for any one of the agencies' three objectives.[119] This distinction, which constitutes a prima facie breach of the freedom against discrimination on the grounds of nationality,[120] was challenged by a number of public submitters, including the New Zealand Human Rights Commission.[121] It has its origins in an earlier provision prohibiting the private communications of New Zealanders from being intercepted for intelligence purposes.[122] In 2013, that provision was significantly eroded amidst outspoken public protest. In light of that political history, maintaining a higher level of protection for New Zealanders seemed to be taken as a given by parliament when it adopted the 2017 Act.

One interesting feature of the legislation is its elaboration of 'general duties' governing all intelligence agency activities. Section 17 of the Act provides that the agencies must act 'in accordance with New Zealand law and all human rights obligations recognised by New Zealand law' and 'in a manner that facilitates effective democratic oversight'. Section 18 creates an accompanying duty on the Director-General of an agency to take all reasonable steps to ensure that the activities of the agency are limited to its functions, and that the agency's performance is 'kept free from any influence or consideration that is not relevant' to the performance of those functions, and is politically neutral. The Director-General has a further duty to take all reasonable steps to ensure that any co-operation with foreign partners is also in accordance with New Zealand law and all human rights obligations recognized by New Zealand law. This provision appears to be intended to respond to public concerns that cooperation with New Zealand's 'Five Eyes' partners might be used as a way of circumventing the constraints placed on the agencies under New Zealand law. Section 19 of the Act specifically recognizes that:

> The exercise by any person in New Zealand or any class of persons in New Zealand of their right to freedom of expression under the law (including the right to advocate, protest, or dissent) does not of itself justify an intelligence and security agency taking any action in respect of that person or class of persons.

This provision echoes an earlier provision contained in section 2(2) of the New Zealand Security Intelligence Service Act 1969. Its meaning has never been tested and quite what it adds to the protection already given to the freedom of expression under section 14 of NZBORA remains unclear. The boundaries of the freedom of expression and lawful dissent have yet to be clearly defined in the New Zealand context.[123] The point at which 'advocacy, protest or dissent' becomes a 'threat ... to the operations of the Government of New Zealand' or its 'sovereignty', entitling the agencies to take action, will be largely defined by them in secret, albeit under the gaze of the Inspector-General. Whether section 19 will act as a substantive legal restraint will thus only become apparent over time.

## Conclusion

The post 9/11 war on terror era, with its seemingly omnipresent threats to individual safety and ever-increasing security responses, has had less of an effect on New Zealand's law and wider social practices than in most (perhaps even all) comparator societies. In large part, this is due to accidents of geography and history; the country's place on the periphery of global politics has helped it to avoid experiencing the sorts of attacks that drive policy change elsewhere. Long existing criminal law and policing responses have largely sufficed to address the problem without requiring any great extension of state power.

However, even in this backwater environment, the threat of terrorism has caused ripples. No government, nor its security services, want to be seen to be 'asleep at the tiller' in the unlikely event of an attack. Such sensitivities resulted in the 'Operation 8' overreaction to what was, in hindsight, little more than armed role playing by a group of non-threatening fantasists. Just as important, however, is the fact that New Zealand keenly values its international connections and is eager to demonstrate that it is a good global citizen. Consequently, legislation has been implemented to affirm the nation's commitment to UN anti-terrorism resolutions, as well as practices adopted to reassure our intelligence allies of our commitment to the global cause. The nation's courts have been co-opted into sending that reassuring message, even at some cost to rule of law values. And the country's security agencies have been overhauled and made fit for purpose in a new era by being expressly required to balance 'national security' and individual liberty concerns in their every action. These developments may be minor compared to much of the rest of the world, but they do demonstrate that concerns about global extremism have spread even to its furthest corners.

## Notes

1 A Young, 'New Zealand's terror-risk watch list remains steady at 30 to 40, spy chief tells MPs' *New Zealand Herald* (21 March 2018) www.nzherald.co.nz/nz/news/article.cfm?c_id=1&objectid=12017499

2 The 2018 Global Peace Index ranks New Zealand behind only Iceland as the second most peaceful country in the world; see Institute for Economics and Peace, 'Global Peace Index 2018: Measuring Peace in a Complex World' (2018, Institute for Economics and Peace, Sydney) http://visionofhumanity.org/reports

3 However, the accuracy of this portrayal has been seriously called into question by N Hager and J Stephenson, *Hit and Run: The New Zealand SAS in Afghanistan and the Meaning of Honour* (Nelson, Potton & Burton, 2017).

4 At the 2013 census, 46,149 individuals (or approximately 1 per cent of the total population) identified as being of the Muslim faith.

5 A Beaglehole, *Refuge New Zealand: New Zealand's Response to Refugees and Asylum Seekers* (Dunedin, Otago University Press, 2013). Indeed, such policies have

been applied overly zealously in at least some cases; see *Zaoui* v. *Attorney General (No 2)* [2005] NZSC 38; [2006] 1 NZLR 289; M Hassan, 'I just felt like I was a criminal….' *RadioNZ News* (28 June, 2016) www.radionz.co.nz/news/national/307416/'i-just-felt-like-i-was-a-criminal-'

6 See, for example, the Department of Corrections 'Combatting Violent Extremism' working group; J Walker, 'An introduction to combating violent extremism', *Practice: The New Zealand Corrections Journal* 5, no. 2 (2017) www.corrections.govt.nz/resources/research_and_statistics/journal/volume_5_issue_2_november_2017/an_introduction_to_countering_violent_extremism.html

7 B Greener-Barcham, 'Before September: A History of Counter-terrorism in New Zealand *Australian Journal of Political Science* 37, no. 3 (2002): 509, 509–10.

8 A Conte, *Counter-Terrorism and Human Rights in New Zealand* (Wellington, NZ Law Foundation, 2007), 59–81.

9 Crimes Act 1961, s269.

10 Ibid., s306.

11 Ibid., s307.

12 In 2003, however, New Zealand introduced a separate offence to cover what might generally be called 'terrorist threats'; see Crimes Act 1961, s307A. No person has been charged under this provision.

13 Crimes Act 1961, s66(1).

14 Films, Videos, and Publications Classification Act 1993, s124.

15 New Zealand Bill of Rights Act 1990, s5.

16 Ibid., s4.

17 Ibid., s6. See A Geddis and M Rodriguez-Ferrere, 'Judicial Innovation Under the New Zealand Bill of Rights Act – Lessons for Queensland?' *University of Queensland Law Review* 35, no. 2 (2016): 251, 269–76.

18 Crimes (Repeal of Seditious Offences) Amendment Act 2007.

19 *Boucher* v. *R* [1951] 2 DLR 369.

20 *R* v. *Selwyn* (8 June 2006, CRI: 2005-004-11804, District Court Auckland).

21 New Zealand Law Commission, 'Reforming the Law of Sedition' Report 96 (March 2007) at 9.

22 However, material directly intended to motivate specific terrorist actions may give rise to a charge of incitement to commit a criminal act, while material intended to recruit members to a designated terrorist entity may be prosecuted under the Terrorism Suppression Act 2002. See below at n. 36.

23 Films, Videos, and Publications Classification Act 1993, s3(2)(f).

24 Ibid., s3(3)(d).

25 Ibid., ss123 and 124.

26 *R* v. *Patel* [2016] NZDC 11454.

27 *Patel* v. *R* [2017] NZCA 234. Notably, the decision to classify the publications in question as 'objectionable' was not challenged.

28 Ibid., at 41.

29 Ibid., at 49.

30 Ibid., at 52.

31 D Clarkson, 'Kiwi teenager radicalised online planned mass killing in Christchurch 'for Allah'', *Stuff* (16 February 2018) www.stuff.co.nz/national/crime/101480988/kiwi-teenager-radicalised-online-planned-mass-killing-in-christchurch-for-allah

32 D Clarkson, 'Supervised golf for Christchurch teenager who planned terror attack' *Stuff* (17 April 2018) www.stuff.co.nz/the-press/news/103168707/supervised-golf-for-christchurch-teenager-who-planned-terrorist-attack

33 These include the Aviation Crimes Act 1972, the Crimes (Internationally Protected Persons and United Nations and Associated Personnel, and Hostages) Act 1980, and the Maritime Crimes Act 1999. See generally Greener-Barcham, above n. 6.

34 Terrorism Suppression Act 2002, s5.

35 Ibid., s6A.
36 Ibid., s8.
37 Ibid., ss12–13.
38 Ibid., s13A.
39 The background to this operation is described by the Independent Police Complaints Authority, 'Operation Eight: The Report of the IPCA' (May 2013) www.ipca.govt.nz/includes/download.aspx?ID=127984
40 D Collins, 'Media Statement: Solicitor General', Scoop Independent News (8 November 2007) at 2 http://img.scoop.co.nz/media/pdfs/0711/SolGenTerror.pdf
41 Ibid.
42 Arms Act 1983, s45.
43 Crimes Act 1961, s98A.
44 *Hamed & Ors* v. *R* [2011] NZSC 101.
45 Independent Police Complaints Authority, 'Operation Eight: The Report of the IPCA' (May 2013) at [374]; [375]; [378]; [379]; [383]; [387]; [390] www.ipca.govt.nz/includes/download.aspx?ID=127984
46 N Mankelow, 'Police apologise to Tuhoe over raids', *RadioNZ News*, (13 August 2014) www.radionz.co.nz/news/national/251999/police-apologise-to-tuhoe-over-raids
47 Terrorism Suppression Act 2002, ss47A, 48.
48 Ibid., s43.
49 Ibid., ss9, 10.
50 Ibid., s12.
51 Ibid., s13.
52 Ibid., s33.
53 Ibid., s38.
54 Ibid., s4 (definition of 'designated terrorist entity'). At present, this list encompasses IS (Daesh), Al-Qaida and the Taliban and associated individuals and organizations.
55 See Cabinet Minute CAB (03) 34/15A.
56 A Conte, *Counter Terrorism and Human Rights in New Zealand* (Wellington, NZ Law Foundation, 2007), 297–316.
57 J Ardern, 'New Zealand adds to list of designated terrorist entities' (4 April, 2018) www.beehive.govt.nz/release/new-zealand-adds-list-designated-terrorist-entities
58 See, for example, B Hurley, 'The jihadi and me: Conversations with 'bumbling' Kiwi jihadi Mark John Taylor' *Sunday Star-Times* (18 December, 2016) www.stuff.co.nz/world/middle-east/87592895/the-jihadi-and-me-conversations-with-bumbling-kiwi-jihadi-mark-john-taylor
59 The Bill was finally enacted as three separate amendment Acts: Customs and Excise Amendment Act 2014; New Zealand Security Intelligence Service Amendment Act 2014; Passports Amendment Act 2014.
60 Foreign Affairs, Defence and Trade Committee, *Report on the Countering Terrorist Fighters Legislation Bill 2014 (No 1–2)* (2 December 2014) 6–7.
61 Passports Act 1992, s27GA.
62 The NZBORA, s18(2) states 'Every New Zealand citizen has the right to enter New Zealand.'
63 Passports Act 1992, s23(3).
64 Search and Surveillance Act 2012, Part 3.
65 See, for example, A Geddis, 'Kurdish Bombs over Kobane' *Pundit* (9 December 2014) www.pundit.co.nz/content/kurdish-bombs-over-kobane
66 C Finlayson, NZPD Vol 702, Pg 1207 (9 December 2014).
67 By ss4, 5 and clause 8, schedule 2 of the Passports Amendment Act 2014.
68 New Zealand Law Commission *National Security Information in Proceedings (Issues Paper 38)* (2015) at [2.47].
69 New Zealand Law Commission *Supressing Names and Evidence (Issues Paper 13)* (2008) at [1.1], citing *Re Victim X* [2003] 3 NZLR 220, at [51], per Hammond J.

70 The New Zealand Law Commission recommended in 2015 that the government should develop such a procedure: New Zealand Law Commission *The Crown in Court: A review of the Crown Proceedings Act and national security information in proceedings (Report 135)* (2015). The government has yet to respond to the Law Commission's recommendation.

71 Under: s27(3) of the Crown Proceedings Act 1950; ss52(4) and 70 of the Evidence Act 2006; and ss13, 14, 16, and 30 of the Criminal Disclosure Act 2008.

72 See, for example, the summary of the procedures adopted by the New Zealand High Court in two high profile proceedings set out by the New Zealand Law Commission in *National Security Information in Proceedings (Issues Paper 38)* (2015).

73 As protected by the NZBORA, s27 (implementing article 14 of the United Nations International Convention on Civil and Political Rights 1966 (999 UNTS 171)).

74 See advice prepared by the Ministry of Justice for the Attorney-General in relation to: the Telecommunications (Interception Capability and Security) Bill (3 May 2013) at [11]–[15]; and the New Zealand Intelligence and Security Bill (12 August 2016) at [88]–[97] www.justice.govt.nz/justice-sector-policy/constitutional-issues-and-human-rights/bill-of-rights-compliance-reports/

75 See Human Rights Commission, *Report to the Prime Minister: Government Communications Security Bureau and Related Legislation Amendment Bill; Telecommunications (Interception Capability and Security) Bill; and associated wider issues relating to surveillance and the human rights of people in New Zealand* (9 July 2013) at [33] www.hrc.co.nz/your-rights/human-rights/our-work/

76 See New Zealand Law Society, *Submission to the Law and Order Select Committee: Telecommunications (Interception Capability and Security Bill)* (13 June 2013) at [7]ff. www.lawsociety.org.nz/news-and-communications/law-reform-submissions/submissions-on-bills

77 R Harrison, 'Fundamental Freedoms and the "War on Terrorism"' (2005) 8.1 Yearbook of New Zealand Jurisprudence 141–62; L Inverarity, 'Immigration Bill 2007: Special Advocates and the Right to be Heard' *Victoria University of Wellington Law Review* 40, no. 2 (2009): 471.

78 Terrorism Suppression Act 2002, ss32, 38 and 40; Customs and Excise Act 1996, ss38M and 38N (introduced by s15 of the Customs and Excise Amendment Act 2004); Passport Act 1992, ss29AA–29AC (introduced by s24 of the Passport Act Amendment Act 2005); Immigration Act 2009 ss240–4 and 252–71; Telecommunications (Interception Capability and Security) Act 2013 ss101–13; Health and Safety at Work Act 2015, s162 and Sched. 4.

79 Law Commission *supra* n.68 at [5.15]. See also the discussion by the Law Commission in its Issues Paper *supra* n. 70 at [4.27]ff.

80 Immigration Act 2009, ss263–271; Telecommunications (Interception Capability and Security) Act 2014, ss105–110; Health and Safety at Work Act 2015, schedule 4, cl. 6–11.

81 New Zealand Law Society, *Submission to the Law Commission: National Security Information in Proceedings* (7 July 2015) at 10–11 www.lawsociety.org.nz/news-and-communications/law-reform-submissions/submissions-on-bills

82 [2017] 3 NZLR 247, [2017] NZHC 746 per Dobson J. See also the subsequent judgments in the same case: [2018] NZHC 1328; and [2018] NZHC 1797.

83 Ibid., at 41.

84 Ibid., at 84.

85 Ibid.

86 See, for example, the definition of 'classified security information' in Passports Act 1992, s29AA and, in particular, the grounds in ss(6)(c) and (7)(a).

87 See www.gcsb.govt.nz/about-us/ukusa-allies

88 New Zealand Law Commission *supra* n. 70 at [2.27].

89 [2017] 3 NZLR 247, [2017] NZHC 746; [2018] NZHC 1328, at [44].

90 [2010] 4 All ER 91.

91 Ibid., at 44.
92 Ibid., at 46. See also Lord Neuberger MR at [160] and [172], and Sir Anthony May P at 287–8.
93 [2018] NZHC 1328.
94 Ibid., at 51 and 82.
95 Ibid., at 52.
96 Ibid., at 82. See also the discussion at [55]–[56], [60]–[69]. This contrasts with the English Court of Appeal's approach in *Mohamed* supra n. 90, which considered that: 'There is no "disclosure" of "US intelligence information" if one publishes information which has already been placed in the public domain …' (at [197] per Lord Neuberger MR).
97 Ibid., at 40.
98 The New Zealand Intelligence Security Service (which focuses on human intelligence) and the Government Communications and Security Bureau (which focuses on signals intelligence).
99 M Cullen and P Reddy *Intelligence and Security in a Free Society* (2016, Wellington, New Zealand).
100 Intelligence and Security Committee Act 1996, s21 (repealed).
101 M Cullen and P Reddy *Intelligence and Security in a Free Society* (2016, Wellington, New Zealand) at 1.34–1.45.
102 Ibid., at 1.2–1.3, 1.19, 1.33 and 1.56–1.58.
103 Ibid., at 1.13.
104 Ibid., at 1.5.
105 Ibid., at 1.7.
106 *R* v. *Hansen* [2007] NZSC 7, [2007] 3 NZLR 1 at 101–4 per Tipping J.
107 M Cullen and P Reddy *Intelligence and Security in a Free Society* (2016, Wellington, New Zealand) at 5.78–5.85.
108 Ibid., at 5.85.
109 Ibid., at 3.42–3.47.
110 Ibid., at pp. 5–12.
111 Intelligence and Security Act 2017, s9.
112 See, for example: the submissions by the Inspector-General of Intelligence and Security, the Legislative Advisory Committee, the Privacy Commissioner and the New Zealand Law Society www.parliament.nz. A definition had been included in the initial draft of the legislation, but was removed during parliament's deliberation.
113 Intelligence and Security Act 2017, s59(2).
114 Ibid., s48.
115 Ibid., s49.
116 Ibid., s158(1)(i).
117 Ibid., s163.
118 Ibid., ss53, 58 and 59.
119 Ibid., ss54 and 60.
120 Protected by the NZBORA 1990, s19 (implementing articles 18 and 19 of the ICCPR). Note that this prima facie breach of s19 was not addressed in the advice prepared by the Ministry of Justice for the Attorney-General: 'Consistency with the New Zealand Bill of Rights Act 1990: New Zealand Intelligence and Security Bill' (3 August 2016). The 2016 review justified the distinction in terms of the reciprocal obligations inherent in the relationship between a government and its citizens (at 5.61–5.62).
121 See, for example: the submissions by the Human Rights Commission, the Legislative Advisory Committee, and the New Zealand Law Society available at www.parliament.nz
122 Government Communications Security Bureau Act 2003, s14 (repealed).
123 See A Geddis 'The State of Freedom of Expression in New Zealand: An Admittedly Eclectic Overview' *Otago Law Review* 11 (2008): 657–81.

# Index

For Product Safety Concerns and Information please contact our EU representative GPSR@taylorandfrancis.com
Taylor & Francis Verlag GmbH, Kaufingerstraße 24, 80331 München, Germany

www.ingramcontent.com/pod-product-compliance
Ingram Content Group UK Ltd.
Pitfield, Milton Keynes, MK11 3LW, UK
UKHW021302190926
475701UK00009B/615

*9780367670955*